# OMAR ALI-SHAH

## THE

## RULES

## OR

## SECRETS

## OF

## THE

## NAQSHBANDI

## ORDER

# OMAR ALI-SHAH

# THE
# RULES
# OR
# SECRETS
# OF
# THE
# NAQSHBANDI
# ORDER

TRACTUS BOOKS

# RULES OR SECRETS OF THE NAQSHBANDI ORDER

This book was first published by Tractus in 1992 in a shorter version edited by Paul Barrett and Augy Hayter. The present edition includes about 75% of new material.

Cover design by Alain Jacob.

Library of Congress Catalogue number 98-61227

**ISBN 2-909347-09-5**

TRACTUS
P.O. Box 6777,
Reno, Nevada 89513 U.S.A.
phone/fax (702) 345 - 7585
and
TRACTUS BOOKS
43 rue de la Gaîté
75014 Paris FRANCE
fax (33) 01 44 07 12 07
tel (33) 01 40 47 63 63

# CONTENTS

# EDITOR'S FOREWORD

Before launching a book like this onto the marketplace, a few words are required, not as a warning on the packet along the lines of *Esoteric literature can be damaging to your mental health* but to establish a kind of guideline for people who have not yet had the chance of familiarizing themselves with the Sufi Tradition and thinking.

The knowledge the Sufi Tradition seeks to inspire is a way of feeling and doing rather than the western idea of a body of intellectual information. This means that the person who comes along with no previous formal knowledge of the subject need not feel inferior to people like myself who have been trying to do it for more than thirty years. The reason is simple: most people grow up in the context of a biological or surrogate family, and manage willy-nilly to develop some form of personal vision as they grow into adulthood. Everyone is hence already in possession of some form of learning equipment even though from the point of view of the Sufi Tradition, this can be either rusted or under-used.

The techniques of the Tradition, of which this book is but one amongst others, are thus designed to make use of and maximize on what a person already knows.

The basic idea of such techniques is that they are to be used in conjunction with one's own experience and the daily context of life. This means that you key them into your everyday life, as opposed to placing them on a metaphorical "altar" for purposes of worship.

Why it is considered necessary for a teacher to supervise such an activity is that people who start off in anything they have not done before will always be somewhat disoriented. After a while they may not be quite so lost but they can still pursue one possibility or avenue of research to the detriment of another, which leads to an unbalanced apprehension of real phenomena. It is the presence of a teacher, whose job is to monitor the learner's work, that enables less time to be wasted in a possibly fruitless quest.

To a certain extent, one can consider that this apprenticeship is similar in nature to that of a manual craft. My father was a teacher of itaglio printmaking, and he was sorry when, from the fifties onward, the black ink used on the plates began to be sold pre-mixed with linseed oil. In the old days, one had to grind the ink from dry cakes and mix it into the oil using a grinding-stone on a piece of plate glass. Getting a properly smooth texture of ink was not an easy thing to do, and most apprentices would have to grind the ink for a long time (a process known in French as "broyer du noir") before being allowed to even begin using it themselves on the copper or zinc plate.

When I asked him whether the ready-mixed ink was not as good as the other, he replied "Oh no, the ink itself is fine. It's the relationship with the ink that has changed for the worse."

I don't think it is stretching the imagination too far to say that this book should be considered as one might consider that dry cake of ink, a basic component to a great deal of work to come. There is no label on the side of the ink-cake telling you how to turn it into a beautiful image: the image must come from oneself. The burin won't make a line by itself, but the conscious hand can learn to use that burin. Or, as Omar Ali-Shah repeats over and over again, knowledge must be usable to exist.

# EDITOR'S FOREWORD

There can therefore be no possibility of using this book as a sort of formulaic cookbook for esoteric wisdom. Nevertheless, the possibilities of use to which this book or that ink can be put are infinite, so that there is no point in becoming discouraged. One finds one's own way.

If one treats this book with the respect and attention it deserves, it can help almost anybody, so long as they key it into their overall life context without becoming obsessive over details, because that is when the consciousness becomes inflexible. One has to bring the whole of one's own life to bear on the concepts contained in the book, and it is only from this point on that the concepts themselves will acquire some meaning. If one tries to reduce this book to some kind of "how to" manual, this type of thinking will, of itself, render it useless.

A word on the framework of thought within which this is all taking place. To quote Omar Ali-Shah in his preface to *Sufism for Today*:

> *The Sufi Tradition is not a religion, nor is it a cult. It is a philosophy of life, and its purpose is to offer to man a practical path to enable him to achieve a measure of higher consciousness, and through this elevated consciousness, to be able to understand his relationship with the Supreme Being...*
>
> *This philosophy has been handed down throughout the ages. It has retained the ancient quality and has guarded its ancient secrets so that it may be available, unchanged and untarnished, to those who seek deeper wisdom through deeper consciousness.*

This is therefore the frame within which the present book must be considered. If you believe that such a thing is possible, read on, or take this book to the check-out counter and take it home with you. If you don't believe that such a thing is possible, don't waste your time: put this book back on the shelf of the bookstore and go to the movies.

The *Rules or Secrets* are instruments to this general end, no more and no less. When used for lesser ends, they will at worst turn against oneself, or at best become totally useless. The intention with which one uses these techniques will very precisely define the level at which they can work—in other words it can be all or nothing. They are in no sense threatening, but one should just remember that one is handling powerful instruments. Those of us who have some experience of the Tradition know that the acquisition of inner weight makes our mistakes heavier as well.

The rules in this form were in fact laid out many years ago, in the sixteenth century. The first eight of these rules are said to have been drafted by Sheikh Kwaja Abd al-Khaliq Ghujawani who is buried in Ghujawan on the road between Bokhara and Samarkand, and the last three by Bahaudin Naqshband, founder of the Naqshbandi Order of Dervishes, whose recently restored shrine is also near Bokhara.

As Omar Ali-Shah explains in one of the chapters, the word "secret" in the Tradition implies less something which is confidential than something which is of an intimate nature. It is therefore more useful here to consider secret as being of the nature of intimate, something which addresses itself to the most secret part of the self. If one allows them in, this is the area where the rules can develop and flower, and it is in fact the only place where they can grow. If one tries to use them in any other way, say for impressing people with one's knowledge or for establishing domination over others, they will dissolve, or worse still, turn against one.

The various concepts expressed through these rules are

almost infinite in their possible and varied applications, which is why Omar Ali-Shah does not reduce this flexibility of application by giving many precise examples. As he says, if one prescribed a recipe-like usage, such as "use *alone in a crowd* when you're in the subway during rush hour" one runs the risk of limiting its usage to the subway. The possible situations in which one might use this and other concepts are so varied that people trying to develop themselves by using this technique could conceivably have their horizons narrowed by too many suggested applications.

For this reason, if anybody feels that what is stated in this book appears to be vague, it is because Omar Ali-Shah is subtle enough to realize that there has to be enough room left over for the reader to be able apply his or her own options and experiences to these concepts. He is addressing himself to the feel of the rules' use, rather than to the passing personal situations and events one uses them on.

Comparing notes or talking over how one applies them with someone else can be useful, but when this is done outside of a context where people have a similar intention, distortions usually develop. There is a certain narrow efficiency in dogmatism, and people can go off on this kind of tack, dragging others with them. This is one of the reasons why the supervision of a teacher is considered necessary in the Sufi Tradition, which tends to play down the importance of so-called "powerful personalities."

One of the most important things a teacher does in the Sufi Tradition is to judge when something—if anything—is required. You don't get stripes for length of service, but after a while you do get a bit more sense of how long things take, call it a feel for pattern. We are talking here of decades, not of hours and minutes. Yet some important things do happen quickly, which makes it impossible to generalize.

A few words on the way Omar Ali-Shah works with his people may be in order here, since there is much fantasizing about gurus and teachers from the mysterious East, and anyone reading this book becomes *de facto* his pupil, insofar as these talks were all delivered to his students over the past fifteen years.

He does not invade his pupil's lives, create dependency or use systematically shocking tactics to achieve his (and their) ends, although he is capable of doing so. All family ties and relationships are to be respected and built on, recourse to all artificial stimulants discouraged. He uses the normal time-frame within which we live, which means that progress will often take longer than one would have hoped, and a shock or a provocation will be held in reserve for exceptional cases, for instance when a pupil is falling into a rut of some years' duration. A Sufi teacher doesn't walk into a room with his 'guns blazing' unless there is some teaching point to the operation, but he still has to keep it in reserve as an option if nothing less is adequate for the situation.

The notion of time and appropriateness to the situation is paramount, as well as the 'keying in' factor. One can say that, generally speaking, people have a tendency to be impatient, and western education feeds this tendency by promoting the illusion that you 'know' a subject when you have assimilated a certain amount of basic information about it. In the *Fihi ma Fihi*, Rumi likens a man who says "I understand" to a person who has just filled a skin bottle with sea water, and who then holds it up saying: "This is the sea."

This tendency also means that people won't consider they have learnt something unless it has taken a very heightened or dramatic form. In other books Omar Ali-Shah has pointed out how people get drawn towards cathartic-type experiences where they are torn apart, the better, 'so the assumption goes, to be rebuilt again afterwards.' Certain therapists and many false teachers batten onto this kind of attraction by working in terms of conflict rather than towards harmony, and there is a certain pattern in the western world, where people have been naive about this kind of abuse, in which this kind of thing has been used as a technique.

My own short observation of Idries Shah and longer observation of Omar Ali-Shah as teachers, leads me to think that they do arrange things, but within a certain limitation. They are highly respectful of the pupil's own rhythm of assimilation over time. Omar Ali-Shah works through small groupings of people, but there is no trace of the high-pressure and money-grubbing tactics one associates with "cult" situations.

It should not be forgotten however, that the discipline required from a teacher who really does respect the capacity and rhythm of his pupil, and who carefully works with and around it, is of an exceptional nature. Working this way requires immense patience. This patience can be learnt from a teacher, but not quickly, insofar as this discipline within an overall flexibility takes a long time to assimilate.

If one can develop something analogous to this kind of patience towards oneself, it will help one to make powerful use of this book. The key to this book's use is familiarization: the closer one gets to these concepts, the more one can apply them to the various inner and outer circumstances in our lives.

The more one does this, and the more transparent one makes oneself to these concepts, the more these developmental modules can then work through us; almost—but not quite—in spite of ourselves.

# RULES OR SECRETS OF THE NAQSHBANDI ORDER

In the earlier version of this book, the editing was "harder" in the sense that we tried to get as close as possible to proposing a single version of each rule. Time makes one more modest. In this expanded edition of the first book I have gone back to the original transcripts and have followed the original extracts more faithfully, which means that there is a certain amount of overlap.

Some may consider this repetitious: my feeling is that it is useful to watch Omar Ali-Shah considering and reconsidering a subject at different times, as one might look at the work of a painter returning to the same scene throughout his life, throwing a slightly different light on the subject each time, because he knows that the essence of his life's work is in that place.

Augy Hayter
1992 & 1998

# THE MEANING OF NAQSHBANDI

The word Naqshbandi is made of two words: *Naqsh* is painting and *bandi* are the people who do the painting. You could therefore say that Naqshbandi means the *painters* or the *designers*.

Now do we design the past or the future? We design the future because the past is already designed. It is also known in the Tradition as the mother-order, as well as *Kwajagan*, which means the *guardians of the Tradition* throughout history.

The Naqshbandi Order has always been commanded or guided by a Sayed, that is a descendant of the Prophet Muhammad. It is an orthodox Order in the sense that it follows the main line which we hope can lead us as close to the truth as we can hope to be.

For us, there is only one total truth, and that is God. There is only one fear in the Tradition which you or I should have, and that is the fear of God, nothing else.

Study the rules and learn them. Allow these rules to become part of your life, just as you breathe, just as your heart beats. Let these rules become equally a part of your being. Invite them to help you.

The way of the Tradition is long, but the encouraging point is that many people have followed this way. It is not a way that is restricted to people with an enormous intellect or anything like that, in fact a huge intellect is possibly a handicap rather than a help. What counts is faith and effort. If a person is not prepared to have faith and use effort, do not take this path.

When I say that this path has been followed successfully, I can cite Rumi, Hafiz, Jami, Saadi and Ibn Arabi, none of whom were superhuman, but they certainly tried more than average.

Rumi kept a diary which was never published, and one day he wrote "I came home dead tired and couldn't even lift my head up, and I asked myself "What is the point of all this?" I work like a donkey, and at night I am just tired, what is the point?" And then he wrote after that : "The sun rises in the morning."

5.12.87

# SECRECY

There are eleven rules, or what are called "secrets" of the Naqshbandi order. Within the Sufi Tradition, as you probably know, there are different schools of teaching. The senior school is the Naqshbandi.

These rules or "secrets" are not secrets in the sense that we are a secret society. If you like, we are a society with secrets: there is a difference.

People who join together to do something, to try and attain a personal and common goal, must do it by using certain precise tactics. These can be called secrets or "hidden" things because you don't go and shout them from the housetops, for the obvious reason that you will get into interminable debate with everybody on their "interpretation" or "why you are doing it" or "who do you think you are"—only if one has an argumentative bent does one go ahead and do it this way.

If one betrays these secrets, nobody is going to be angry, because they are by no means incredible: in fact they are very basic and simple. They are secrets because we keep them privately.

Every activity in the Tradition comes from one of these points, therefore if one is doing an exercise, participating in a group exercise, listening to some music or somebody talking, you can find how that activity applies to this or that rule for one very simple reason: each of the rules is part of the human character.

# RULES OR SECRETS OF THE NAQSHBANDI ORDER

If you are told to do something, a part of you would either like to know why, or what will happen if you do it. If you can say "Ah yes, this activity comes from this particular rule" then you won't waste time in thinking about it, you'll just do it.

Certainly, there are occasions when a person might be asked to do an activity or an exercise which they can't relate to one of these rules. Maybe they will go through the rules again and again to find "which one relates to this" or worry that they might have "forgotten one part of the rule"—then they will blame themselves for being stupid and me for not telling them and the world for not being fair to them. They will be wasting their time. It is better simply to do it.

Learn what is the basis and what is the spirit within each rule, i.e., not only the words but also the spirit behind it. Don't say to yourself "Ah this comes from rule number 5" because at that point you're getting into numberings and not contexts.

Each rule has a name, and when you associate what you are told to do with that rule, you are repeating that rule to yourself and understanding it better each time.

For convenience and efficiency, numbers are sometimes used, but the problem with numbers is that a number is somehow less human than a word. There's a very old and stupid joke which deals with numbers, and since it's one of the only jokes I can ever remember, I'll tell it to you.

Apparently there was this American jail, and every Saturday night the prisoners had a theatrical show. Now a new prisoner went to his first performance, and he was astonished, because a man would get up on stage and say "twenty-four" and everybody would laugh for five minutes. Then he would say "nineteen" and everybody would laugh and clap.

# SECRECY

After the performance he went to an older prisoner and said: "What is this? I don't understand."

The old lag said: "Well you see, in the prison library there is one joke book, and all the jokes are numbered. Everybody has read this book a hundred times and they all know the number of the joke, so they don't have to tell the joke, they just say the number."

So the new prisoner said: "Very good, I'm going to be here for twenty years, I will also get this book." So he got hold of the book and he learned all the jokes and all the numbers.

Some months went by, and he was given the opportunity to take part in the next performance. He was a bit nervous to begin with, but he got up on stage and he said "twenty-nine" and nobody laughed. Nobody clapped and nobody said anything.

Then he said "forty-two": there was no reaction. So he thought: the funniest one is "a hundred and four!" and by this time people were saying "Ssssh, Booo!"

So he was very ashamed and went back to his friend and said "What happened? I know these jokes, I learnt them all, and they are very funny."

And the man said: "Well you see, it's not the number that counts, it's the way you say it."

21.11.85

# RULES OR SECRETS OF THE NAQSHBANDI ORDER

## REFRESHING THE SUBCONSCIOUS

Generally speaking, there are two states of being people recognise; the conscious and the unconscious. Of course, this is a very broad outline, and there are other states in between, but when talking simply, one can say the conscious level of existence is supposed to be one in which a person learns, records, acts, and assimilates knowledge, and uses that knowledge in a conscious and deliberate way.

Apart from sleep, when to all intents and purposes the person is nonconscious, the unconscious state is one which is at the root of many of the problems which people face, especially today.

The unconscious mind or the unconscious being is considered here to be distinct from the inner being, which is on a different level. We will say you have the level of consciousness, of unconsciousness, and the level of inner being.

The unconscious—or subconscious, as it is sometimes called—takes on terms of reference and conditionings without very much scrutiny, without much care.

This is very often because it is the unconscious or subconscious mind which is recording these conditionings. A person can absorb them without being conscious of the fact that they are being recorded.

For instance, a person might be consciously exposed to a certain type of conditioning, certain terms of reference or certain ways of behaviour, and consciously, they might examine it and reject it.

# REFRESHING THE SUBCONSCIOUS

But the effect doesn't necessarily just end there, because very often, after they have considered it consciously, it has left a mark on the unconscious or the subconscious mind in such a way that it becomes part of their behaviour, in the sense that this part of their conditioning comes to the surface when it is exposed to certain influences.

The unconscious or subconscious mind can therefore influence a person's behaviour and thought pattern to a very deep degree, and even actually become their reaction.

As a result of this conditioning, their reaction is something they come to accept as normal or as an integral part of their personality, and they often allow this conditioning to come to the surface and influence their thoughts and actions in a form of instinctive reaction without any conscious thought at all. It is also because their conditioning has sometimes not left them with any choice in how to react to a certain situation—they have a set reaction based on conditioning, and, to a certain degree, based on their personality—they have certain sets of cards, if you like, which in a given circumstance, they play automatically.

This conditioning may be of a political, sexual, national or any other nature, and by the time a person reaches the age of twenty or twenty-five, they have acquired twenty or twenty-five years of conditioning on all sorts of levels, in all sorts of circumstances.

If they react instinctively from the unconscious or subconscious, and they have a problem or get into trouble because what they did was the wrong reaction to a particular circumstance, they feel they have to blame their conditioning, and they can always pass it off as "Oh, that's me"; "Oh that's my conditioning"; "Oh that's my background"——but it is no excuse.

# RULES OR SECRETS OF THE NAQSHBANDI ORDER

In the context of the Tradition, you have a set of rules which plainly state how a person sets about watching themselves, examining themselves, and getting to know themselves.

For what purpose?

One of the purposes is obviously that the person replaces certain conditioned terms of reference by new terms of reference which are more positive and useful—i.e., terms of reference which they have understood and accepted, and which have not been imposed upon one by years of conditioning.

If the person in the Tradition ignores the terms of reference which are in the rules, and reacts in the same old and set way to certain circumstances, the reason is laziness and lack of self-discipline.

None of the rules will claim to make you into the perfect person under all circumstances—but what they can claim to do is increasingly prevent you from repeating the errors which commonly occur in people's lives because of conditioning and/ or because of habit.

Learning to know and understand oneself is only the first step. True, it is a long step, and it takes a long time.

The second step is: having then learnt a little, or much, about oneself—to motivate oneself then in the directions which are indicated by the rules.

Remember, the rules do not make a person into a machine. If a person says "There is such and such a situation, I will react according to rule number five"—this is a form of mental indiscipline.

# REFRESHING THE SUBCONSCIOUS

Certainly a person should have the rules at the back of their mind at all times, and under whatever circumstance, in order to find one which they can apply to that given situation—but this should become part of their thought pattern. Again, it does not prevent them from falling into errors which, as I say, are usually accountable to lack of mental discipline and—very often—laziness.

"I'll just do that and see what happens"—no, you follow it up, because if you are yourself already involved, or going to become involved, in a situation—if you have some reasonable idea of what your conditioning is, and in which way you might perhaps make an error—by then going through the rules and through your knowledge of yourself, the new terms of reference you are using should form part of a mental discipline which you henceforth follow.

You don't impose a mental discipline upon yourself just for it's own sake or form. You do not impose it on yourself in order to escape your own laziness or stupidity. You have to understand that adherence to the rules requires your commitment on a very deep level—and not merely occasionally reading the rules, or reciting them to yourself.

You have to allow them to become part of you, so that, in a given situation, you can react in the best possible way for yourself and for your inner being.

Yes, it takes time—yes, the temptation is to react instinctively, or react as one is used to reacting, rather than in the form of a thinking reaction. On the other hand, if the thinking reaction means that your decision-making or your powers of decision are slowed down because you have to go back through all the rules to see which one applies, this means that the person involved has not fully understood or appreciated the rules.

# RULES OR SECRETS OF THE NAQSHBANDI ORDER

In their own way, they are all dissimilar—as well as being harmonious with each other. One can consciously apply one or two rules simultaneously—but when they have become part of your pattern of thinking and behaviour—i.e., part of your pattern of understanding yourself—then, in a given circumstance, it is most likely that one or other of the rules will be predominant in your mind when you think about a particular situation.

You have to give an opportunity to this new thinking, and give yourself the opportunity of deliberately applying it.

Sometimes, life being as it is, one is obliged to make a hurried decision about something. These types of situations are inescapable, given that in some places or in some situations life is lived at a very nervous or tense pace, and perhaps it doesn't allow one enough time to make a mature choice or harmonious judgement about a particular situation.

Before the rules can become really part of your behaviour, you will inevitably make certain mistakes, or consider that a particular rule applies, when it in fact doesn't. Or else one will use conscious evaluation rather than a deeper evaluation of a situation, and cause confusion to oneself or fall into error.

In every circumstance, whether there be error or success, one should examine the circumstance and see what precipitated the error, or what encouraged the success. Every situation is, after all, a lesson, and if one can say to oneself: "Yes, I consciously used a particular rule, I followed a particular discipline, a particular train of thought throughout this activity, and the result was positive"——then one can say that one has mastered at least one of the rules.

It is a question of being realistic as well. There are, obviously, certain situations in which the rules do not apply, and there are times when one should not attempt to force a situation to comply with a particular rule. But in the more profound areas, involving one's family, one's career, and things of a more valuable nature; you owe it to yourself to think usefully and positively—allowing the rules to flow into your thinking, harmonising with your thinking as a matter of course, as a natural event—not as an imposition, not as a law which must not be broken, but as something which you feel the need for, which you invite to act upon you—and you then act together with it.

You flow with the rules; you use the rules. The rules are there to be learnt, to be used, to be followed. If one does not pay enough attention to them, one is doing a disservice to oneself, because in this area there is no question of either intelligence or intellect being involved. It is a feeling.

To flow with a rule, applying a rule and seeing it functioning—to see it working within oneself and the situation—is a reward in itself.

So remember—divide up the conscious and the unconscious. The unconscious can assimilate, and also gather up a lot of garbage and rubbish, a lot of terms of reference which you don't need, but which—because of conditioning—you can't avoid.

One refreshes one's unconscious or subconscious mind by using the rules, which go into the subconscious, and on into the inner being, and crowd out the inessential or negative forms of reaction or thinking a person may have developed—it is as much a question of habit as of conditioning.

The question is not and should not be "Why or how do I use the rules?" The question should be: "Why not?"

# RULES OR SECRETS OF THE NAQSHBANDI ORDER

The answer is because they are there, they are coherent, available, and applicable, and there is no degree of harmony which can properly be achieved if there is a struggle between what you consciously feel and what your subconscious is trying to feed to you.

If the conscious and the subconscious are in harmony, then you are in harmony with yourself.

If there is something which is a negative charge or influence in the unconscious or subconscious, this will be a cause of creating tension and creating confusion.

All aspects of life looked at with the rules in mind can be clarified, and the confusion can be replaced by a harmonious process of feeling within oneself.

4.02.93

# LOOKING AT YOURSELF

It is important to understand the function and the composition of the group in the Sufi Tradition.

It is possible for a person to work in the Tradition alone, but it is more difficult to do so because the person does not produce and receive the same amount of energy.

The number of people in a group is not important, so you cannot say a group of a hundred people is more important than a group of ten. The question is one of quality of activity, not of quantity.

When we talk about a group in the Tradition, we use the analogy of a carpet, because a carpet is composed of hundreds of thousands of knots. You therefore cannot say that a big carpet is more important, as such, than a small one.

As far as I am concerned, it is the individuals coming together and working harmoniously which make an important group, because people working together harmoniously, in and with nature, produce a special energy.

When they are working harmoniously with nature, they have the energy they produce themselves, the energy which comes from working in a group, the energy which comes from the natural surroundings, as well as the energy which comes from the source of the Tradition.

Each individual should be able to use all four energies together, and in order to use the energy correctly they must first learn how to do so. That is why we have a discipline of action in the Tradition, which is there in order to help you use the energy better.

It is very important for you to feel that you are receiving the energy and using it. You have to feel what we call the circle of energy passing through you, and as you receive, so you harmoniously use the energy. That is why we use another analogy when we call it the chain. Each individual is one link in that chain.

If a number of people want to move a large object and put a chain round this object, they will only move the object if they pull harmoniously. If they pull without discipline, they will be pulling against each other.

What weakens the use of this energy are things like competition or jealousy. If you show me a person who is jealous of other people, that person is at war with himself.

It is for us in the Tradition to try and influence the society in which we live. The individual is influenced by the Tradition and one then helps and influences one's own family and friends. Gradually and hopefully, that influence and energy spreads in what is called the oil-spot technique: if you take a piece of paper and put spots of oil in different parts, the different spots of oil will gradually cover the whole paper.

What we have to do is to allow the energy to come into us and look for opportunities to use this energy. A person in a group shares the energy. A person cannot hold onto more energy than they can usefully use. This means that if for some reason he or she has more energy than can be used, rather than helping the person, it stops one, because one is not taking it, using it and passing it on—one is then stopping its natural flow.

# LOOKING AT YOURSELF

When the person receives it, uses it and passes it on, you have the complete circle being accomplished.

There is one basic secret to being able to use the energy correctly, and that is the intention of the person. If the intention is either not clear or weak, then the harmonious rhythm will be slowed down. What you must therefore do is regularly examine for yourself and repeat to yourself what your intention is. There should be a constant effort of examining your intention.

This does not mean that you are worrying about it all the time—it means only that you are thinking and reminding yourself of it. Always be conscious of your intention: mention it and discuss it with friends in the Tradition, as well as making it clear to yourself. Repeat to yourself: "I want to improve, I can improve, I should improve."

Who is watching you all the time? You are. But watch yourself harmoniously, and with kindness.

24.05.92

# RULES OR SECRETS OF THE NAQSHBANDI ORDER

## USING THE TEACHING & THE RULES

For hundreds of years, one of the functions of a teacher has been to explain the teaching and how people can best make use of it.

This teaching has been carried on continuously in the East for hundreds of years, but it has been available in the western world for only five or six hundred years.

Teaching the Tradition in the West is very difficult because people in the East have had a much longer contact with teachers. This means that some of the words and instruments we use are already familiar to people in the East, whereas in the West, these words and instruments have to be taught to people very carefully.

If you use the phrase "the energy of the Tradition" in the Eastern world, people understand what it means, because the energy which comes from the Tradition is used for particular things. It helps you to learn and develop. This energy can be used in many different ways, and one is taught by the rules of the discipline how to use this energy best.

If you have learnt and are conscious of the Naqshbandi rules, you will find situations in your everyday life in which you use one or other of the rules. The moment you take one of the rules and use it, you are making contact with the energy.

Every person in the Tradition is responsible for their own actions. In any situation, one should therefore always be thinking: "Which of the Naqshbandi rules can I use in this situation?"

# USING THE TEACHING & THE RULES

There are people who say that using and following these rules is a form of conditioning. This is not quite true, because the amount of conditioning carried by the average person is considerable. When I say that much of the conditioning you have must be overcome, it means that you are consciously following a discipline which you feel is right, whereas the conditioning you may have at the moment is one which you didn't have the choice of accepting or rejecting.

Part of the system of removing this conditioning and putting in something more positive lies in the use of books. Just as you regularly do an exercise, you should read texts from the Tradition regularly.

You never read the same text twice in the same way because your knowledge has increased. In fact, you are getting deeper and deeper into the text every time you read it.

Similarly, every time you do an exercise, you are getting more and more into the actual use of energy. This process of learning and developing is very slow and gradual, because you are struggling—in a way, you are fighting against the conditioning which has been imposed upon you. You are therefore trying to overcome a negative energy which exists all around.

Some people say that in order to develop in the Tradition, people have to fight against themselves. In fact, it is not really a battle, but it is an effort. Everybody has a certain amount of negativity within them. Nevertheless, this quantity is in fact very small, and it is just that they are sometimes surrounded by the negative.

This negative energy acts in a way to disturb your developmental thinking, but nevertheless this negative energy cannot control you or take you over.

# RULES OR SECRETS OF THE NAQSHBANDI ORDER

You must learn to do something which you may remember from the Naqshbandi rules, which is learn to look at yourself. You know within yourself when you are acting or thinking in a negative way, and if you see and feel that negative coming up, you must take some action to stop it.

I repeat, this negative cannot control you, it can only annoy you, and there are clear ways indicated to you of getting away from this negativity. The simplest way is to use your own personal zikr, because the power of the zikr is much greater than the negative in a situation. Ibn Arabi put it well when he said "To use a zikr is to wash your soul with words".

You must always be conscious of the fact that because everyone lives and earns a living outside the Tradition, we are all subject to negative influence—but your protection and refuge is the Tradition. If you use the books which have come down to us, you will find this repeated again and again.

You have to be very strong and very firm in using the techniques of the Tradition. Use any activity in the Tradition, but use it carefully, firmly and directly. Whether you are reading something, doing an exercise or a zikr, do it properly, correctly, and clearly—because, as I have already said, the moment you initiate a positive activity, you have the influence and energy of the Tradition coming into it with you.

If you really are in contact with your own feelings, you will know what to do—you repeat your intention to yourself, you ask for help, you do your zikr, you read a book.

You can also do another thing which is sometimes helpful, which is ask your Teacher.

Asking me is quite simple: the problem is getting an answer. In fact, I do read all the letters I get, and as I've said before, I welcome these letters because during the winter they keep my fire burning—but I do read them first.

Sometimes I reply quickly and sometimes I take a long time to reply. There are two very small and secret reasons for that: one is that people will sometimes write a letter, say of several pages, and then when they finish they reread the letter and find the answer. The other one is the question of when they can use the answer.

Some people think I have a crystal ball and write to me signing themselves "José" or "Enrico" without putting an address or street number on the letter. I can think of two reasons for doing this: either they give me some sort of magical credit or they think they are so well known that I will know automatically who it is.

You can understand why it takes a little bit more time to answer such a letter. I can tell from the postage stamp which country it comes from, but it is difficult to write a letter back to "Eugenio-in-Brazil".

There is a Nasrudin story about writing letters because there is a Nasrudin story about everything. A man went to Nasrudin and said, "Will you write a letter for me?"

"I'm sorry, I can't" said Nasrudin.

"Nasrudin, you write the letter and I pay you for it, so why can't you do it?" said the man.

"Well, you see, my foot hurts" said Nasrudin.

"You don't write the letter with your foot."

"Yes" said Nasrudin, "but my writing is so bad that I have to go to the man and read it to him."                25.05.92

# RULES OR SECRETS OF THE NAQSHBANDI ORDER

## WORKING WITH THE RULES

Working and being in the Tradition commits one to following certain rules and having certain terms of reference. Since the Tradition lives within and because of people, the absence of people would obviously mean the absence of a coherent Tradition and vice versa. Therefore when one is committed to acting in the Tradition, one should examine what this commitment means.

Apart from having certain terms of reference which you are encouraged to use in place of other terms of reference you have used before, you have a number of rules which you read, and it is expected that your attitude or behaviour should be a reflection of various aspects of the Naqshbandi rules.

When you have read the Naqshbandi rules, you can clearly see that they cover a vast horizon of social, personal or professional activities, because the Tradition essentially exists to influence or nourish, as we say, the inner being of the person. In this process, we are convinced that the assimilation by the person of certain rules and the following by them of certain disciplines will also produce an external action/reaction within the person, in the sense that their conduct or thinking will be mirrored by some aspects of some of the rules.

You don't take one or two of the rules and say "I will follow this specific rule today under all circumstances," because those circumstances will change throughout the day, whether they are personal, family or professional; or whether it is your state of health, being, or alertness that is continuously changing.

# WORKING WITH THE RULES

If you have decided to abide by one specific rule today, you are imposing a sort of burden on yourself. Rather than using the rule as a functional tool, the rule then becomes a self-limiting factor because your own interpretation of the rule becomes too narrow.

The answer to the question "How do I then impose these rules upon myself?" is quite simple. As the situations change throughout the day, and as your contacts, thought patterns, and the way you feel also change, so you try and make them harmonize with one or other of the rules you know, or even two or three of them at the same time.

If you know beforehand that you can take a day off, you can say "I will sit at home and meditate upon one of the rules or some other particular aspect of the Tradition," and that is perfectly all right.

You are then giving yourself the time and the freedom of choice as to which rule you are going to mull over during that day. But in the normal course of events, your contacts, your life, your situation and your feelings change so much that if you try and bring them into a context you have previously decided upon, it will not only have an inhibiting effect on your professional, social and other activities, but also on your practice of the Tradition.

"How can I fit this situation into this context which I have already decided upon?"— the answer is that you don't.

You find yourself in a context of need: supposing you have to take a decision, do something, undertake an activity, and for that reason you run through the rules in your mind and pick out one or another which you think could best help you, guide you or stimulate you in the particular circumstance you find yourself in.

# RULES OR SECRETS OF THE NAQSHBANDI ORDER

This also applies to a predictable circumstance : "I have a meeting with somebody in the afternoon. It will possibly be good, bad or indifferent, and I want to be able to influence that situation."

There is no question here of any sort of magic or jiggery-pokery business of casting spells or anything like that. You can influence a future situation, whether it is tomorrow, next week, next month or next year. You don't do it by rattling old bones, sticking pins in a doll or any weird things like that, but very simply, if you are going to be in a situation, you go into the situation prepared for it in the sense that you are carrying a positive charge into that situation.

Now you may have decided beforehand that the situation or interview or whatever may be difficult or problematic, and you will probably be tense or get angry, or something like that. If you go into the situation prepared for any of these eventualities, then an imbalance, which is getting scared, angry or becoming violent, will be negated by the fact that you have brought a positive charge of energy into the situation.

As the situation unfolds, if you allow yourself to react without reference to the Naqshbandi disciplines, then you are just a reactive person.

Before one acts in everyday life, one sometimes takes the opportunity to think before one acts. Then again, acts are sometimes impulsive—one does or says something on impulse, or for instance one buys something. One sometimes reacts to something in the form of what one would call a "normal reaction."

Having a normal reaction doesn't mean that you take five minutes to react to something someone says to you, because the person will not generally give you credit for the fact that you think before replying. Apart from the fact that you will get a reputation of being somewhat slow as a thinker, it also disturbs the harmony and possibly enrages the person even more. Thoughtful reaction is therefore that you are putting an influence on a circumstance by being positive, rather than being controlled or victimized by one or more circumstances.

If you are positive, well-disciplined and well enough trained, you should not just react on the spur on the moment, in a tit-for-tat way. People have very often said to me that they were discussing something with somebody and "suddenly the discussion turned into a quarrel or fight" or something like that. I don't believe that—I think this is an under-interpretation or under-evaluation of a situation.

Things do not "suddenly happen" like that. Two people may have opposite points of view and they may be capable of debating until one of them says the wrong thing or acts in the wrong way, and that enrages the other person, puts the spark into the bonfire, and up it goes. These things don't just happen for no reason.

If a person is following a rule which we will call *thoughtful reaction*—one can't and one is not expected to foresee every little circumstance which will occur during the next 24 hours.

Nevertheless, if such persons are aware of the way they think and react, and aware of what their tendencies, strengths and weaknesses are; they can bolster themselves up and diminish the strength of the others. This may sound like Dale Carnegie's "How to Make Friends and Influence People" but in fact it is nothing more than common sense.

If you ask nine or ten people "Have you ever been downhearted, disappointed, angry, frustrated or fed up?" and they all say no, I'm afraid they are not telling the truth.

# RULES OR SECRETS OF THE NAQSHBANDI ORDER

Everybody has felt this way at one time or another, but it is the way they have reacted that has made the difference.

Even a negative situation contains a learning factor, and if a person is defeated by someone else's political rhetoric in an argument, they have still learned something. Even if they limp away, they've paid for the lesson by the beating which they got, therefore something has been learned.

If someone says "We have no common sense: how can we avoid just being ourselves?" Well, who else are you going to be? The whole function of the Tradition is to help people evolve, not to make them into puppets. The way I react to things myself is because of my background, training, and other genetic and personal features which you all have and which are all perfectly normal. There are different circumstances under which you all become provoked or angry or nervous.

If I offered any one of you rabbit pie, you would probably not refuse it, but if you offered me rabbit pie, that would be an insult in Afghanistan—we're just strange like that. We are all composed of these reactions, and sometimes we can bring out a selective reaction.

If I am offered rabbit pie I should normally not get insulted and smash the pie into your face. I should be kind, patient and understanding about your foolishness; you don't understand my little ways, and I end up smiling and taking the rabbit pie and not eating it. My thoughtful reaction would then be : "Oh is that rabbit pie? I'm sorry, I don't eat rabbit on Fridays"— which is a useful way of avoiding things.

Of course, you cannot foresee every possible combination of circumstances before it arises within a situation. Nevertheless, you have a rough idea of what could lie ahead in the next 24 hours, so you say "At moments of tension, problems, disappointment or frustration, I will try and look around within myself for how I can best use one or two Naqshbandi rules, and apply it."

I guarantee that this works and I can make it work. A person can make it work because they are holding onto something that exists. The connection they are making exists. If they say "Poor little me"—no. It's "poor little me" plus the backup of the Tradition.

This does not make one a captive of the Tradition. It means that one becomes a part of the living Tradition as it is as and as it should be. People's dependance on the Tradition does not make them addictive, so that they cannot think of anything or do anything on their own without first asking and then doing as they are told. It simply makes them aware of the existence of an energy to which they can connect and from which they can receive nourishment.

It is essential, especially in this day and age, for people to be able to maximize on the time of quietness during the day they have available to them—for instance a period of calm for even five or ten minutes, a lunch break, or the evening.

People are turning over at too high a rate of revolutions because this is a civilized society and everything is supposed to be done fast. Everything is quick, so there is an element of tension which always exists.

As I have said so many times, tension is not attention. Tension in itself produces negative energy. Attention is focusing calmly and clearly on what one can do, on what one is going to do, on what one should do and on what one evokes and asks the energy of the Tradition to help one to do. Nowadays, any moment in which one can connect with a meditative, energy-generating or harmonic aspect of the Tradition and which one can then use in order to either remove oneself from one's exterior self for a moment, or to remove oneself from a tense or anguished situation that can sometimes be produced—not only can a person use these moments to do this, but they have a duty towards themselves to do so.

If someone has a headache and ignores an aspirin saying "I am going to conquer it by myself," praise be to their courage—but if there is a way to do it with an aspirin, it is all to the good that they should use it. The Tradition is not an aspirin in the sense that an aspirin produces a chemical effect, because contact with the Tradition means that people bring in a thought pattern through osmosis which harmonizes better with the Tradition, and which enables them to be less subject to the tensions, problems, questions, quarrels and difficulties that exist all around them.

You are not unconscious of what is going on around you— you are still sensing everything. What you are doing is maximizing on the time you have which is of a positive nature, or which you can convert into the positive.

Time has no colour. Time has no positive or negative charge, as such. People say time is what you make it. In a sense you can influence it. If you say "I have ten minutes," you can take a brick and hit yourself on the head for ten minutes, you're perfectly free to do so. You can also have a bath in ten minutes. You can also meditate or read something useful for ten minutes.

Those ten minutes depend on you, so in that sense you control time. We are all controlled by time in certain senses, but in others, if one asks "I have ten minutes, what shall I do?" —do something useful, something positive. Not only does that enhance the person, but it builds up one's confidence and ability to be able to switch to a positive note in a negative situation.

# WORKING WITH THE RULES

Like attracts like.

You cannot go around saying "I'm trying to obey such and such a rule, but it is so difficult because my circumstance is such-and-such"—have you ever considered whether the rule you are looking at harmonizes with the situation in which you are trying to use it?

Take the idea of *Khilwat dar Anjuman* (*Alone in a Crowd*)— if you are somebody who works in constant contact with other people, you may have the impression that there is no way you can distance yourself from them, unless you go away and crouch in a cupboard. So you don't do that. You say "It is impractical for me to try and use this particular aspect today, I'll try another one."

This means that a part of the person is working on one of the other rules while still remaining in contact with a number of people. One is not thinking "I wish they would leave me alone so I can go into a state of *Khilwat*."

One is one's own master. If one is constantly in contact with people and one wishes to absent oneself, there is a perfectly normal way of going off to smoke a cigarette or something for five minutes, and then coming back, but making good use of that five minutes. If you make use of those five minutes within the context of the Tradition, you will find that it builds up, and that it becomes easier to get back into that state and identify which rule you should use.

Living by the Tradition does not mean that you are surrounded by walls which inhibit your thought. On the contrary, the rules are supposed to encourage you; but don't choose them in a rigid sense. See what the situation is, see how a particular one might be applied or should be applied, and under what circumstances, and it may change even three

41

minutes later.

Unless you are conscious of the rules, unless they are familiar to you, unless you harmonize with them, and only if you do not think of them as alien and arbitrary entities which have been sent down to control your life—only then will you ever feel at ease with them.

They are not outside entities which "click in"—because they are all part of the same energy.

They are only divided into different rules for the sake of clarity, and they are all beads of the same tasbee.

So you have to learn to think of them as part of your own thinking: not as an imposition but as an encouragement.

30.04.92

# USING INFORMATION FROM A TEACHER

I don't expect everybody to remember everything. I would like to think that they do, but this is somewhat utopian. In fact, people forget more than they remember. However, as long as they remember certain things, it will always be valuable.

As I have said before, I repeat things in different forms with a different emphasis according to the need of the circumstance, the time, and other factors, so even if I give things out in a pretty concentrated form, one shouldn't think that it represents a sort of one-off opportunity in which one is forced to commit it to memory all at once.

If information has really been forgotten, or if one can't recall it within a certain pattern or context, then don't try and "put it together"; because at that point you are relying on memory, and memory is not always constant. You can get interpretation of the "Did I remember this or that?" or "Was it this or that?" type, which sets off a process of false memory.

I repeat things over and over again because it is necessary for people to understand certain fundamentals, without the listener or reader becoming involved in over-interpretation, under-interpretation or anything of a spooky or supernatural nature. I do repeat things. Much of what I say is on cassette or has been transcribed and will remain available.

You don't just try and remember everything I have said, every indication I have made, or every technique, tactic, instrument and piece of reading I have ever mentioned: first and foremost you try and learn to use them.

# RULES OR SECRETS OF THE NAQSHBANDI ORDER

I don't talk for the pleasure of hearing my own voice. I do it when I am required to do it and I am required to do it in a functional capacity, in order to teach people.

If one gets uptight after a meeting, saying "I've forgotten such-and-such a thing" or "Did he say this or that?" and so forth—if this way of thinking produces tension, then it is counterproductive. People have enough tensions without adding to them.

If one forgets a thing, for whatever reason, it will come back. Relax and don't push it. Don't drag a thing out kicking and screaming, because it can very possibly manifest itself in a different form.

You can also bring out something which you want to recall, which is either convenient or nice, or which accords with your particular mood at the time of your recalling it—and which is not always truthful. "Oh, I wouldn't lie to myself!"—Wouldn't you? People do it all the time; call it basic laziness or something else. But anyway, as I say, we're not looking for victims and we're not blaming memory, because all memories have faults—people are more or less alert at different times.

Try and remember things within contexts. This is why, in initial stages, I tend to break things down into concepts. It is true that they are basically theory, but your responsibility is to put them into practice, and my responsibility is to monitor the way you do it, and also help you to do it while pushing you to do it.

The bases are clear, the terms of reference are clear—it is the amount of effort and energy you put in that makes the thing fruitful.

21.11.85

# USING DOCUMENTS FROM THE TRADITION

As you probably know, there is a lot of documentation about the Tradition. You have translations of basic works and there are updated writings of people's experiences, voyages and studies.

These are all books of reference, and as the term implies, it is something to which one refers, for instance to explain or to go further into a particular concept—perhaps to examine one's own personal terms of reference and see whether they are akin to the Tradition's basic terms of reference.

If you read them in their entirety, most of these books are indigestible in the sense that if you start at page 1 and plough through to page 612 in one sitting, it is a tribute to your ability to read, and little else.

One works through them. You don't hop in and out in the sense that you do ten pages and then think "Right, I've understood that, I will jump lesson 7, 8, 9, 10 and 11. I'll go on to 12 because that must be more important and highly charged." It won't work, because the Tradition is constructed on a technical basis. You need lessons 2, 3 and 4 before you get to 5 because they introduce you to ways of thinking, terms of reference, and new points of view.

If you really try to jump the queue you may find yourself in a situation where you are examining a value, a point of view or a context, without certain terms of reference which you should have picked up along the way. And not only should you have noted and assimilated them, but you should have actually used them so that they are familiar to you.

The terms of reference and tactics we use in the Tradition are familiar because they are not and should not be alien or hostile to you—I mean alien in the sense that they come from somewhere "out East and I don't know."

The basic common denominator of all developmental paths or schools is the development of the human being. Geographical, racial, and other considerations are really not important.

If a developmental path or thesis is projected in a way which totally reflects its origin—i.e. by demanding that the people speak and understand the language of the founder; or that they are induced to dress, behave, think and eat exactly like the founder—it is not functionally efficient.

Many people have spent lifetimes learning Persian, Arabic and other languages in order to read things in the original, which is perfectly laudable. There is nothing wrong with this, except that it is very time-consuming.

If a person starts at a reasonably early age, takes a language as a degree course, and then is gradually able to read in the original, this is perfectly good: but there is a very complex area involved in a philosophical or developmental school.

The point here is that by definition, the language, terms of reference and nuances of the language are always further exploited by the person writing in Persian or Arabic.

The old teachers were masters of their craft in the language as well as within the Tradition, which means that there is no room for a sort of half-baked knowledge of the language. It has to be really known and fully understood with all the nuances, and that includes which particular nuance is implied in a particular context. This is not easy at all.

One therefore takes advantage of the correctly made translations of these books of reference, and one reads through and establishes a rapport with them.

One does not read them through with a notebook at one's side, copying out little notes or phrases which seem interesting, evocative, impelling or whatever, because all one will possibly get is a long list of words, contacts, phrases, terms of reference, which will tend to maintain a sort of adrenalin "high."

This is a situation devoutly to be avoided. I don't know what the equivalent of a philosophical adrenalin high is, but I'm sure that if there isn't one yet, somebody will invent one — but the point here is that an adrenalin high is a transitory phenomenon.

In the Tradition, this means ploughing through a great deal of material. Once again, it should not be assumed to be hostile or alien, it should become a part of you.

This material will not necessarily be tedious, but a lot of it is complex, and it does require application from the participant. It will require understanding, and above all it will require the development of an affinity towards the teacher.

undated 1985-90

# PRESCIENCE

Much has been said from time to time about a sort of prescience or precognition which people working in the Tradition employ under certain circumstances. This prescience has to be defined: what we are talking about is not the ability to choose the winning number in a lottery or the horse that is going to win tomorrow's race; it is a feeling that one should do a thing which is indicated by certain feelings which one has.

It is not an impulse. An impulse is something that happens because of certain circumstances coming together, and the person is impelled by the way they feel or by some outside circumstance to do a particular thing within a particular set of circumstances.

Prescience in the Tradition means that a person feels a distinct impulse to do an exercise, to read something, or to perform a certain function within the Tradition, in the almost certain knowledge that it is the correct thing to be done at that time, that they are in the correct state of mind or being to do it, and the circumstances are such that they will achieve a breakthrough or benefit from doing it.

There is no such thing as forcing this precognition or prescience upon oneself. One can sit down at a particular time and examine what one is doing, or what one should or could be doing, and then do something as a result of a mature and reasonable decision: say perform an action, a zikr, an exercise, or read something as a result of what one calls a thoughtful activity.

# PRESCIENCE

When prescience comes into action and when a person uses it, it is generally a result of the fact that they have been or are in the process of functioning correctly according to the Naqshbandi rules.

If a person has got these rules at the back of their mind and is examining them and their ramifications from time to time—without tension and with a certain amount of ease—then they will find that a particular rule suggests itself to them. That is the first step.

As I have said before, you do not decide in the morning which rule you are going to follow. You can follow one or two or even several of them during the day according to a change of circumstance, but if this feeling of prescience comes, it goes a little bit beyond merely recommending a rule. It recommends a course of action or of thinking, or it acts as a sort of indication, not of what is going to happen in the future but what one should be aiming to achieve.

There is a fine distinction here—some people say that prescience has to do with looking into the future. This is indeed one meaning of the word, and semantically speaking, this interpretation is correct. However in the Tradition, prescience is more a distinct indication or feeling than looking into the future in terms of hours and days.

One doesn't get the feeling that one is "looking into the future." What one is doing is looking into one's future being, in other words the capacity which one has within oneself to develop, and occasionally under the right circumstances, one will, if you like, get a glimpse of this person which usually represents oneself.

One is not seeing phantoms, nor is one seeing oneself in a week's, a month's or a year's time—one is getting a sensation of understanding. It is not so much a *déjà vu* or a feeling of something familiar, it's a feeling of having achieved a certain degree of development using certain deliberate and distinctive techniques, and arriving at a situation where one is projecting one's knowledge forward.

That may sound like something which is magical or superstitious, but it isn't.

In everyday life one can project oneself forward when planning one's work for the day or for the week ahead. As a living person on this planet, one is then projecting oneself, planning forward. It is also projecting forward, but a feeling of prescience in the Tradition means that a person projects their being forward toward a goal to which they aspire, and that goal is a certain deep and permanent consciousness—i.e., a deep and permanent feeling that they are working on themselves and with themselves in a correct way, to a correct measure.

When I say "to a correct measure," this is exactly what I mean. A person cannot push themselves into understanding or into development as a result of getting over-intense about it. There are certain steps a person must take and certain paths you must climb in order to achieve a certain degree of ability to understand your own being.

Once people have understood their being—in other words when they have a fairly clear idea of the strengths and weaknesses of their being—they can then make a fairly clear assessment as to how much, or to what degree, they can exercise or 'load' that being. No useful function is performed by forcing such a process.

There are books which have dealt with certain mystic brotherhoods in which—and mention has been made of some Sufi brotherhoods in which a person has physically isolated themselves from the world and indulged in a very severe diet, or even abstained from food or drink completely—and have created a certain state within themselves by means of constant zikr and repetition.

Physically of course, this is possible. Isolating oneself from all contact with human beings and following a very simple diet, or in fact fasting and constant repetition, under certain circumstances, can produce something useful.

However in many circumstances it will produce hallucinations—because the actual physical separation and lack of nourishment, plus certain rhythmic breathing or rhythmic movements, can cause a form of catalepsy, and a person can imagine things or have visions.

This is not what we are talking about. We are talking about knowing oneself to the degree that one knows what one can achieve under certain circumstances, whether these circumstances be an exercise, a visit to a place, listening to some music or reading a particular book.

A person should be able to feel that he or she is making some sort of progress, without necessarily putting a name to it. What form does it take? If they feel that doing a particular thing is becoming more familiar to them and they seem to handle it better or feel more in tune with it, this is a form of breakthrough which can also be called consciousness on the level at which they are at the time.

You can try and push yourself harder, you can try and load yourself with more activities, more information, more reading, more exercises, but there is a limit, and beyond that limit it becomes counterproductive because the person can get into a state of tension from trying to do too much.

# RULES OR SECRETS OF THE NAQSHBANDI ORDER

So the knowledge of oneself is one of the essential steps and one of the basic products of following the rules. These rules, which include *travelling in the homeland* or *travelling within oneself*, also mean that one is keeping oneself in tune with one's degree of development and harmony.

You are best placed to know if you are in harmony with a particular object, place, piece of music, text or exercise.

The feeling of prescience that you latch onto should therefore be measurably detectable. You should be able to say "This is right thing I am doing at this time—it is the right thing for my degree of knowledge and capability, and I feel in harmony with it"—but having felt or achieved that state: mark it.

This is an important thing to do. Just as when you do an exercise or perform a zikr you achieve a certain elevation of being, so you should try to remember that circumstance and how you then felt—because the next time you do an exercise you can start it off as near as possible to that point, which means that you are hopefully always starting from where you left off the time before.

Equally, if you get this feeling of prescience or "breakthrough," as some people call it—this term is only an approximation—one should remember the particular feeling or impact, whether it was physical, emotional or psychological.

Try and remember that, and remember also the circumstances under which this feeling occurred, so that at a future time, when one is able to examine oneself, one tries to look at oneself in the light of the feeling that one had before, and that one has already marked. It is often difficult to do this, because the feeling is not something which can be easily explained.

11.06.92

# CHANGING THE BEING

I think it would be useful to go through the various rules, so that people can understand more fully how they are applied and in which circumstances they can try and apply them.

In some versions they appear numbered in different ways, so I'll take the numbering which is most familiar to you. The order of numbering is not always exact in the sense that you have to apply number one before number two, or anything like that: the numbers exist simply to divide one from the other, because if you didn't people would seek to classify and differentiate between them in an artificial manner.

Learning the rules should not mean that one says "The other day I was doing number 4 and then I went on to number 8" and so forth—either to oneself or with anybody else. Referring to them by numbers is better left to discussions about bus routes, and not things like this.

When going through the rules, you don't have to feel forced to begin with 1 if you want to think about number 3 or number 4. You can start with any particular one, but don't think of them in terms of numbers, think of the actual phrase which describes them, because the phrase which is given to them has a meaning—it describes a state of being at a given time.

A digression about "being": in the past there has been a habit I suggest you devoutly eschew which is to think a lot about the "being," i.e., "What about my being at the moment? What or who is my being?" and that all gets wrapped up with things like "identity crisis" and that sort of thing.

# RULES OR SECRETS OF THE NAQSHBANDI ORDER

When I say that this particular rule applies in a particular form, it indicates the state of being into which you should put yourself at the time you are thinking about, or doing, that particular exercise. It is no more than the state of being which you are conscious of at that particular time.

Questions like "Is the whole of my being involved in this particular thing?" mean that we are getting into the area of debate so beloved of café philosophers, as in "Which of my beings is drinking this coffee?" It doesn't matter, as long as some part of the being is in contact with what one is aiming for in that particular circumstance.

If one says "My state of being at the moment is such-and-such," it is a total statement.

Now part of my being may be distraught, hungry, tired, worried or painful; but speaking about the totality of one's being implies that one actually knows what the totality of one's being is at any given time, and that one is able to involve it in a particular activity at a particular time.

It is in fact possible to do this, and a person can eventually arrive at that point—but to say off the top of one's head "the state of my being at the moment," is not only inaccurate, it is an arrogance. It implies that I can move the state of my being from A to B as if I was just changing my position in my chair.

You change the subject of your conversation, you change your thought pattern—you do not, without considerable time, effort, and years of practice, change your entire being from one given moment to another.

What you do is change a part of the being, a part of yourself: that part which happens to present itself on the surface. The part of you that you are more conscious of at a particular moment is the one which can and hopefully should accord with the rules you have here.

You might say "If I'm not supposed to judge what state of being I'm in at the moment, how can I judge something which you are telling me I'm not supposed to judge, in order to accord with something I only vaguely understand?"

It's just like when you have a number of familiar words or phrases like the zikrs. A particular moment, circumstance, train of thought or feeling might lead you to select one particular phrase, word, or zikr which accords with your need or your intention at that particular moment. Like attracts like.

One can therefore say "All right, in a given circumstance, let's say I would like to be "alone in a crowd": *Khilwat dar Anjuman.*

This is perfectly all right if it means that psychologically, physically and socially, in a certain ambiance, you can absent a part of yourself from what is going on. You detach yourself from the tensions, worries or confusions of the situation and "do your own thing" at the same time as appearing to be smiling and nodding at whatever is going on.

That is an obvious process. But if you apply another rule which requires more concentration, it would be the wrong one for that type of circumstance, because it would mean you are no longer participating in your present social situation.

You're absenting yourself too much, so that if somebody addresses a remark to you, you would have to say "I'm sorry I wasn't with you."

This can happen, and it's not a sign of anything seriously wrong, it's probably only that the conversation is penetratingly uninteresting. You choose which particular rule you might want to consider at a particular time, whatever the form it takes.

One needn't be worried by this. As long as one knows which particular rule one is trying to work on or use in a particular circumstance, then it's all right.

16.06.88

# DEFINING ONE'S TERMS OF REFERENCE

Whether professional, personal or otherwise, everyday life and circumstances provoke and produce questions.

Some of these questions are perfectly reasonable and normal ones a person can try and answer for themselves—in the sense that, say in one's profession, one asks "What am I doing"; "What am I aiming for" or "Where am I going"—or for instance, in a particular area of interest, say writing, poetry, or anything connected with the arts or crafts: "What am I aiming to achieve? What am I trying to do?"

Some questions which come up in these areas can be answered, explained or examined fairly easily. Nevertheless, they may not always be capable of being answered immediately, and sometimes they may not even be answered to the satisfaction of the person asking the question.

You might say that this sounds funny, because if one is putting the question to oneself, how is it that one can come up with an answer which is not satisfying to oneself?

The reason is very simple. If the question is about one's own achievement in a professional or other area, one may not be capable of looking at oneself or at what one is doing objectively enough to be able to produce an answer which may be unpalatable.

The answer may be one that a person isn't happy with, but if it is a reality, then they will have to accept it and do something about it.

# RULES OR SECRETS OF THE NAQSHBANDI ORDER

So that would therefore be an area where occasionally a person, faced with a question of where they are going professionally or so forth, having objectively looked at the situation, might come up with an answer which doesn't necessarily satisfy them but which could nevertheless be correct and encouraging, and which could either direct them or at least enable them to direct their own attention and activities in a more useful and positive way.

Of course, other questions come up which are subject to fairly easy answering. For instance, there is the economic question: one either has the money to do something or one hasn't—one has got to borrow it, or one can't. So there are certain situations where the answer to a question like "Shall I do this, can I do this or that?" can be plain and simple, providing the person looks at the situation with as much objectivity as possible.

I would call these questions worldly questions which relate to a person's everyday life, profession, or activities.

But there are other questions which increasingly come up with a lot of people about their own selves in relation to their development, their degree of consciousness, their place in the scheme of things, and also their general, shall we say, spiritual level.

These questions are very often provoked by certain doubts, fears, or reservations people may have in regard to themselves. Questions like "What is my place in the scheme of things? Why am I here? What am I doing? What is my degree of development? What is my degree of religious faith? What is or should be my relation with God?"— all of which, as I say, are of a spiritual level, and which frequently come up in different guises.

# DEFINING ONE'S TERMS OF REFERENCE

People can and do consciously or unconsciously ask themselves these questions, and they can sometimes be confounded by the answer.

It is not that the person wants to lie to themselves and produce an answer which will automatically confuse or distress themselves, because one isn't hopefully in the business of trying to confuse or distress oneself more than ordinary worldly things and worldly activities do. But what is important here is: a)— the way in which the person asks the question of themselves, and b)—that it depends on the terms of reference that they use, either in asking the question or in answering it.

A person can say, for instance, that one of the required characteristics of being a Sufi or dervish, is to be humble.

Apart from the fact that if you have twenty people you'll get possibly ten different definitions or explanations of what humility is—out of those twenty people, you will also get ten or fifteen different ways in which a person thinks that they should show humility: i.e., is humility bowing and scraping, walking along and tugging one's forelock, or stepping out of the way and being polite to everybody, no matter how they treat you?

Is humility to consider to oneself that, by comparison to the universe or galaxy, one is nothing?

So first, it's the term of reference or definition of "humility" that counts, and second, the way in which a person considers that they should demonstrate or show this humility, either to their own satisfaction or according to certain criteria which are established.

Here you can have a problem, because one's own definition of humility, i.e., "How I should behave in a humble fashion" and what might be called the accepted western idea of humility can be quite different.

A person, for instance, may say "Because of my personality, job or habit or something, I behave, if not in a rude way, at the very least in a fairly pushy or extravagant way" or something like that, and "I will therefore reduce this pushiness, this arrogance I am manifesting, and it will make me more humble." So that is one definition. One is saying to oneself: I am "too pushy" or "too arrogant" so I will become less pushy and less arrogant, and therefore more humble.

Now of course, that may be one's own judgment, and the judgment of the society in which one lives can be a different thing. People can say: "He or she is less pushy and arrogant than they used to be, but they are still pushy and arrogant." So even when one may be satisfied with one's own degree of humility, society may not accept that degree.

Everybody accepts the fact that many orders of monks wear coarse garments and subject themselves to long periods of fasting, abstinence or cold weather, and by that means show their humility to others. This is widely and perfectly normally accepted. But to get back to the spiritual level, the aspect which concerns us here is: how much of the humility a person is showing is truly coming from their own humble self?

I'm not attacking the monks and saying they are actually living the life of Riley—that they just come out occasionally to show they're humble, and go back and carouse—I am sure they live very austere and simple lives. But by my measurement, and by the measurement of the Tradition, it is not only the humility that one shows that matters, it is also the humility one feels that is a major factor in establishing humility.

# DEFINING ONE'S TERMS OF REFERENCE

In fact, one is in the best position possible to view oneself clearly. You can put on a patched robe and wander the streets, then come back and have a champagne bath—nobody will know except you.

So when people say, for instance, in a complaint one often hears, that something is wrong and "I can't live with myself" because of this thing or other, we come to point number three—in case you've lost count—which is "defining your terms of reference."

Your terms of reference may be on a different scale and of a different nature than the terms of reference employed in the society in which you live.

Defining one's terms of reference is an essential part of following the Naqshbandi rules, because if one knows what these rules represent and how they should be applied, there is no flexibility, in the sense that there should be no margin of error.

If you are engaged in an exercise or an activity which is concentrating on, or using, or trying to bring out, or follow, one particular rule—you should have defined your terms of reference to yourself in relation to that rule. You cannot and should not redefine your terms of reference each time.

27.02.92

# RULES OR SECRETS OF THE NAQSHBANDI ORDER

## CHOOSING A RULE WITHOUT WASTING TIME

Any degree of useful conscious or subconscious contact with the Tradition, builds up.

Unless you familiarize yourself with techniques, and work out how you can use them within the context of your job, family responsibilities and other things, and unless you feel satisfied that they are correctly working, you will not feel at home with them. You will always feel that they are perhaps some form of, shall we say, alien discipline which one does not really and truly understand. This would mean that one perhaps doesn't fully welcome it, and one would be therefore unable to put it fully into use.

If it is put into use in a halfhearted fashion, say because one doesn't really know how one can apply it, or under what circumstances it could or should be applied to oneself, then again, this can be a cause of agitation, in the sense of "Should I be doing this? Should I be doing that? I could be thinking of this or that rule, doing this one or the other."

Don't fall into the trap of choosing what one "should" be doing, because this can become an end in itself. If one is sitting for fifteen or twenty minutes in a train or a bus and running the various Naqshbandi rules through one's mind, thinking or deciding which one to think about, which one to act upon or how to act upon it, very often that fifteen or twenty minutes can be completely occupied by the process of looking through and deciding. By the time you have come to your decision, perhaps you've reached your destination and it's too late to actually do anything.

# CHOOSING A RULE WITHOUT WASTING TIME

So you have to try and keep these rules, as it were, running through your mind. There is no particular circumstance in which the particular rule should be applied, "and if one doesn't apply that particular one, one would be wrong." A black and white attitude—seeing it in terms of 'right' or 'wrong'—is false. There is never a wrong time to apply one of the rules or apply a technique based on one of the rules. There are better and better times to use them, but they are times provoked, produced or taken advantage of by you.

Say you see a situation developing, which may be of a personal, family or of a spiritual nature. First you see it or feel it developing, and then you work out which rule or rules, could or should best be applied under that circumstance.

As I say, there are better ways of applying certain rules under certain circumstances, but the choice has to be yours and it is a choice made by you alone. This choice is, as we say, drawn out of your inner being. It is attracted out by the circumstance.

You might think it's a piece of guesswork, but if you are thinking "I think this should apply in this circumstance" or "This could apply in that circumstance"—fine, apply it. Don't wait to sort of dip your toe in the water before jumping in.

Equally, don't jump in without knowing how deep the water is. There is such a thing as going into a situation and introducing one of the rules or an aspect of one of the rules without fully committing oneself to following through.

For instance, one may find that a rule can apply in the initial stages of a situation, and part of the way or halfway through the situation another rule could or should be applied.

There are no "hard and fast" situations—there are clearer or less clear situations.

# RULES OR SECRETS OF THE NAQSHBANDI ORDER

So again, when you're looking over the rules, define what you understand them to mean. I know you've got them all written down and more or less explained, but they should be part of your conscious thought process as well.

Also, a very familiar thing you should not do is embroider on them, in the sense that people tend to add little bits of something else—i.e., "Half of one rule plus half of another makes a new rule"—it doesn't.

There are certain very fixed parameters of the rules. If they are circulating within your consciousness, the particular rule which best applies or could be applied in a circumstance is attracted out; it is attracted to the surface.

In making the choice, you have to trust yourself. You hope you understand the parameters of the particular rule in question, and you trust your understanding of the rule well enough to be able to apply it in a particular circumstance.

Again, if there is a circumstance which seems to fall between two rules, don't debate with yourself about it. You can perfectly well say "I will use one or another" or go into one, and then phase into the second one. There are, in fact, very few circumstances where only one of the rules can apply.

The rules, after all, abut—in the sense that they touch on each other. They are part of a whole discipline, and just as circumstances within a situation are modified and become positive or negative—as circumstances within a situation change, so do the application of the rules, but not the definition of those rules.

You do not redefine the rule each time you think about it or each time you use it. You should know what you are applying, just as a painter or artist using a particular colour is

CHOOSING A RULE WITHOUT WASTING TIME

committed to that particular colour. If they want to modify the colour they know how to subtract a certain part of that colour's spectrum or add another colour to modify it.

So the use or application of a rule, based on the direct defining of your terms of reference of how you use it, is important, and it works on a harmonic basis.

"Harmonic" here means that like attracts like. If there is a situation which indicates a particular course of action to you based on a particular rule—and if you are fairly satisfied and confident with yourself—use it and apply that rule within certain very rigid limits.

It is better to apply a rule rather than to spend a lot of time worrying about which one to apply or not, or applying one for fear that something will go wrong. Nothing goes wrong if there is a reasonable harmonic coming from the rule and from oneself into a situation.

Only half of the skill is in learning the rules—in fact, even less than half, say twenty percent.

One can learn them parrot-fashion and run through them, look at them and apply them or not, but the skill which really comes in by experience and knowledge and feeling for them, is that you have defined them to yourself. You have defined how you, in particular, as an individual, apply a particular rule in a positive and useful way, in a given circumstance.

Familiarity with them is an indication that you are not afraid or worried about using them. They should not be used in such a way that one says, "Well, something awful might happen if I use the wrong one or make the wrong choice."

Even if you are not using the correct rule there will still

be a positive influence on a situation. It may not be the best one, it may not be the correct one, it may be out of place, but it will not be inharmonious.

If one feels a disharmony with certain events or circumstances, one should try and define the reason for this lack of harmony, and try and introduce a positive harmonic into the situation.

To sum up—you should make it a task to understand how you understand things.

It is no good saying that this, that and the other thing is "written down." If it is not understood, it can't be applied properly. Nobody in their right minds picks up a bottle of something unknown and swigs from that bottle without reading the label or without knowing the ingredients.

They say that knowledge is power. Yes, in the sense that if you know how to use your knowledge and use your being— if you know how to bring its latent qualities, spiritual and otherwise, to the surface—then that is power indeed. Power which gives you power to look at yourself and to develop yourself.

If it is power over other individuals, or over society in general, you're in the wrong business.

Unless you know the secret of transmuting base metal into gold, which would make you a millionaire overnight, you can't really claim power by knowledge. Nobody ever has.

Whether it be Jami, Hafiz, Rumi, Saadi, or anybody else, nobody has ever claimed power over anything other than aspects of themselves, because that was something they could indeed control, develop, modify and elevate.

# CHOOSING A RULE WITHOUT WASTING TIME

So be careful how you explain yourself to yourself. Don't go too deep. Don't make it too complicated. Don't project to yourselves an image of some immensely complex, intractably stupid or lazy, or for that matter, brilliant, personality.

Look at yourselves critically, kindly, carefully.

Unless you do that, you cannot apply certain techniques, because you will be applying them to a part of you that you don't know about, and therefore cannot operate. Just as, if you find yourself in a strange city, you need a street map; you can't just find your way by inspiration.

Equally, any knowledge you have which gives you an insight into yourself, into the way you react or can be influenced, into the way that you can develop yourself—into the way that you can maintain that elevation of consciousness—this is the power to which you should aspire.

27.02.92

# RULES OR SECRETS OF THE NAQSHBANDI ORDER

## 1. HUSH DAR DAM
### or *The Awareness of Breathing*

*Breathing is an important ingredient in exercises, either personal exercises or in a group. Breathing should settle down after a while to a certain rhythm. It settles down naturally, it should not be forced into being fast or slow. If you force the breathing you are using energy which can be used usefully in other ways. Allow the breathing to stabilize itself. Be aware of the breathing without being preoccupied with it. Breathing deeply is valuable and can and should be learned, or it can be taught by the Master.*

*The awareness of breathing in a certain manner.* Of course breathing is common in many meditation and other schools. Normally—commonly, I suppose—people breathe with the top one-third of their lungs: they basically pant—and occasionally there is a sort of a yawn or a deep breath.

Breathing has a very important function, because not only does it keep people alive, but the exhalation of stale gases and so forth clean the system, and the correct breathing, the deep breathing, tones the system.

When one does this, another one of the basic exercises the Lataif—is concerned also with breathing.

Deep breathing should not be artificial breathing. It is not breathing in, and then sort of holding the breath until one gets slightly giddy and then breathing out, because you can have hyperventilation, which is breathing very quickly and over-breathing, and that can precipitate a certain state of giddiness or dizziness and that sort of thing, which sometimes in some curious fashion, people equate with a sort of esoteric "high"— which is all very good if you want an esoteric high.

If you're doing an exercise, your breath is measured, it's correct. It's not laboured, it's not short; it is taken in and out, inhalation and exhalation; correctly and simply and slowly. There's none of the theatrics of the great sort of rasping; but there are some schools of the Tradition who do a sort of rasping and howling and that sort of thing, which is perfectly all right in its place.

One works out a tempo of one's own being with an exercise, convenient to oneself, and together with the de-tension which accompanies an exercise. These are just the basic things: there is a lot more about this which can be learnt and can be worked out.

21.11.85

In all of the various texts, you always find the first rule as *Hush dar Dam*; the *Awareness of Breathing*. This comes first and there are very good and fundamental reasons for this.

Firstly, from the physiological point of view, breathing is obviously a necessary function. The function it performs at a very basic level is that it takes in oxygen which is used for the system.

Now *Awareness* or 'taking note' of one's breathing does not mean becoming fixated with one's breathing, it's the opposite. Throughout our various texts it has been stated that when one is doing an exercise or a zikr, one's breathing should take on a certain rhythm, and that it is not necessary to use a metronome to breathe according to a particular speed. One's breathing slows down naturally and this is why one should allow a period of time for one's breathing to settle down to a certain rhythm before one does an exercise or zikr.

If there happens to be a rhythm or music in the background of this exercise, the tendency will be to try and follow the rhythm of that music in the breathing. This is all right, as long as one is conscious of the fact that one is trying to develop deep breathing.

Physiologically and psychologically speaking, deep breathing is more beneficial; one is taking in more oxygen. There is also a limit to that : you don't want hyperventilation, when a person is taking on more oxygen than the body can process and one is then getting a sort of "high" on it. Psychologically, furthermore, deep breathing is symptomatic of calmness, quiet, tranquillity, lack of worry, lack of anxiety.

Having established a moment of calm around oneself and within oneself, one then aims to achieve the physical calm associated with deep breathing : a feeling of warmness, quiet and relaxation.

Being aware of one's breathing is not the same as being wary of it or watching it, because there you've got the element of anxiety: "Am I breathing right, is it too fast, is it too slow?" Let it find it's own specific rhythm given the particular circumstance under which it is being done. Apart from any waste of energy which one might later miss because one was over-watchful in one's breathing, there is a degree of attention which is being taken away from what one is doing.

When establishing this breathing rhythm, one should obviously try as much as possible to establish it for the purpose of going onto another activity, which is the zikr or exercise. The focus of the intention is firstly on establishing the breathing, and then doing the zikr or the exercise. Any physical or psychological energy spent on worry, or any degree of tension or anxiety, detracts from the second step of the zikr or exercise.

As one gets into these rules, one is aiming to establish a sort of ideal situation. Everybody in their own mind has an idea of the ideal situation in which to sit down, think, or do a zikr : "Go and sit in a corner of a tekkia where everything's nice and calm and quiet."

That's fine, except that there's not always a tekkia near at hand. One then selects a place in one's own home or somewhere else, and one creates an ambiance of calm around oneself as far as possible. If you cannot choose an ideal place or circumstance, choose a circumstance which is as good as possible, and then create a more beneficial ambiance around and within oneself: not only to encourage one's ability to do certain zikrs or other activities, but also to cancel out any external disturbance, noise or other things which can cause a lack of concentration.

What you're doing in achieving this *Awareness of your Breathing* is preparing a fertile situation for another step.

A person should obviously aim at achieving a certain rhythm of breathing that they themselves know. They don't need anybody hovering over them saying "Ah, you're breathing too fast" or "You're not breathing enough," because in most circumstances a person will do a zikr or an exercise by themselves, and therefore they have to be the judge of their own breathing or activity.

If one's intention before doing it is sound and correct, and if the place is reasonably quiet, then one will be able to judge for oneself, by experience, whether one feels comfortable in this breathing or not. This is something one has to judge for oneself.

# RULES OR SECRETS OF THE NAQSHBANDI ORDER

It is possible to be taught how to breathe, but before anybody picks me up on that, there are only certain circumstances under which particular types of breathing can be taught. These are specific forms of breathing which accord with certain specific activities or exercises. So just take record of the fact that it's possible to be taught, and don't worry about putting in your application.

16.06.88

## 2. NAZAR BA KADAM
### or *Watching over the Steps*

*"Watching over the Steps" means attention to the times and opportunities of action and inaction, action being when you should do something positive. A movement, exercise or piece of reading which is positive and useful. Inaction means pause or halt. Pause , halt or patience can be equally useful. To say it is better to do something rather than nothing is not always correct. There are moments when positive inaction is valuable. When you try to use the energy when the moment is not right you get frustration and confusion. The right action at the right time is the secret. If you are watching your steps you will get nearer to doing so.*

The second one is : *Watching over the Steps: attention to times of action and inaction.* Now *Watching over the Steps* implies a certain amount of caution in one's activities in the Tradition; a certain amount of thought.

*Attention to action and inaction*—when does one feel that this is the right time, circumstance, to do a particular thing? Action is not always profitable in the sense that doing something is inevitably better than doing nothing.

Sometimes it isn't.

If you're in a rowboat in a moderately rocky sea and you have no oars, the worst possible thing you can do is to get up and try and balance yourself, because you will tip the boat over.

73

# RULES OR SECRETS OF THE NAQSHBANDI ORDER

If you indulge in inaction at that time—which is huddling down in the bottom of the boat and hoping that somebody has noticed and will come and tow you in—then that is inaction, by definition, but it is the correct action for the time. So therefore, in the circumstance, you work out what is the correct action or inaction. So the two, in a sense, are the same.

21.11.85

*Watching over the steps* does not mean a tension situation, as if one was telling oneself: "I'm going to watch out in case I fall over my own feet."

If the ground has been marked by saying "My intention is to do this" and if, as far as possible, one has arranged the circumstances, the timing and one's own availability, one is then able to concentrate on what one is doing without watching oneself.

People are notoriously quick to fall into negativity, and say "What am I doing wrong?"

Very often they are doing a lot of things wrong simultaneously, but by the law of averages they are probably also doing something right. If they judge themselves from a conditioned viewpoint, they may find themselves to be a disaster and fall into a complete depression.

If one is being constantly self critical, this leads one to a self-antagonistic attitude: "Oh, I hate myself"; "Oh what a fool I am"; "Oh poor old me" and then after that, you go on to: "Oh well, I'm just like that" and then one excuse follows after another.

A constantly nagging, critical or hostile attitude will either provoke a hostile reaction, or else excuses. Once one gets away with one excuse to oneself, then there's another excuse, and a

74

third, and then you look around and you find justifications.

Watching oneself, watching one's behaviour, watching what one says or does is perfectly all right. There are normal civilized social or legal norms and requirements, and one accepts them.

One uses a certain amount of caution when crossing the street, driving or doing anything, and one can perfectly well be moderately critical of one's own performance in a situation. One can analyse it and think how one could have done better or what one should have said. One can ask why it went wrong, if it did go wrong: "What could I, what should I have done?" in a reasonably quiet and harmonious way.

The self-critical examination in the sense of: "I will tear myself to pieces every evening to find out what went wrong" becomes an end in itself, and you end up chasing your own tail.

People even become hostile towards themselves and blame themselves for mistakes because they very often won't put it down to something simple—they prefer to find a sophisticated or intellectual reason, because it's "more important." Such people would consider that saying something like "Well, I had just better watch it in that area" is not good enough.

So *Watching over the Steps* means one is watching circumstances while feeling when is the right time for action, when is the right time for inaction, and when is the right time for pause.

Action is doing something, inaction is doing nothing, and pause is a sort of suspended state, as in "pause for thought." Perhaps one is in the process of doing something and one needs to consider the implications or the results of following this particular course of action. One can say "I'm going to stop what I'm doing—I'm not going to go into inaction, which is the "doing nothing" phase, I'm just going to go into neutral, as it were, pause for reflection, and see what I am doing."

In what context? Again with these rules, one is talking about the context of the Tradition, but many of these rules are very valid in ordinary life and can be applied.

However the implications of applying these rules both to one's inner life and to one's exterior activities can be difficult, because you can have a situation where a person is inclined to look at a situation from two seemingly different points of view, and occasionally from two completely opposite or even hostile points of view.

An example is the famous question which somebody did ask me: "I have inherited a few thousand dollars—which is better for my being, to open a hamburger stand or to sell kilims?" This question is more properly addressed to one's bank manager.

If it is near a cinema, sell hamburgers, and if you are in the middle of Teheran, where there is a lot of competition, selling kilims won't do you much good.

If the question is wrong, it's because it is based on a false premise, as in "If one has two thousand dollars, should one give it to the poor or gamble it away?" Well, that is not the sort of question which is properly addressed to me.

I don't get angry, but there are questions that people have asked me that you wouldn't believe. It is just that simple common sense or market research provides the answer to the question about kilims and hamburgers.

# NAZAR BA KADAM

So watching over the discipline of one's thoughts is just as valid as *watching one's steps* because *step* or *kadam* in the Tradition means step or pace, but it also means the different stages in one's thought process.

Given the human mind, if there is a possibility of spending endless time debating with oneself over various different harmonious or hostile possibilities, the person will spend inordinate amounts of time supporting one, and then going and looking at the other one, and then going back and looking at the first one, and then hopping about. This can simply be a way of avoiding a decision.

Using the Naqshbandi rules only becomes complicated when people try to apply them to a situation which should be capable of being solved by normal experience, horse sense or past history.

When one detaches oneself from everyday life and activities and makes time during the day or after the day's work—that is when one can usefully benefit from reading and doing things of an active nature.

*Watching over the steps* is not just watching oneself "to catch oneself out." One is watching for opportunities, circumstances, or what are called coincidences: "Oh wasn't that strange, I met so and so, I saw such and such a thing." Right—build on them.

Part of *watching the steps* is also being alert and aware. As I am sure you know, alert does not mean tense and anxious, any more than aware does not mean swivelling one's head round 360 degrees.

It means being open to positive impacts, situations and energies, latching onto them, holding onto them and using them.

RULES OR SECRETS OF THE NAQSHBANDI ORDER

One is watching in a relaxed, not in a critical way as when one says: "I'm going to make a mistake and then I'll catch myself out." That is not its function.

It is rather "I am going to act and behave in such a way that I can hopefully prevent myself from making a mistake"— in doing that, I am not looking over my shoulder watching myself creeping along and trying to catch myself out, because that leads to paranoia.

It is a situation where you are watching, alert, and prepared to capitalize on a positive situation, to enhance or develop a situation further. It means that you are always producing a positive current of yourself and within yourself: like attracts like.

It doesn't mean to say that one goes out and wanders the streets swivelling one's head behind oneself looking for something, because the problem then is that one will find it. A man in a white coat will probably come and lead you gently away. This is counterproductive, it is not *watching*, it is being unaware.

What happens when we sleep and we are unaware?

There is no anxiety factor in the sense of: "Have I missed something?" Like attracts like. If one is emanating something of a positive nature and one comes into contact with a person, a place, a thing or a current of a positive nature, the contact will inevitably relate. Being on the alert for a situation is being watchful.

This is thrown in as a sop to the people who say that "If you try and use an energy when the time is not right, or the situation not propitious, you lose energy."

# NAZAR BA KADAM

A person won't lose any energy in the sense that "I was in the wrong situation and I was all hyped up and full of energy, and there was this situation which I thought was good, and then all my energy suddenly disappeared." The energy one was likely to have had at such a time was probably a superfluous or nervous energy, which is normally discharged in any number of different ways.

The watchfulness, the being alert, is not being anxious in the sense of: "I must find a positive situation, otherwise ..." Such anxiety is a recipe for confusion, because you will have people crashing about looking for positive situations, colliding with each other, thinking that the fact they walked into a tree has a superior meaning. Walking into trees is not to be recommended.

The example of walking into trees is hopefully a bit of an exaggeration, but the analogy here is that there can be a pseudo-situation, in which a person is all hyped up and yet convinced that he or she is really full of useful energy, and they are looking so hard for a situation to absorb this overflow that they then produce the situation themselves.

There is nothing wrong in that except for one thing: if a person gets into the habit of confusing a pseudo-situation with a real situation, how does one come to know the difference?

The basis of all situations, experiences or harmony is of course that very word, the harmonic of a situation. If you like, one can imagine a harmonic existing: this is where a person's knowledge of themselves, however fragmented it may be, comes into play.

If one says "I'm not going to confuse myself or lie to myself" and one then examines oneself with self-knowledge during an activity, and one finds that what one is actually doing is standing in Hyde Park banging one's head against a tree trunk—and that there is nothing galactic about the headache one is experiencing—one should then say to oneself "This is not a correct situation."

Yes, this is a caricature, but people do think like that. They don't often do it willingly, but they sometimes counterfeit or imagine experiences to suit their convenience, or to suit their particular fixation of the moment, or simply because they are daydreaming.

None of these situations are particularly negative or obnoxious, providing one recognizes them as being such. And if one is watching one's steps or watching one's behaviour, and also being alert to circumstances and opportunities of using energy, then the possibility for this kind of pseudo-experience to express itself becomes smaller and smaller.

If one deludes oneself into thinking that a pseudo-experience was of some transcendental nature, then one is satisfied with accepting counterfeit coin.

Of course, in the outside world of trade, commerce and industry, since it is a necessary commercial activity, all companies and individuals project themselves as being bigger and more important than they are. The hard-nosed industrialists or public relations men, the people whose job it is to build an image, know the facts in the balance-sheet of the company they are selling: they know how much it is worth and they know that their business is to make it look bigger. This is their profession, and there is nothing wrong with it: it's the name of the game in industry or commerce. Nobody with a dress shop in Bond Street says to customers "Come and look at the lousy old rubbish I had made up in Cyprus and which I've marked up five hundred times" because this is going down-market to an unnecessary degree. They project an image and people buy the label.

# NAZAR BA KADAM

The difference of course is that in commercial and industrial activities, this is a known fact. You say to the finance director of ICI, "How much are you worth?" and he says "Billions and billions and billions and billions." He knows that he has exaggerated by one billion, but since he knows it himself, it's all right. He only gets into trouble when he thinks he has actually got billions and billions and billions and billions, and then some body else with a billion more comes along and takes him over: he's made a mistake.

In commerce and industry a person does not or should not delude themselves into thinking they are worth billions more than they actually are, because the result is simple and plain. They go out of business. It's not the end of the world, it's just the end of their business.

In a person's own inner life and personal judgement of themselves, everybody should have a reasonably high estimate of themselves: their ability, their intelligence, their looks, their dress sense, their cars, their general tenor of life. This is certainly tempered by humility and, as far as possible and as far as they have learnt, knowledge of what they really are.

But this positive estimation of oneself should be tempered by a real knowledge of oneself, however deep or superficial it may be. It doesn't mean to say one is constantly judging oneself: one is *watching over one's steps* in the sense of: "Did I take advantage of that situation?" or "Am I deeply and consciously trying to be harmoniously in tune with a certain situation?"

Again, which situations—where? "Oh, I will harmonize with the 31 bus"—not necessarily. It is enough to pay your fare and take your ride.

Watching and being aware is different from carping, criticizing, finding fault with oneself, self-abnegation, hanging one's head low, or strutting around like a peacock. There is a harmony between the two. If one aims for that harmony, it is a watchful state in which one becomes quietly confident and convinced of the fact that one can, and will, attract and benefit from the positive.

You don't convince yourself of it, you just believe it; because look at the other side of the coin: "Oh, I can never do anything"; "Oh, nothing good ever happens"; "Oh, all the people I know are horrid"; "Oh everything is awful"; "Oh, they're polluting the atmosphere." This attitude of lamentation is possibly the other side of the coin.

Now why should a person have to go all the way from one side to the other? "I am quite content with myself but they are indeed contaminating the atmosphere"—both of these things can be true, but they have to be looked at in a balanced way.

If one's whole energy or thought processes are taken up with earning a living 18 hours a day, then the priority is earning a living. One can certainly tear oneself apart and say "I should be using more time on myself" and this may be perfectly true, but even if one is working 18 hours a day, I defy anyone to say that they cannot find 5 or 10 minutes from those 18 hours for themselves.

One minute, spaced out every five minutes, is still time: "One day I'll take a week off and I'll walk in the moors and talk to the moorhens"——Yes, but there are other things which conspire to prevent one from doing so, like paying the gas bill.

So *Watching over the Steps* is also watchfulness over one's priorities: don't set them against each other. There should never be a situation where one says "Is it better for my inner self to have a meal or do a zikr?"

# NAZAR BA KADAM

Such a question should not propose itself. If you are hungry, eat—and on the basis of the energy you get from the eating, do a zikr immediately afterwards or at some subsequent moment.

You do not find contradictions in a proper cosmological system. Man produces contradictions because, since he is "free" and "rational," he produces alternatives, and given half a chance, the alternatives will be poles apart.

"Shall I drink this cup of coffee, or smash it on my head?"

No rational being thinks like that, but in certain ways people do think that way, although not quite so abruptly. Yet if a person wasn't "supposed" to be rational, they wouldn't even actually think of the possibility of smashing it on their heads.

You might say "Ah, but no, drinking the coffee and then smashing it on their heads is irrational" but man is basically rational, not irrational.

It is only because he has thought it all out too much in terms of "What can I do with that cup of coffee" that he has produced the second alternative of "I'll pour it down somebody else's neck" or any further permutation of this sort of thing, such as "I'll look up coffee in the Encyclopaedia Britannica and then go to Brazil to see whether it actually grows." You might call it the "I'll get back to the basis of everything" sort of thinking.

So *Watching over the Steps* is thinking a little bit less and doing a little bit more, in a useful way.

16.06.88

# 3. SAFAR DAR WATAN
## or *Travelling in the Homeland*

*In this case Watan or "Homeland" means inside the person themselves. This is distinct from travelling 'outside' themselves for the purpose of learning, making contacts or visiting places to experience the Baraka. Travelling in the Homeland means observing oneself in a detached, tranquil, non-critical way— gently critical, not self-accusing—and learning from one's errors.*

Let us consider *Safar dar Watan* or *Travelling in the Homeland*.

*Travel in the Homeland*, or *the observing of one's own self.* Now we use the context of *Homeland* to mean 'within oneself.'

It's called the *Homeland*; it's also called the *Heartland*, meaning that one examines oneself, again, from an objective point of view and yet also with a certain amount of sympathy and patience—again, without continually seeking to fight oneself or blame oneself. And when examining oneself, as it were, travelling around.

Acquainting oneself with oneself, as they say, in the sense of "What makes one react?"

What area of the body influences one's thinking or one's actions is all part of knowing oneself and knowing one's reaction to circumstances.

21.11.85

84

# SAFAR DAR WATAN

Now *Travelling within one's self* or *Safar dar Watan* means just that. It's a simple definition and it should not be subject to change or modification each time one does it, for the simple reason that, firstly, if it is properly understood and used, each time it is used one is building up the ability to use it further.

It is like any muscle. You are using a faculty more and more, and knowing it better enables you to do it a little bit better each time, because you take off, hopefully, from the point at which you left it last time.

If you impose upon yourself, shall we say, a new explanation, or re-examination of the term of reference of *travelling within oneself*, for instance by adopting a different form of travel each time—well, we all know that this travel is a spiritual journey, a spiritual travel. It is not by bus, train, airplane, bicycle, horse or donkey.

You don't therefore say, "Right, this time I will use the number 88 bus. Last time I used a donkey" because the actual basic fundamental of travelling within oneself or examining oneself, is happening on a spiritual level.

Therefore, having defined that to oneself you hold onto that. You don't say: "This week or next week, I will do it in a different way", because if you do that, you lose time. You lose impetus and momentum and concentration. In that particular way, you lose your investment of time.

27.02.92

Travelling inside oneself and observing, is different from the second rule which is *Nazar ba Kadam* or *Watching over the Steps*. *Nazar ba Kadam* implies a state of observation with caution, being careful, watching. Not apprehensive, not worried about doing anything, not afraid to do anything, but literally *watching* and observing. Feeling the situation, and feeling what is the right thing to do under the right circumstance if the intention is right.

*Travelling within oneself* implies examining oneself, observing oneself : now this is a noncritical observation. One can and should observe oneself, one's actions, one's impulses, and the results of one's actions in a reasonably critical way.

The word "critical" is very often used to imply a sort of hostile atttitude: this does not necessarily need to be so. If one watches oneself or examines oneself with certain terms of reference in mind at the same time, this is examining in a useful way: it is critical, yes, but in the sense of analytic.

Generally speaking if you say somebody is being critical, it tends to mean in a pejorative or negative sense: the person is going to produce criticisms. Almost any person, activity or situation can be criticized—it depends whether this is objective or subjective criticism, whether it is friendly or hostile criticism.

When *travelling within oneself*, examining oneself, examining one's motivation, or examining the results of what one does; one's aim should be critical only in the sense that it is analytical, i.e., looking at something—it is not trying to find fault.

In a given situation—supposing you are doing something with three or four other people and working with those people produces a certain result. If the result is bad and the activity has been a failure, people will gather round and examine the situation and everything in a critical way, usually to apportion blame or find fault: "Who was responsible? Who did it?" so they can then blame the person or blame themselves.

Equally, if an activity succeeds, they may gather together

and apportion the benefits along the lines of "You did well, you did less well, that person did more, that person too" in the sense that everybody is happy uncritically: "It worked, wow! It's great, therefore we don't have to examine it any further."

Both of these attitudes are incorrect, if one focuses on oneself, if one is travelling within oneself—because they are the two extremes. If you do something and it turns out badly, you most certainly examine it in a reasonably level and calm way: "What went wrong, what did I do, what did I say?" This is not criticism in the sense that you are trying to find yourself totally responsible and then feel guilty. You are simply trying to see what happened : you examine it, find out and learn.

Equally, if you do something and it works out well, there is also a lesson to be learned from it.

So examination, when it's a gentle self-criticism, is not a sort of do-it-yourself psychoanalysis, it is actually *travelling*.

Now to travel implies going from one place to another, and during such travel a person will usually observe things like the fauna and flora, the houses, the road, animals, other travellers, other people, as well as traffic, weather conditions and various other things. They will sometimes observe such things subconsciously and sometimes by actually taking note of them, not necessarily giving them any great importance—but afterwards they may sit down in the evening after travelling from A to B and play back in their mind what they saw, who they spoke to, how they felt, what it was like.

Some people rely on their memories, some people write everything down in diaries so that they can go through it, remembering and recreating situations or experiences—this is why the word *travelling* is used here.

# RULES OR SECRETS OF THE NAQSHBANDI ORDER

One could equally well give it another name, but the technical names of the Naqshbandi rules are specifically chosen to mean exactly what they say. The word *Watan* is a very familiar word which has a very special meaning, it is *Homeland*, not any land—it is not travelling in the countryside, nor is it travelling in a state or travelling anywhere—it is *Travelling in the Homeland*.

In Naqshbandi parlance, when you talk of *Watan* in such a context, it means oneself, because one is an entity, just like a homeland, and travelling is just that: moving from A to B, observing, recalling, examining, not in a completely subjective way. When I say "Don't be critical," it means don't be hostile or systematically negative in the criticism. In one's *Travelling within Oneself*, if one finds adequate cause or reason to level some criticism against oneself, then it is right and proper that one should do so. Whether recalling that particular event makes one feel guilty, ashamed, sad, stupid, foolish or something else doesn't really make a difference.

If one is *Travelling within Oneself*, i.e. face to face with oneself, one can and should be honest. One knows what one saw, heard or experienced in a particular travel: it's all somewhere in the memory. Conveniently and understandably, the memory is selective: it tends to remember things which it liked better, or which were more pleasant. The memory associates situations with feelings.

If a person has had a particularly uncomfortable trip in a car, a coach or a train, some days, months or years later they can recall that particular voyage and recall the fact that it was uncomfortable—say it was hot, stuffy, the vehicle or whatever was shaking and the seat was uncomfortable and tight—one does not recall exactly the degree of discomfort because the pain or suffering which one experienced is in fact not a positively useful feeling or sensation to be exactly remembered.

# SAFAR DAR WATAN

It was a suffering, a pain, and uncomfortable: one doesn't want to recall the exact degree of pain.

It's a familiar phenomena—if any of you share my phobia for dentists, you will understand that if one could conjure up exactly what happened the first time the fellow said "This won't hurt" and shoved the drill straight into a nerve and one went through the roof—if one could exactly summon up that degree of pain, not only would you never go back, you would never even go down the same street as a dentist.

Fortunately, such a degree of pain is not retained, firstly because it's not necessary. The experience itself—you went and knocked on the door and somebody said "Come in" and he reached back for the drill—all you have to do is remember that, and it makes you brush your teeth three times a day and not eat sweets. The useful factors have already been learnt from the experience and you don't have to re-experience the whole thing.

So you remember the goings-on and that is enough. You've got the essentials of the situation and you hopefully don't have to say "Dentist? What's a dentist?"— if you have blanked it out to that degree, good luck, tell me how—but I don't think one does.

Therefore one doesn't have to replay everything—"I remember, it was dreadful!" is enough. You take the valuable things, the necessities, and as time passes, the mind or capacity of recall goes through the files and pigeon holes, looks and takes things out, looks at them, keeps the ones which are valuable and dumps the ones which are not necessary.

The memory retains selectively. Memory can also be helped to retain more strongly and vividly by a simple trick from elementary school, and that is by using an image of something.

This can be used to recreate or re-experience a sensation in one's mind which one might have felt in a particular circumstance.

You might say "If that is so, is it not possible that I could play back my encounter with the dentist and experience the same degree of suffering?" The answer is no, because the mind, the memory, doesn't want to hold pain and suffering.

Also, the image, ambiance or feeling one wants to recreate is one of happiness or feeling at home in a circumstance, in an ambiance, in a place: these things are all positive. So every retention cell in the mind which keeps the sounds, the feelings, the taste and everything are all available—they're all in there, stimulated, getting ready to push their memory-piece out into that situation.

So you can recreate the ambiance, and, assuming that it is positively useful, all the memory banks will become involved in that process, and they will put in the most seemingly inconsequential things. Now, why and for what purpose have they remembered them?

If one went to a particular place which had a very significant effect upon oneself, if you think it over and sort of put your mind back and walk through the place again—again the travel factor comes in—you walk though the place and replay it in your mind, encouraging your mind to bring out other things which were occurring at the same time—you will find, as I say, that there are so-called inconsequential things.

You might remember "Oh yes there was a bird singing" or "A cat crossed my path" or "A bird flew low"—now these are inconsequential in the sense that they are not the major important factors in that situation—but they do go towards putting the whole thing together, and they do show that the mind is not only capable of retaining, but of filling in details as well.

# SAFAR DAR WATAN

Now why this happens and how this relates to *Safar dar Watan* is that when you are recreating, or imagining, or remembering, you're also travelling within yourself in the sense that you are going to various parts of yourself which retain the feeling, the touch, the heat, the smell, the sound or the sight of all these factors.

If these factors can be consciously called up to fill in the picture and run it over, going back, again, in the sense of "What was it like there? What was on the right? What was on the left? What was in front?" and one can then work it through, playing it through again—you can fill in, as I say, a lot of seemingly inconsequential factors. That is on a conscious level.

Now imagine that for every level of conscious retention in which you are consciously remembering a particular situation or ambiance with a little bit of effort—for every conscious level you can pull up, there are many interior or subconscious levels which are much more firmly implanted into the person, and which work together with the other deeper levels.

You have a situation where you are looking, if you like, downwards—if you have four or five levels there, you look at them and they appear. However there are situations which are valuable, and you look down on those situations as if you were on the top looking down—each level is, in a way, transparent or translucent, like so many layers of thin plastic, each layer bearing some sort of outline or imprint—and looking through all of them from the top, you see the whole pattern emerging.

The whole pattern is already there, imprinted on the deeper memory cells. In the context of the Tradition, the skill is to be able to look at this picture, this situation, and take those portions on which you want to work at the moment out of it.

# RULES OR SECRETS OF THE NAQSHBANDI ORDER

This is where both the conscious and the unconscious *travelling* works—the travelling within yourself, examining yourself. You're not regressing yourself back, and you're not looking for any kind of predefined psychological or psychometric profile or any rubbish like that—you're looking at your actual person, yourself.

There are areas where the picture may not be as clear as other places—one can examine such places and try and explain what their function is, or one can leave them. I'm not talking about "hidden secrets" or "dark corners of the mind" and all those sort of novel-type situations, I am talking about areas which are not familiar to oneself.

If they are not familiar, again, it doesn't necessarily mean they are objectionable or hostile. The human consciousness—and a little bit of the subconscious—is afraid of the dark. If one is travelling along, and a small road leads off in another direction, and it's narrow and has trees and things like that, one doesn't say "I must go down that road and find where it goes." Equally, one doesn't say "Oh, all dark, narrow and leafy roads are dangerous"—again, the two extremes.

One is travelling, so one examines, at the same time as one is making use of one's experience and feelings and intuition. And every seasoned and experienced traveller uses something else, which is a compass.

Now your dependance on the compass depends on how fast you are travelling or how erratic your voyage is. But for a traveller, it is enough to occasionally check the compass and make sure that the direction is right. If then one is then obliged to make a detour as a result of circumstances or a change of time or something like that, one can always then check to make sure, and come back on the path.

# SAFAR DAR WATAN

Travelling within oneself, looking at oneself, examining oneself, criticizing oneself should be done in a useful way—there is destructive criticism and constructive criticism—examining oneself in a useful way means using terms of reference as the compass. If you're in a situation where there are one, two or three alternatives, if you find or if you feel that you can't make a decision, you come to the equivalent of a crossroads on a map with three roads leading off, and you want to go one way or the other way.

At that point you can either look at the compass, look at the map, flip a coin or you can spin round three times and whichever way you are pointing, you go : you can do any one of these things. If you don't know the road, what is functionally useful is to use whatever terms of reference you think apply in that situation.

I repeat this often because it is the basis of a useful activity—you stop, and you repeat to yourself what your intention is. Why are you travelling at all?

Having done that, and having affirmed to yourself that your intention is to try and reach a particular thing, then you bring terms of reference into focus. These terms of reference range from the completely stupid Neanderthal thought to the most refined esoteric involvement and aberration.

Neanderthal-type terms of reference are things like "The three roads available to me: one goes uphill, one goes straight, and the other goes downhill," so that the Neanderthal vote might be "Going downhill is easier, going straight is all right, going uphill is a sweat, so therefore we vote for either downhill or the straight." Okay, but you're thinking like a horse here.

Other terms of reference should also be applied which involve observation: this is a very important thing because many actions and reactions depend on observation. If the observation is correct, it should not be a guess—there's an enormous difference between a guess and a decision based on observation.

I'm sure you're all familiar with the classic story of Nasrudin, who took a job as the doorkeeper at the Palace. He had a little cubbyhole of a room just next to the door, and it was nice and warm. He was lazy and he used to sit there and occasionally open the door and close it and go back to sleep—it was warm and he got regular food, and it wasn't too bad, so he was quite happy.

One day, the Grand Vizier came to him and said "Nasrudin, the Sultan is going to the Mosque for Friday prayers, what is the weather like outside? The Sultan is going in full dress and with all his retinue, and it's important that we know what the weather is like."

Nasrudin said: "It is raining heavily."

The Vizier went back and the Emperor and all the Court put on protective clothing and hats, formed up in the courtyard and threw open the gates, and outside it was blazing sun. They rode for a mile and a half, sweating like dogs, and when they came back they beat the daylights out of Nasrudin.

As he lay there in a broken heap, moaning, the Vizier came up to him and said "What made you say that it was raining?"

"Observation," said Nasrudin.

So he said "What observation, halfwit? If you look out of the door, you can see it coming down. What sort of observation is that?"

"I observed from my room," said Nasrudin.

SAFAR DAR WATAN

"It has no window to the outside, how did you observe?" said the Vizier.

"As a matter of fact, I saw this cat come running in from outside and since it was absolutely soaking wet, I deduced and observed that it was raining outside."

The Vizier said to him "Nasrudin, you know that just outside the palace gate on the left-hand side there's a butcher's shop?"

"Yes," said Nasrudin.

"You know that cats like meat?"

"Yes."

"Well that cat has a habit of going out and trying to steal meat from the butcher, and the butcher has a bucket of water which he then throws on the cat, and this happens regularly."

So Nasrudin went off and got into a fight with the butcher, and put all the blame onto him.

You see, observation can produce a theory or a result, and misinterpretation of observation can produce an equal and opposite result.

So one's observation should be careful because, when one puts together the results of observation with one's feelings and experiences to come to a decision; if those observations you have put together are harmonious, if they all more or less agree—the chances are that this decision is correct for that time and for that place.

Now watch it—you don't trot out the same justifications and experiences in every situation. You may use the same intention, the same terms of reference or point of view—but you don't use exactly the same explanations and justifications to yourself.

A measure is a measure is a measure—no, it isn't. You go into a garage and ask for two metres of gasoline, and they'll say "It's in litres, mate" and if you say "Look, one measure is the same as another measure" see what happens. Measurements are terms of reference: one is used for length, another for volume, a third for weight, and you make intelligent use of the right measure in the right circumstance.

Equally towards yourself—a person, by examining themselves, travelling within themselves, knows their own strengths and weaknesses. They know it to themselves. They are conscious of them, they are also conscious of their limitations, but remember, a limitation can be self-imposed— "Oh I could never do that"; "Oh, I haven't got a chance"——it's always possible to say that and it's possibly true. "Everybody can do anything" is not true. Everybody can do some things and some people can do a lot of things, and some people can't do anything. Okay.

But if there are limitations, these limitations, again, are encountered in the voyage within oneself. If one says "Oh I could never do that" and if it is important enough to spend time on it, one must certainly examine it. Is there a physical, economic, social, political, geographical or other absolute block and limitation? If there is, forget it. If it is "I could never buy that because it costs five hundred pounds and I've only got three hundred and fifty"——well, either forget it or save.

Certain limitations are imposed by conditioning "Oh, we such-and-such (English, French, Afghans, Turks or whatever) don't do this" or "can't do that" or "shouldn't do that"——some limitations are imposed by conditioning and some of them are good, if they are indeed limitations. If someone says "We will never accept any foreign domination"— you can say "that's not a limitation" but some people think it is because they think things like "All the world should be one" and "Everybody should be the same" and all that garbage.

So there are certain racial, linguistic or historical reasons for saying "This is not possible", "This we will not do" or "This we should not do"—that's perfectly all right.

But examine other limitations and see whether they are self-imposed. Maybe a person is afraid of doing something— there may be a very good reason. It may not be good for them, it may be dangerous, it may be disturbing or basically they know that somehow, for some reason, they don't have the capacity to do it.

If they discover that there is some sort of inhibition, some sort of limitation, by all means, if it is important enough, if it's something which stops them from doing something—examine it.

Again, if it is because they are afraid of it, this is no reason to become terrified, ashamed, and to close it away and that sort of thing. Examine it—it may very well be that the fear is a protective device, that a person should not in fact do that particular thing because their being is telling them "You are not capable of doing it".

But they don't then go around thinking of themselves as second or third-class beings, or stopping every second person and confessing how dreadful or deficient or wanting they are in this or that area, because then it becomes a self-indulgence.

Examine during the travel, look for the truth . Everybody in the world has said "Truth is not always palatable" so therefore you had "better not examine it." Well, you don't necessarily have to examine it constantly—I mean if you have a dead fish in your cupboard, you do not have to remind yourself constantly of its presence, it will do it for you.

If you think: "Oh, it's actually the smell of cooking from the restaurant down the road," more fool you. It becomes quite manifest after a time, and you can spray anything you like all over the place, but it will still be there.

You throw open the cupboard door and face it—preferably with a clothespeg on your nose—and you take it out and drop it in the bin. You do not close the door and go limping off, sniveling, and confessing to everybody that you have a rotten fish in the cupboard—it has probably become apparent to your neighbours in any case—you do something about it.

It certainly could be a source of shame or social anathema and everything like that, but if it is transparently and patently obvious, then do something about it using authentic and correct methods and terms of reference.

If you have a rotten fish in the cupboard, it is really not efficient or useful to do a zikr at that moment, however laudable an action it may be.

The circumstances dictate the action. While you are doing the zikr, you may be unconscious of the presence of that fish for the moment, but you are not removing the presence of the fish, you are removing yourself from the presence of the fish: it's not the same thing.

"I am, therefore I think" or "I think I am" or whatever, but the fish doesn't have to think both to smell and to affect you. You can hide from the fish and hope it will go away—it's already dead, it's not going anywhere.

# SAFAR DAR WATAN

So go for the practical aspect: there's nothing esoteric about a dead fish. A person possibly might get high on the odour of dead fish—some people get high on mushrooms—but as a tactic, the "fish trip" is really not defensible.

Therefore in a context of being inside oneself making use of the useful conditioning one has, whether it is religious, racial, educational or whatever: separate the wheat from the chaff, separate the ones you use in particular situations and the ones you use in other situations.

You do this consciously every day in ordinary life: when you get on a bus to get to Oxford Circus, you do not give the man cowrie shells. You can try, it won't work. They used to be currency, so I am told, in the South Pacific: you wouldn't even think of doing such a thing today.

You may say "Don't be silly" but on the inside of themselves, people do exactly the same thing in various different circumstances.

"Oh I thought it was a good idea"—No, you didn't think—actually, it's not true. You reacted, there was an impulse to say: "That's probably a good idea," and then, having "made a decision," willy-nilly, a person will "go for it," and sometimes go further than they intended—but in order to save face they then refuse to admit they were wrong rather than bring themselves to a full stop and say "No, this isn't the way," and retreat and take another line of attack. This is called admitting defeat, and there is a certain degree of pride and things like that, in the sense of "One should not admit defeat"—certainly, in some circumstances, one shouldn't—but in some circumstances wisdom dictates that one backpedals fast.

Which situation? Well you know, you can produce a book with an index and record every conceivable situation in the world, and people will suffer enormously as a result. They will suffer physically, economically, strategically, politically, and every other way, because by the time they've looked it up, the situation is already past, and while they were looking up "wolf-pack," it's too late. All that will be found is the book, and a few bones. Once on the bus, by the time you have worked through all the bus routes, the right time has gone by, and the key factor is time.

The right thing at the right time—success. The right thing at the wrong time: the wrong thing at the right time.

All Naqshbandi rules are concerned with getting to know yourself better and better. Getting to know yourself, because you have to live and exist with yourself, so it is much more convenient, useful, rewarding to know with what you are living, whether it be good, bad, indifferent.

By knowing yourself, you can see the strength and weaknesses, defend one, use the others. By learning to know yourself, you can start to get answers, or get near to answers, of the questions like: "What am I doing in this existence? What is my relation to the universe, to the cosmos, to God? How shall I look at myself? From what point of view or from what points of view?"

This all has to do with knowledge. Many schools of philosophy, Buddhists and whatever, are concerned with meditation in order to understand, for instance, the nature of God. Certainly, this is the objective of every person, or should be. But we, in the Tradition, have to start by knowing ourselves and knowing what we are—and not constantly producing "What", "Who", "When", "Why", "Wherever", "How" and so forth. Take one or two questions and try to get close to the answer.

# SAFAR DAR WATAN

"What is the meaning of life?" Supposing I knew—if I told you, you might not believe me: and even if you get the answer and say "Yes, I accept it" I will have to go through exactly what I am going through now, which is explaining to you how to try and understand about yourself to start with.

Some truths can be unpalatable, such as "We don't want to know about all this travelling, let's get to the clouds and harps and happy bits." Yes, clouds, harps and happy bits are very nice, but a cloud has no substance, harps are fine for those as like harps, and happy bits are happy—yet a constant pounding of harps surrounded by clouds and the happy laughing of angels doesn't seem to me to be an adequate aim, or an adequate reward for effort.

You might say "Come on mate, what do you want?" Well, I do know exactly what I want, as a matter of fact, and it doesn't involve massed harps and things like that. I'm not knocking it, mind you, but I mean, one has one's aspirations.

So functionally, what one does is put these rules into operation at a particular time, basing one's activities, thoughts and action on one's intention; using the tools, which are available, having a flair, developing a nose for circumstance, for when to use them, to what degree, and with what emphasis.

In *Travelling within Oneself*, one should not start a sort of "traveller's diary" and write down events as they occur as "inner experiences"—you simply remember them, because don't forget, one of the other rules is *Remembering*.

It doesn't mean to say you remember "everything which ever happens at any moment" irrespective of anything "in case it might be worthwhile"—no. Remember things. Be alert and sensitive to things which are meaningful, useful and positive. If you get into the habit of doing this, you will find that the "recall" works, because the positive things fall into place—you attract them.

You don't remember every single piece of information you've ever heard. You aim at attracting out the useful things from a whole data bank, a whole memory bank—you take the thing which applies, and use it correctly.

The tactics or techniques, whether it be one zikr or another, one activity or another, visiting one particular place or another, should and will be harmonious with what you want to achieve. It is not, and should not be, a thing which is so separate that there is an effort to put the two things together.

Admittedly, those of us who teach, can and do, use different methods and techniques, some of which may be surprising, shocking or confusing, but they are all for the purpose of stimulating a person into a train of thought, or into a direction or context which they can then use. The operative word here is "use" because it is no good putting a person into a situation which they can't handle, because then they panic.

Unless you're asking for trouble, it's no good giving a one-year old child a hammer. A hammer belongs in the hands of a person who knows how to use it: when and as they get old enough and accustomed to using a hammer, they use it.

Among other things, my function is to train people in the use of techniques, and if necessary, impose on them a technique, situation or context which they themselves should be able to learn from.

But as you know well, I don't do anybody's thinking or actions for them—I push, pull, encourage and suggest terms of reference, certain attitudes to take up, and indicate ways and means of harmonizing with these terms of reference or

# SAFAR DAR WATAN

attitudes. If you look at the whole context of all these Naqshbandi rules, in one way or another, they harmonize. There is not one that you can take, and say "When I am doing a particular one, I can't be doing the other one, because they are incompatible." No, they are mainly compatible, they mainly complement each other.

When you find one or two which are difficult to follow at the same time, it's because one or the other is exclusively needed. All that means is that it needs all your thought, feeling and attention behind it—it's not that you are ignoring or rejecting the other ones, it means that particular one needs your whole attention in the moment. You don't have to keep three balls in the air at the same time—you're aiming for quality, not quantity.

So when you come to *Safar dar Watan*, firstly make sure that you know what you mean by that. It's not just a tourist trip—it is a learning trip to learn about yourself, to know about yourself, to know how you react, to know your strengths, your weaknesses, what you know and what you don't know—it's not a constant self-examination and the "Oh dear" syndrome.

You do and should feel and have a sense of what my father would call adequate humility. Adequate humility means just that. "Oh I'm so humble, it isn't true" or "Humble, me? No"; as in the well-known story of the three monks: the Jesuit, the Benedictine and the Dominican, who were debating as to which order was best. The Dominican, after hearing the Jesuit and the Benedictine, said "You know, the Jesuits, for logic and argument and thought and planning, they are really the best: and the Benedictines make their nice liqueur and they are very nice people, but when it comes to humility, we are the best!"

So humility is what you make of it, or what it makes of you.
3.06.88

103

# RULES OR SECRETS OF THE NAQSHBANDI ORDER

One of the most difficult of the Naqshbandi rules is probably *Safar dar Watan* or *Travelling in the Homeland*; which means travelling within oneself, looking at oneself, examining oneself, and looking at how one's reactions are, and how they impact upon one.

It is very easy and sometimes very convenient to take up some sort of attitude based on background, conditioning and other factors, and to say that one is 'like this' or 'like that' and 'there is nothing to be done about it.'

This is a point of view I do not accept, because to start off by saying there is nothing that can be done about one's activities, reactions or attitudes to certain things, is, I believe, incorrect.

I believe that there certainly is an opportunity, and even many circumstances, in which one makes up one's mind according to the situation which applies at that particular time.

Saying "Oh well, I am just like that" or "Things are like that" or "Life is like that" is avoiding the issue. It is avoiding the importance of using certain things from the rules which one is not looking at.

When one is making the voyage within oneself or when one is looking within oneself, this is, again, not a critical view in the sense of "negatively critical"; where one is looking for something negative. No, one is looking for something positive which one can enhance, which one can improve, or add to.

If one is looking for a negative aspect or negative thoughts and influences, there are plenty of them around. But there is no reason why a person really committed to a proper useful path should look only for the negative.

One can, of course, look for the negative, identify it, and

then do something about it. Yet to say that one is constantly influenced or attacked by things of a negative nature may be true—but what about the energy one is putting in to overcome these things which are of a negative nature?

True, there are many things a person in different circumstances will find which will be negative, disturbing or confusing, but they have to be looked at from a positive point of view, in other words, from the point of view of "What is one trying to do about these things?"

One just doesn't say "These things are there and I will accept them, go along with them, and bear them."

Of course, with certain things, one has to. Because of work or other conditions, one has to put up with them or bear with them—but other things which are of a personal nature can be looked at from a positive point of view and should be. The positive being: why should this not be a positive situation? Why should it be a negative situation?

People too easily fall into the pattern or trap of thinking in a negative way—sometimes because of laziness, lack of foresight or lack of conviction—but such factors which are of a negative nature should not be ones that influence one's ways of action.

They may be ones which a person thinks about, and they may be ones which a person passes by and looks at—but they should not be factors which cause a disturbance in a person's way of being. For goodness sake, there are enough factors in one's everyday life which cause confusion, doubt, and even problems which a person asks themselves about—but the person should then face these things, within oneself, looking at them in terms of the Naqshbandi rules and saying: "Are these actually valid, in the sense that, should I give them any importance?"

# RULES OR SECRETS OF THE NAQSHBANDI ORDER

"I might think about or look at them, I might pause to look, but are they really confusions, doubts or problems which are valid enough to give me cause to stop what I'm trying to do—in other words which give me cause to divert from a positive way of believing, a positive way of thinking?"

When looking at oneself, there are many ways in which a person might think: I will look at myself in 'this' way, in 'that' way or in 'another' way. Go through the rules and look.

The most useful place to start from is a feeling of being convinced, being solidly happy. This requires that a person should go into the another rule which is *Khilwat dar Anjuman*, being *Alone in a Crowd*. Here, being *alone* means withdrawing under certain circumstances, as far as one can, as much as one can, and then, when one is out of the crowd—i.e., out of the tension, out of the confusion—one can then look at oneself valuably and usefully and think of what one is doing.

There are certainly many temptations when one is thinking about what one is doing, what one is wanting to do, what one is interested in doing or what one thinks one could do. All these things are perfectly possible and valid, but the question here is: what can one do best for oneself and for the group one is in?

This is not a selfish or unselfish decision which one makes, in the sense of "I will do everything for the group and nothing for myself"—no. But if one is part of a group and a member of it, then the activity one performs under a given circumstance has to be with, together and useful to the group, because this then reflects back upon oneself.

To say "I am alone"—yes, under certain circumstances, one is—but under other circumstances, one can also say "I am alone under certain rules, which I impose on myself, in which

# SAFAR DAR WATAN

I believe, in which I put my trust, and which I hope will influence me in a useful way."

Many negative thoughts come from sources which are under one's control. Many are not, but in fact, many are.

If they are under one's own control, one should take a positive attitude towards those negative thoughts one can influence, and say "No, these are aspects of myself which can be influenced by me, and I will indeed influence them in a positive way."

To say: "These are all things which I don't know about, and I don't know if I can influence them and I'm not sure about them" is a negative way of thinking. One should always think of what one can do in a positive way, in way which is useful to oneself.

Otherwise one is becoming a servant of chance. If things go right, one is happy. But if things go a little bit more wrong, what then is one? What situation is one in? In a situation of confusion, of difficulty, of problems.

Nothing can be solved by allowing oneself to be on the receiving end of problems or negative thinking all the time. Within oneself, one has to think and be, and use, the positive. This means one uses a positive way of looking at oneself in order to find some positive solution to situations or problems.

I talk about problems; but such things are not always problems. There are situations which are not necessarily problems, which are good. One should look at those situations in a way that one affirms that they are positive, that one has produced them oneself—possibly with help—but that one has indeed produced them, and one has then influenced them in a way that they have become positive.

# RULES OR SECRETS OF THE NAQSHBANDI ORDER

If you begin by saying that there are "so many problems which are not capable of being explained" or "not capable of solution"—then you are starting from a negative point.

You have to start from a point that at which you say "there are problems, there are situations and confusions" and that "they are capable of being explained, examined, combated and overcome."

The Tradition is not about always telling people the good or nice things, but it certainly is about telling people what their capacity is. Nobody should be in the Tradition without understanding that there is a capacity they have, which they can enhance and use, which they can understand and develop.

Without that feeling, that belief, what are they doing? They are merely passing their time in believing something and hoping.

Yes, hope is necessary, but action is necessary also.

It is not enough just to say "I hope something will happen." One has to say "I hope this will happen, with the help of the Tradition, in such a way" and to make that point firmly.

Take that point on, and from that point, move forward.

Otherwise the Tradition is just a loose combination of hopes, fears, beliefs and partial understandings, which is not good enough. It has to be firm, strong and enduring. It has to be something which will move a person, guide them, and bring them to an understanding of themselves.

Without a real understanding of themselves, people will look inward and will think that they already have an understanding of themselves, but it is not a true understanding, only a partial one.

# SAFAR DAR WATAN

It has got to be a useful understanding.

Why?

Because if they are looking at themselves in a useful and constructive way, this "why" leads them to look at themselves and find out why a certain pattern of thought and action is a certain format they have developed within their thinking, and which then guides them and motivates them.

The motivation has to be from within them—how do they think of themselves? They look at themselves, they think about themselves, and they find some way, some direction which they can follow in a useful way. Otherwise they are embarking on a pattern of thought or a pattern of action which will produce confusion within them.

It has to be something which has some dedication, and that dedication has to be based on some useful feedback from themselves. None of the rules lead the person to an "instant understanding" of themselves or the way they think.

What this direction does all the time is indicate a way to them in which they can think in a more useful way. By thinking in a more useful way, they can then act, behave and understand themselves in a more useful way rather than saying: "I'm like this" or "I'm like that" and "I've been brought up to believe this or that."

Don't take such values as being lifelong. Look at them, understand them, and take them as things which can and should be usefully used—otherwise they are merely indications one can ignore. One looks at them, one examines them, one sees in which way they can influence one in a useful way, or in which way they can usefully move, modify or influence a person's thinking.

# RULES OR SECRETS OF THE NAQSHBANDI ORDER

*Safar dar Watan* is one of the most difficult forms of activity, because it means you are both looking at yourself, and also having to look at yourself in a way that will produce something. You are not just looking at yourself as if you were something abstract or something which doesn't relate to you.

It is something you are looking at which has an importance for you. It has an influence upon you, and you then ask yourself: how does this influence or impact move you? Or again, how can you use it in such a way that it will be useful for you?

So *Travelling in the Homeland* is a very important aspect, because you are doing that travelling within yourself and you have to bring up certain realities to yourself when you do so.

Such realities may sometimes be embarrassing, sometimes not very nice, sometimes confusing, and sometimes difficult. But equally, they are real, and they have to be looked at from the point of view of reality, because they come from the real person.

So *Safar dar Watan* is, as I say, one of the most difficult rules in the Tradition, but it is one upon which a person can rely—if it is done in a correct way, in the correct format and under the right conditions.

It means looking at oneself in a critical but not hostile way, in a gentle, reasonable and sensible way, and to try and find what is the motivation in certain activities which one may find confusing or contradictory.

So look and find.

24.10.92

# 4. KHILWAT DAR ANJUMAN
## or *Retirement in Company*

*Khilwat dar Anjuman: the ability to detach oneself from a situation which may be noisy, disturbing, confusing and frenetic. One should be able to retire into oneself for a short time. This does not mean to cut off from everything that is going on, it means the ability to distance oneself from tension and disturbance by using a zikr for a short time: the detachment is qualitative and not quantitative. It can be used as a defence by oneself or with the help of the Master.*

*Retirement in Company* is the ability to detach from surroundings and from tensions or problems or activities which are hostile to a certain tranquillity of mind.

It's a form of switching-off and slowing-down, a closing-off of circuits which are not necessary in a particular situation. One can demonstrate this quite easily to oneself. The tactile sense operates—when one is using this hand one is thinking: "Ah, this feels like that" and so forth.

Now there's a certain amount of attention and energy used when one is exercising the tactile sense. If you don't need to exercise this other hand—and obviously you don't use all your senses all the time to reassure yourself that it's still there—because not exercising the tactile can itself become a preoccupation—therefore the amount of attention and energy which you will be expending or using on that is conserved.

111

# RULES OR SECRETS OF THE NAQSHBANDI ORDER

Equally, if you're not using taste, that circuit is running at a sort of minimum rev turnover. It can be in gear; it's not switched off so that a great effort is needed to restart it. At any given moment for instance, if it's running at the lowest possible revolution, and you put a drop of vinegar or something in your mouth, it is reactivated instantaneously. So you're closing down circuits you don't need at a specific time.

In *Retirement in Company,* you're closing down as many of the circuits as possible, without going into a sort of hibernatory state or something like that. You're just closing down the unnecessary circuits by attempting to achieve relaxation and tranquillity. Any muscular or physical tension you might be expending unnecessarily is conserved—so the ability to detach goes along with that.

You aim at achieving this type of detachment for three minutes or five minutes, for ten minutes, for twenty minutes—given almost any situation. It can be in a tube, a train, a bus, or anywhere.

If you're sitting in a traffic-jam, rather than sitting there drumming your fingers on the steering-wheel saying "why the hell doesn't the light change"——switch off a few circuits.

Don't switch them off to the point that somebody's leaning on the horn behind you because it has changed to green three times, and you've been 'gone' or something; because this creates social problems, especially if you have passengers.

So *to detach* means: given the circumstance, the situation—whether for three minutes, a half an hour or something like that—you switch the unnecessary circuits off.

21.11.85

# KHILWAT DAR ANJUMAN

*Khilwat dar Anjuman* or *Retirement in Company* can be both a defensive and also a singularly developmental characteristic one can use.

In our everyday lives we all experience moments, places or things which cause tension or frustration—it is like noise. It may be the noise of constant traffic or machinery, the noise in an aeroplane or at an airport, or else general noise which intrudes upon one's peace and quiet. They can all obviously attract a certain amount of one's attention—unless one is wearing earplugs or something—and, measured in terms of the Tradition, such things can create tension as well as waste energy.

These noises therefore take the form of something that can waste energy—albeit very little—by attracting one's attention away from what one is doing, as when a mosquito is humming round and buzzing. One is then slightly disturbed and one is using a certain amount of concentration and energy to keep it out of one's thinking, but subconsciously it is there.

If what is involved is a situation fraught with negative emotion, which then comes out on the surface in the form of tension and fear, a person reacts towards it either by being fearful, and then by hiding their fear and becoming aggressive, or else they themselves are caught up in the tension of the situation itself, and you have a 'dog chasing its tail' syndrome.

I have always said and will always maintain that tension is a negative factor which is present in almost every circumstance of everyday life, and it is a factor one must guard against.

So *Khilwat dar Anjuman* or *Retirement in Company* does not mean running away, locking oneself away in an ivory tower, retiring to a cave in the mountains, or stuffing one's ears with cotton wool. If one can insulate oneself from unnecessary frenzy, noise and other things, this is perfectly reasonable: but to run away from such things is, a) a defeat, and b) under our rules in the Tradition, a person is not allowed to go and sit in a cave in the mountains.

The tension imposed upon one in everyday life situations has to be handled, and *Khilwat dar Anjuman* helps one to do this. If one is in a situation or ambiance with another person or several other people, say in a noisy, negative or dirty place; one's reaction is likely to be negative. Perhaps one has a feeling of hostility towards a person or towards certain people.

In ordinary polite society, if one has a feeling of hostility towards another person but one is obliged to work or talk with them, or something like that, one goes through the normal polite ways of hiding one's distaste, getting the job done as quickly as possible, and vanishing: but at the same time one is thinking somewhere "Damn and Blast! I don't want to do the job with this person, I don't like this person" or something like that. One is then building up a certain amount of tension within oneself.

One can of course be blasé and say "It doesn't matter, I can deal with any sort of bad situation, and come out smiling." If one can do that, one certainly should, but one should also know how one is doing it. This is how: one is using this *'absence'* from the situation as a defence.

One is not closing it all down, becoming unconscious, closing one's eyes or screaming inside. One is removing a convenient portion of one's conscious mind and thought-process from the situation, which is a nervous, neurotic, negative or frenetic one. One is removing a part of one's consciousness from that condition while remaining in the situation, meanwhile nodding, smiling or putting in whatever word is necessary, while at the same time one is in fact 'absent' from it.

# KHILWAT DAR ANJUMAN

In doing this, you are not only retiring into yourself and defending yourself against the negative, the frenetic and confusing; but by using your zikr at the same time, you are also producing a certain amount of very useful energy.

So you see the value of this particular rule: not only is it a defence against confusion, disturbance and tension, but it is actually enabling you to amass positive energy under difficult circumstances.

I must repeat that the positive energy you generate and amass by following the different rules is a qualitative and not a quantitative type of energy. It may be generated in a period of five minutes of retirement, or else in 10, 15 or 20 minutes, or even longer. The measure of how good it is cannot be calculated in terms of minutes or time. The measure is how deeply and how reasonably you retire without completely absenting yourself from company.

How much you can retire, to what degree, or for how long you should retire, is, of course, your own decision.

For instance, if you know that you are going to be in a meeting, and there is going to be a person there who is going to drone on for a half an hour about things you already know, or on some subject which is exciting to them, like themselves— you might then be able to say to yourself "I will sit there and programme myself to nod and smile: meanwhile I will detach as much of myself as I can and repeat my zikr until that person sits down, at which time I will then be able to fully commit myself to a situation in which I have some interest or something to say."

This is a perfectly reasonable situation.

Another example: if you are travelling by bus or taxi and

are caught in a traffic jam, your attention does not wander, especially if you are driving.

But if you're a passenger, if you are waiting or queuing for something, or have some time, however little, during your daytime or evening activity—say when you are invited to a dinner, a dance, or even a theatre or cinema show—rather than daydream, you can put your mind into gear and connect with your being by reciting your zikr with the intention of 'absenting' a certain part of your conscious mind from the activities you are involved in at that moment.

*Khilwat dar Anjuman* is therefore a defensive, and also a productive exercise in terms of energy. Furthermore it has the faculty—which should be developed—to buffer or insulate oneself from frenetic and negative situations which may be producing negativity, confusion or tension.

You are not going inside yourself like a snail crawling into its shell in order to shut everything off. The snail, by definition, sees or feels danger and does the only thing it can do since it can't run—it curls up in its shell. It closes itself off physically and in every other way, but as soon as the sound or movement which has frightened it goes away, or when it believes it is safe, it puts its head out. It is now either right or wrong: if the bird is still waiting there, zap, and it's finished. If the bird has gone, it's safe.

Human beings cannot afford the luxury of the 50/50 choice. It would be ridiculous if you were killed every time you made the wrong decision about something, because one would be dead very early in life.

The amount of hassle or problems one gets from a wrong decision is not the equivalent of death, but it is still uncomfortable and annoying: it can produce agony or neurosis and it most certainly does produce tension. But one can't recoil from every aspect in life, otherwise as I say, one would have to lock oneself away in a cave in the mountains.

One doesn't just "roll with the punches" either. If one says "I'll ignore that"—one ignores it to the degree that one can—one cannot ignore everything.

If one said to oneself: "Okay, I will not talk to any negative, neurotic, obscene, violent, loudmouthed, or otherwise awful people"—the truth is that this would very severely cut down the number of people one spoke to, the number of shops one went into, or the amount of business one did with other people.

"I only want to talk to people that I like" is fine. Unfortunately one does not have this privilege. In one's own private life, in the evening, afterwards, one can certainly indulge in such a luxury, but with the hurly-burly of life, one usually doesn't have this advantage.

One therefore doesn't just "make the best of it" and limp away from a particularly bruising, frenetic, neurotic or tension-making situation, saying "Oh well, it wasn't as bad as it could have been"—one closes off certain parts of oneself as much as possible, so that one is not impinged upon, damaged or disturbed. One will not then be in a state of tension as a result of what one has experienced or as a result of the situation.

I repeat: the time when you use this particular rule of *Khilwat dar Anjuman* depends on you. Nobody can tell you when to use it because it's dependant upon circumstance. If I say to you "Use it exclusively in tubes, buses, planes or trains" this would obviously limit its use.

Also, the skill is not only to be able to use it in a place where you're just sitting as a passenger, for instance, when the bus or train is droning along hour after hour—it is probably easier to use it in this kind of circumstance, and it should indeed be used then, why not?— but the skill is also to be able to use it in circumstances where other people are involved and in which one doesn't need one hundred percent of one's own attention.

So instead of allowing one's mind to drift off into shopping or whatever, one then concentrates one's mind on generating positive energy, with literally, a part of one's mind being absent at that time, and while that part of one's mind is absent, one is also—if you like—"scoring points."

So it's not only defensive, it is very productive. It is not a shield like a piece of plate glass around you, because you are only using the energy of the Tradition to insulate yourself from the circumstances and people that cause you problems, or who have negative outpourings. You're not recoiling within yourself and disregarding everything: you simply switch down the circuits you don't need.

Get onto your zikr; repeat it, get the energy flowing. With the energy flowing, feel your connection with the Tradition, feel the link which exists, feel the interchange of energy. Repeat your intention to yourself, repeat your zikr, don't slip away into a dream.

Keep this a functional activity. It's not putting yourself to sleep and it's not putting yourself out of touch with the situation: you leave a part of your mind to monitor the situation, and—as far as you can—you get another part of your consciousness to move onto a different level and work there in a positive way.

That is how *Retirement in Company* or *Khilwat dar Anjuman* should be carried out.

undated 85/90

# KHILWAT DAR ANJUMAN

If you are following *Khilwat dar Anjuman* which literally translates as being *Alone within a Crowd*; there again, you have to be careful and clear about how you define that 'being alone' and also how you practice it, for the simple reason that you can literally consider that it can be beneficial to be able to close oneself off from all the impacts, negativities or other disturbing factors, and retreat into yourself in order to, say, concentrate on an activity, think about yourself, or do a zikr.

But if you want to do this, you obviously have to first define what *'being alone'* means. If you take this rule literally, i.e., every time you find yourself in a crowded place or with a large number of people, you 'creep away into a corner,' this can have a number of consequences.

First of all, it attracts people's attention. They'll say a person doing this is 'antisocial', 'paranoid' or 'doesn't like us' and you will be labelled 'unpopular' or something like that. This interferes with normal social activities.

You don't have to wrench yourself away. You don't have to be afraid, in the sense of feeling an obligation: "Oh, I should be 'within myself' among this crowd." Here again, the definition of being 'with oneself' or *alone* is the important one to make for oneself. *Alone* does not necessarily mean physically removing oneself from a crowded place, however much one may be tempted to do so.

For instance, nobody likes walking on the pavements in Oxford Street and being pushed all over the place, bumped around and so forth: "I only wish to stroll along freely without anybody else there"—but when you can't do this, you don't go down a side street and crouch in a corner. What you can do is switch off certain circuits you do not need in a crowded situation, and use those circuits to refresh or rejuvenate something within yourself.

# RULES OR SECRETS OF THE NAQSHBANDI ORDER

In a sense, you may also put yourself "on automatic pilot." For instance, if you know you have to sit in a bus or train for twenty or thirty minutes without being required to do anything or have any conversation with anybody, you can and often do switch off many of the circuits one would normally use, either for conversation, or thought, or for walking, or other things, thus being in a state of relaxation while remaining alert at the same time. That way, you don't miss your bus stop.

By the same token you are *Alone in a Crowd* but not physically absenting yourself. If you can do this and if you can develop this technique—which is something I recommend that you do, since it is capable of being developed further and further—you will find that you can find a lot of time during a single day. I have emphasized this time factor over and over again in Tradition activities, even if it is not always possible to find fifteen or twenty minutes at one time to work on or think about oneself, or do an exercise. There may be professional, family or other reasons which prevent it.

However, if one has developed the ability to be *alone in a crowd* it is perfectly possible to switch off while sitting or standing waiting for a bus, travelling in the tube or doing any other activity which doesn't require physical movement. It is perfectly easy to try and look for two or three minutes, or even one minute, in a day. If you put them all together during that day, you can find eighteen or twenty minutes.

As I say, being alone is a technique, not an action. You can perfectly well be surrounded by jostling crowds, traffic and shouting in Oxford Street and so forth. Of course, you need to have your wits about you, because you'll be pushed into the road or run over, so you don't switch off completely, but you can try and put a part of your conscious, unconscious or subconscious mind to work on something by consciously thinking about something.

# KHILWAT DAR ANJUMAN

This hasn't removed you from the crowd any more than it has rendered you unconscious. It hasn't blunted your senses to the degree that you are incapable of dealing with traffic or other people and you're wandering about in a daze—because that would be contrary to a useful activity, it would produce anxiety. So you don't consciously say to yourself "I am going to walk from Piccadilly Circus to Oxford Street or Hyde Park Corner, and I will put myself on automatic pilot and just think or do my zikr." There is a normal degree of caution and anxiety which is always present in a person when they are in a crowded place.

Whether they were brought up in town or in the country, a normal person is offended by the noise of traffic and people, and the incessant blaring of horns etc., while walking the streets. Normally a person is slightly, if not on edge, at least not particularly happy among a lot of people. It's not a question of whether the people are sympathetic or unsympathetic, it is the fact of there being lots of noise and agitation, and people don't feel happy when they are agitated. This is a normal state of affairs.

Therefore, to say "I will switch off and only become fully conscious when I reach Hyde Park Corner" would be an error of judgment, because there is a part of oneself which remains on alert because of the ever-present danger of traffic, pickpockets or thieves, and a degree of vigilance is necessary.

Pushing against that vigilance, which is there to protect you, would be pushing against yourself. So what you do is this—you are 'absenting' a part of your conscious, unconscious or subconscious mind while—as I say—you are either sitting in a tube, a bus, or waiting for a bus, when you are not called upon to do anything.

27.02.92

121

## 5. NEEGAR DASHTAN
### *Watchfulness* or *Use of special faculties*

*Watchfulness is being constantly on the alert for people, places, music and other things which have a positive energy. It is an openness to things of a positive nature. It means being ready to be open to positive impacts, although they may come in an unexpected way. The exercise of special faculties is developed by contact with the Master and the obeying of his instructions. He knows what you can or should do, although you may imagine or hope for something different.*

*Watchfulness* is the exercise of the special faculties. *Watchfulness* is another term for being alert; being open and 'scanning.' Again, that doesn't imply turning one's head 365 degrees all the time in case you miss anything. No, it implies being sensitive to useful and positive impacts. Again, being open, without the fear of being vulnerable; there is a distinct difference.

So *Watchfulness* is being on the alert, but again, not tense: "I'll notice it if it comes, whatever it is or when it comes or whatever." Halley's Comet is coming this year and it doesn't mean one has to strain one's eyesight all the time—you've seen one comet, you've seen them all. So watchfulness is the development of a special faculty; that innate faculty is developing.

21.11.85

*Watchfulness* is another term for being alert, open and 'scanning.' It means being constantly on the alert for people, places, music, writings and other things with a positive energy.

Being alert should not be confused with being in tense situations, in the sense of looking around and frenetically checking things like music, people or books, because this in itself could be a waste of energy.

A state of alertness means being receptive and open to impacts of a positive nature.

Once again, this means being open without the fear of being vulnerable: there is a distinct difference. Being alert or watchful means that one uses some of the special faculties one is developing. One develops a nose for people, places, music, publications, impacts of a positive and useful nature, so that one can feel their presence, know that they are there, and make a relationship with one or more of them.

It also means that one is ready and open to receiving contacts of a positive nature although they may come in an unexpected way—not only in an unpredictable way, but literally in a way that one may not expect.

If one is expecting a place, a piece of music, a reading or any other factor to give one some sort of impact, and one has already decided upon the nature of this impact—sometimes one's alertness will tell one that there are other further impacts in that place, in that music, or in that reading. At that point, the impacts may be unexpected, but they will be of a positive nature—if the person is ready and open and prepared to receive them and use them.

The exercising, development and *Use of special faculties* are things which are developed by contact with the Master, who monitors how these *special faculties* are being used and how they can be enhanced. He is measuring whether the person has reached a state where these faculties can be put together with other deeper faculties to make a more efficient, more positive and more useful activity.

It is necessary to obey instructions without hesitation and without examining such instructions from any context other than that of the Tradition, because an instruction one receives may be one which can be reasonably understood or put in place—or it may be one which may provoke a reaction, and which will be identified and analysed by using one of the special faculties that are being developed.

The Master knows what any of his students can do and what they should do.

A student may be in a state of alert and feel a feedback from a person, a place, from music or from something they read. They may feel a feedback and they may even be able to increase or enhance that feedback, but they should also be on the alert in the area of using their special faculties, which are developed and enhanced by the Master.

Undated 1985/90

# 6. YAD DASHTAN
## or *Keeping of the Memory,*
## *Sensing of the Being and the Body*

*Keeping of the Memory is an exercise and a rule by which you remind yourself of your being and your experiences. Sensing the being and the body reminds yourself of positive situations. Recreate these situations when you need to feel the positive. Feel the positive energy and harmony with your Master so that he can pass on and you can receive energy which you store in your memory. Examine and remember your positive experiences so that you can use them.*

It is slightly different from *Yad Kardan*, which is rule number seven. For both *Yad Kardan* and *Yad Dashtan*, the *Yad* in the two cases means "memory" or "knowing": *Kardan* is to make the memory, i.e. "memory-making."

*Yad Dashtan* is therefore to "hold" or to "keep" and it's different from *Yad Kardan*, which is *Remembering*, because it means reminding yourself positively, even physically, possibly even saying to yourself: "Remember this particular specific thing and put it deeply into my own memory" i.e. reinforcing, recharging and consciously storing elements and reactions from the Tradition in your memory.

You can bring these things out at a particular time: they also surface at a later stage as you develop this ability, at which time they come out automatically, autonomically: but there are other elements you haven't quite developed, and which take a conscious effort to bring out.

# RULES OR SECRETS OF THE NAQSHBANDI ORDER

Again, it's a familiarization process—the more familiar you are with the use of a particular rule, the more deliberately and sensitively you will try and apply it. Not in a haphazard way—something will dictate to you that the situation warrants the application of one or another rule, or a combination of them. Don't forget, you never say: "I am using this particular rule in a certain context to the exclusion of any other."

You may go into a situation in which, as the context becomes more evident, it may occur to you that this is a situation or context in which one should apply a particular rule or two.

As the situation or context develops further, it gets better or worse or remains static, and an aspect of another rule or another rule altogether may suggest itself to you. This means that you shouldn't think in terms of excluding in the sense of "I am already committed to this, I cannot allow that"—no, these rules are all compatible and harmonious.

Yet this is not an encouragement to go into a situation and become aware of a context, and then just hover around: "Shall I try this, that or the other one?"—going backwards and forwards or up and down. This is a recipe for confusion, for treading water: not for doing anything positive.

Don't swap the rules around: see, feel, and sense which one applies. Don't hesitate to apply a rule, but again, don't begin by saying "I'll try this and see—if it fails, I'll try that." This idea can be in the back of your mind, there's nothing inherently wrong about it, but don't test a rule in a negative sense, as if you were saying "Oh, I've got X other rules if this fails." Yes, you most certainly do, but you don't start off with that attitude.

You say rather that "Something tells me" or "I feel that this context, situation, or state I am in at the moment requires the application of a certain rule or combination of rules"—this is fine. You then go ahead and try it, allowing for modification by subtracting from, or adding another rule to, what you are doing.

This way, you've got flexibility, but not to the extent of wandering about between extremes. You've got the rigid element, which is the backup, as well as the flexibility which allows you to modify your stance, attitude or reaction to a particular thing.

As the effect or influence of certain rules become more familiar to you, the less neglectful you should be. One might say "I am not deliberately neglectful" but the fact that people do not neglect things deliberately does not mean to say they are not.

Very often, people fail in situations or fail themselves by default. Everybody will say "That's nothing new"—true, but examine it. With the benefit of hindsight, after a certain situation or particular context you can say "I could or should have done that, said this" or "changed, modified, that": this is true; this is the benefit of hindsight.

But the experience one has had from the situation should not be lost. With a similar situation or similar set of circumstances, one would not be efficient or true to oneself if one ignored the past and went and committed a similar mistake or similar error to the same degree.

The past doesn't hang around your neck like a millstone: "I won't recall the past, I want to forget it." One normally and automatically uses what is called "selective memory." People remember the good and nice things, and they try and discard the unpleasant things from their memory—it's a normal survival technique—but one should not use selective memory as an excuse for not learning, not doing or not being.

# RULES OR SECRETS OF THE NAQSHBANDI ORDER

People often make the same pattern of errors, and if one makes the same error to exactly the same degree time and time and time again; or if one doesn't interpret a particular book, article, activity or exercise a little bit better each time; then one cannot say that one is using the full capacity of one's being up to the point it has developed.

One therefore brings these things out of the memory, and as they become familiar, so they become more obvious, and one then says "Of course, I can do this" or "I should do that" and one does it—but not as something alien or which one looks up in a book saying "Right, I will now do that." It simply harmonizes with one, it becomes a part of oneself and one brings it out at the right time.

These things which are not entirely familiar to you at the moment require an effort for you to put them into your memory. The effort you make means that you put them in deliberately, using a technique: you don't just read them over and over to the point when if somebody says to you "Tell me about such-and such," you can just reel it out.

You make it enter you so that it gets into a channel as directly as possible without being diluted during the process of going in, otherwise this would mean that all you get, at the end, would be a sort of vague trace of it. If it's put in deliberately, with an effort of mind, memory and will, it will sink in and remain there tangibly, as something real, not just as a vague spark or idea.

*Yad Dashtan* is also *The Sensing of the Being and the Body.* From time to time one sits down and examines oneself without moving, without physically feeling—one examines the body to see how it's generally feeling, and to see whether, by reasonable use of as many senses as apply, one can sense any lack of balance within the system.

# YAD DASHTAN

Obviously, if one stands up and immediately falls down, there is evidence of a certain lack of equilibrium, and it may not need much examination: you smell the person's breath and probably find the reason.

One can examine oneself without actually doing it physically, by a process of detaching oneself, travelling within oneself and looking—not searching for something in the sense that "It must be there" or "I'll find out what it is"—you are simply examining. If you use an awareness of different senses, you can sense a situation in the body which may manifest itself as heat, cold, sensitivity or lack of it, equilibrium or lack of it.

In every context applied to the Tradition, one tries to find a harmonious balance with whatever it is: between one's job and one's home life, between one's work and one's holiday, between sport and sleep, and so forth. To function correctly, the human system should work in harmony.

All parts of the body: the muscles, nervous system, circulation, breathing and so forth, work in a certain harmony with each other. There are variations, naturally, caused by various factors.

One isn't examining oneself as a physician examines you—one is examining one's body and one's being as oneself. You're not trying to find out whether you've got a temperature, a cold, earache or rheumatism, because this is an area for which you naturally see a doctor, or do something about it. You are simply examining to see whether there is any unconscious stress or imbalance within the system. You can wire yourself up to all sorts of systems to check the regularity or otherwise of the heartbeat and get readings, but one is trying to measure and examine the being in a different way here.

If one is in tune with oneself and one has a dialogue and

relationship with oneself, one should be able to feel and tell oneself if there is some conscious or subconscious imbalance—and if there is, whether it can be put down to a tension factor.

This is not a physical examination as a physician would examine you. You're scanning yourself for evidence of possible tension or other factors which inhibit assimilation, development or relaxation. Everybody knows the exterior signs of tension, for instance, tenseness of the hands and that sort of thing following a row. These things can all be overcome, but part of the examination, for instance as when one is establishing a breathing rhythm in an exercise, is to settle oneself down and harmonize with oneself physically.

If, as a result of nervousness or some disturbing thought process there is some tension within a person, one should be able to identify it, and without going into a long psychological or other examination of oneself, see how and if it can be overcome, and if it is inhibiting the necessary relaxation or de-tensioning one is aiming for.

It may very well be that in sensing the being and the body one might find signs of tension which are not necessarily inhibiting. For instance, if one is taking fifteen or twenty minutes out of one's daily activities or job to do an exercise: it is perfectly possible and normal to go into that exercise while conscious of or remembering what one has done in the morning, and planning what one will be doing in the afternoon.

Both of these areas of memory and projection are present in the brain at the same time. So if you are sitting and relaxing, and you find that there is a memory of what you did this morning along with today's planning buzzing about, you do not wipe them out—you don't have to. The two activities are normal and reasonable areas where thought and projection should be going on.

# YAD DASHTAN

Your concern is whether anything at the present moment is disturbing you in such a way that it is preventing you from best using that short period of time you have put aside to do an exercise.

When you do get inside yourself, as it were, you examine to see if there are areas of tension causing the imbalance: then you try to put that balance right, if you can. Try very hard to estimate the degree of imbalance, if it is there—how important is it, how disturbing? Don't give it greater importance than it has, don't consider it as looming over you. It may be something with just a small annoyance factor, and if you give it more prominence, you can make it develop.

Try examining, see if there is an imbalance and see how you can put this imbalance right. Say to yourself "It is within my competence to do so."

You're not putting a time on it, you're not saying "I will do it within fifteen minutes" or whatever, the communication between yourself and your being is such that, after all, you can't divide between your self, your body and your being: you are ultimately on the same side.

You're neither in competition nor are your terms of reference so different—what is different is that the essential being of the person has not been subjected to the conditioning that your conscious mind and human frame has been subject to.

This is why, when the essential being, the deep consciousness of the person pushes against some aspect of conditioning which is being taken on, the essential being sometimes says "Now just a minute!"

Sometimes a person is about to use or is using some

131

conditioning they have assimilated for years, and the essential being will break through and push or jag the memory a little: we call it the "memory factor." It happens when you have established, not only a reasonable communication with the essential being, but an exchange or harmony to the extent that you can tell the difference between a physical headache resulting from tension or eyestrain, and a sort of nagging which is in fact your essential being trying to remind you of your priorities.

So you don't come into collision with yourself, but you obviously have to help yourself to put yourself right if there is an imbalance. You are the only person who can measure as to whether that balance is right or not.

You're sensing—now if you say you are "feeling," how do you feel? One can say "I feel hot, cold, happy" or "sad": this is feeling. If you say "How do you sense yourself?" people will look at you in a funny way because it's not a commonly used word: yet it's perfectly normal to say "On such-and-such an occasion I sensed that something was wrong." Nobody would really take you up on that because at some time in their life everybody has "sensed" things about people, places and so forth, without anybody seeing anything amiss.

What you are doing is sensing yourself—you're sensing your inner being, and you're trying to sense how balanced or unbalanced it might be—and if you do sense imbalance, how to rectify that, or, if there isn't an imbalance, how you can stabilize and develop even better on that basis.

You don't go into the sensing or examination on the assumption that there is an imbalance—however if you do find something in yourself, your pattern of thought or behaviour, that is quite obviously wrong, bad or unbalanced to yourself— at that time you can and should take a few minutes, do an exercise, try and examine to what degree that imbalance exists and why: again, without getting all psychological about it, see how the balance can be re-established.

An exercise, a zikr, is always an opportunity of establishing contact with yourself and re-establishing any lack of equilibrium which might exist. It's not just simply recharging the batteries and getting the energy, or simply getting in tune with yourself: it is also all those contexts together. When you do get in that situation, the "watch and ward" aspect of the inner being suggests to you what can or might be done. But that means taking note of what is coming out as well.

These are all active and positive rules—they are not just 'by-laws' or things which 'one could aspire to.' They all are practical and they should become more practical—to the point of being automatic, as I say, in the sense that one finds that one rule or another applies in a situation, or modifications or aspects of them apply constantly.

You are also examining the deeper or inner being as you know it. You do this by looking at it, and also by measuring it as a result of its reactions to certain things. Your conscious reaction to certain stimuli, to certain contexts or situations is naturally dependant on the quality or type of the situation, the amount of conditioning that you have, and the amount of conditioning which applies in a particular situation.

There is what is called the "studied" reaction: somebody speaks to you in French, and your reaction is to reply in French: you can call this conditioning or what you like; it is a studied or judged reaction to a certain thing. When you're looking at or communicating with the deeper being, you should be conscious of the fact that your conditioned reaction to certain stimuli may be quite different to the reaction of your inner being.

# RULES OR SECRETS OF THE NAQSHBANDI ORDER

People will say "Even though I felt it deeply offensive, I voted Democrat" or whatever "because it was politically necessary" which means that the inner being is not involved in every context. You might say "Since it is part of me, how is it not involved?" It isn't involved in the sense that if you're catching a bus, all of you catches a bus: the inner being is not really involved in the process, it happens to be there and a part of you, therefore it is catching a bus as well.

It's the old syndrome of "Which of me is drinking this coffee?"; i.e. trying to divide up the three or four me's in the sense of "my eighth me on the left is drinking this coffee" is strictly from hunger—it is a fruitless, fathomless and bottomless type of discussion. The context of the being covers the whole spectrum of reaction, action and interreaction on different levels—different levels are involved to a different degree according to the circumstances.

If you're a football supporter, you are probably out there on a Saturday baying like a wolf: why not? I'm not knocking it, I'm sure it's a very amazing thing to do, but I don't think that even the most assiduous esotericist, and I use the word with every prejudice I can think of, would say that the inner being is engaged in singing "Here we go, here we go, here we go" in the stands. One may be saying that, but I don't think that one's inner being is really conscious of the fact. So you cannot say that every level of being is involved at every time and in every circumstance. Certainly it involves itself. it is its responsibility and privilege to do so.

If a person is doing something destructive, dangerous, debilitating or obstructive, or could predictably produce an obstacle in the path of a person's development, then the inner being can and will produce a shock-wave. We call it *takkan*—it means shake.

# YAD DASHTAN

It produces this *takkan*, but there is nothing magical, superstitious or very extraordinary about it. It usually produces it from what might consider a perfectly normal situation which exaggerates itself out of all proportion and turns into a "genie out of the bottle" situation: it becomes a monster. Suddenly the "thing" is there, and it gives the person a shock or shakes them to the soles of their feet. It is, in fact, indicating that the person is on a collision course with themselves or on a collision course with—and here I pick my words carefully otherwise I'll get misquoted—the part they have to play in the scheme of things. Make of that what you will, but just don't use "destiny", "karma" or phrases like that when talking about this sort of thing.

After all, the essential being does have its eyes, ears and feelings, its finger on your pulse, and it knows the different shifts of priority you are establishing by choice, by conditioning or by circumstance—but as I say, it finally does have the right and authority to provoke circumstances, to put you into a circumstance of your own creating, good or bad. Don't forget, I am not just talking about the negative, one can apply the positive to this as well—accentuate the positive, eliminate the negative.

The same thing holds true if one is in a direction which is productive or useful on several levels: then being in harmony with one's essential being does not just add fuel or energy but it also enhances and clarifies the picture, the view: it gives the intention a boost, and it's sort of a green light.

Whereas with the negative, the warning signals will be there and they may illuminate. A person, a group or a country may ignore these, but they ignore them to their detriment. Whether it is a person or a nation, there is no such thing as a person or group so unaware of the fact that their priorities are

135

wrong that they have, as it were, "innocently" gone to destruction or ruin.

The signal lights are always there, i.e. the inner being. The more one develops a rapport and communication with the inner being, the more one keeps the memory developing and operative, and the more direction one will get from it.

This is not a "press-button" thing, as when one says: "Oh well, that's all right, I'll just learn everything there is to know, and then I go on automatic pilot and everything that happens to me is not my fault": it's not as simple as that.

This is only one part of the whole learning process. If one gets a warning light, or if one has the sensation, the feeling that a particular thing is out of tune or inharmonious: what do you do, abandon it? You apply one of the other rules.

Supposing you say "Right, I have got harmony with my essential being, so therefore nothing can touch or worry me"—no. This isn't a fact, because it is only one aspect. Don't forget, you are working on all these rules simultaneously, in different circumstances, as far as you can.

By establishing a contact, a harmony, one reinforces that already existing contact or harmony by exercising the rules. They are not bye-laws you stick on the wall and occasionally look at: they don't oppress you, they don't occupy your entire thoughts, they don't occupy you on every level all the time, but they're always there to be used, and I commend them to you.

23.02.89

# 7. YAD KARDAN
## *Remembering,* or *Recollecting Exercises*

*"Remembering" is an exercise in remembering situations in which one has been. Remembering positive situations in the past which one could have used more positively. "Remembering" is remembering that one is in the Tradition, never forgetting this, and using it as an energy and a source of strength.*

Now *Remembering* is another one. This is a recollection exercise. It doesn't mean recall everything you ever heard or want to remember.

The most convenient way of doing it is to fix on a particular point concerned with meditation, relaxation, use of instruments, use of colours or something like that, and recall to yourself everything that you have heard about that, and how you have either used it or how it has impacted on you and in what way it has become part of you—and also, how you can use it, or how you have used it, or how you might be able to use it.

This is also an aspect of familiarizing yourself with your past—examining your past reaction to things. How a circumstance influenced.

21.11.85

Definitions using 'could' or 'should' are a sort of dependant factor. When you are remembering or examining situations you shouldn't try to make yourself go through every possible topic of conversation, attitude, aspect or everything that you could have used in a particular situation.

The possibilities—that is, your attitude—the way you should have behaved, the way you should have listened, the terms of reference you should have used, to what degree you should have tried to understand, how deeply it should have affected you—these are not things you have to go through exhaustively in order to say "Well, I could have done this, that and that."

All these various things might have applied, they could all have been possible—for instance, physically, because of the time, the situation and so forth—but when one says what one 'could' or 'should' have done, the implication is that one is aiming for something which one could have done, or which one did as a result of properly reacting to a situation, and, having had a correct reaction to a situation, one used terms of reference and applied them, choosing the correct one for that specific situation.

Regarding what one should have done: when one says "In such and such a situation I could have done this" or "I should have done that"—in retrospect, there are an enormous number of things which one could have done, and again with hindsight, one sees or one knows what one should have done.

This is a very fertile area of desperation and horror and blaming oneself: "Oh I should have done this, I should have known better, I should have taken heed, I should have remembered, I should have thought, I should have reacted, I should have felt" and one then feels increasingly stupid, dejected, and generally unfit to be a human being.

This is not useful, because it is also part of looking at oneself. As you recall, the rules are all compatible, they are not in competition with each other. When using one or more of them in a similar situation or occasion, they complement each other and enhance each other's activity.

So if one is examining what one should have done in a particular situation—for instance with me—the possibilities of the "could have done" are enormous, but one narrows down these possibilities to what applies in the present time, i.e. "What can I do now?"

An enormous number of things.

One feels that something is a correct or harmonious thing to do in a given situation, both within the context of the Tradition and in one's normal average life. This thing should reflect outwards.

Regarding 'what one should have done': as I say, one blames oneself afterwards, one feels stupid, one says "Why didn't I think of that?" This is part of another rule which is examining oneself. Examining oneself is not automatically blaming oneself. When you are examining yourself, you are examining your actions or reactions to situation in a constructive, not hostile, way. After all, you are examining yourself with patience, in a harmonious way, as a good friend of yourself—and as such, you do not attack and agress against yourself.

Constructive criticism may be required—and it can even be harsh criticism if necessary—but use the same terms of reference in measuring or criticizing yourself as you would in the case of a very dear or cherished friend. With a very close friend, if you are always biting and critical in your reply when they ask "What do you think of such and such a thing I did?": after the second or third time they won't ask your opinion again. In a way, they will close themselves off from you.

A person can do it to himself or herself. If one says "Every time I look at myself, I show myself evidence of how stupid, ineffectual, or lazy I am"—you will stop doing it because whether it's true or false, there is no necessity to hold oneself up to one's own score. There is nothing useful or functional about saying "I don't like myself."

What this comes down to is that the options may be enormous when dealing with "what one could have done" but with hindsight, what one should have done is to have this sort of dialogue with oneself:

"Okay, I should have done this."

"Why?"

"Because it would have been more constructive, more useful, more harmonious in the context of the Tradition."

One normally examines one's performance during the day in an everyday commercial, political or other context, saying: "I could have made an extra X thousand" or "I could have got X more votes if I had done that." With the benefit of hindsight, this is certainly true.

What really happens is that you're saying "I should have done that, so that next time ..."—this is the promise or threat which is always inherent in one's own activities, and certainly within the Tradition.

If one does an exercise under reasonably quiet and harmonious conditions without being pushed or worried about the time factor, and one settles down and, say, one does an exercise for a quarter of an hour, half an hour, 40 minutes—one might think afterwards "I felt or experienced such and such a thing or I didn't—how can I enhance that state or experience I might have had?"

# YAD KARDAN

One is not aiming, nor is one trying to maintain, a degree of concentration if it equates to tension next time around. What one should do is say "I could have done a large number of things: listened to music, done an exercise, read a book, gone to the cinema, had a meal, gone to sleep or something. As it happened, I did an exercise."

After this period of exercise is over, one examines what one felt, what one thought, what one experienced if one experienced anything—and what one should then do is say "I did the exercise, it was good, it felt positive: maybe I should have shortened it or made it longer." We're not saying: "Was it better for me to go to sleep, read a book or have a meal?" No, the fact that one did the exercise is fine in itself, and in retrospect, one is not picking holes in that. One is simply saying "How could I have enhanced it?"

"Would it have been useful if I had made it longer, added music or used a different music, if I had sat in a different position or used a different zikr?"—always with the idea, again, of maximizing the context of the situation.

If you say "Where does remembering or examining oneself come in?"—Remembering and feeling is very functional, because, as an individual or in a group, if one does an exercise and it is a good exercise in the sense that one feels good and reasonably calm and harmonious with the people— one has a sensation during the exercise.

Now different situations produce a different emphasis of experience—it is a sensation which is somewhat impalpable— it's not warmth, coldness or whatever, it is a sensation. One does not go after assigning a name or a 'degree of' something onto it, but if there is that sensation, that good feeling, that positive feeling—remember it, remember the quality of it.

Don't necessarily try and remember the intensity of it—because again here, somewhere, the simplifying part of the human mind equates intensity with tension—so a person comes out of the exercise trying to remember "the intensity" as much as they can.

What one wants to do is remember the quality of the exercise—for the reason that, then, if one can remember or fix its quality, you can then try and start the next exercise with the same quality, which is already in place as a factor. So you're not starting, as it were, from 'cold.'

One says "I could have done this or that, but as it happened, I did an exercise. In retrospect, part of my attention was distracted because of "a bad position I took up" or "the music I was or wasn't listening to was not harmonious" or "there was some other factor" I either put in, or didn't.

Therefore, where "What one should have done" comes in, is in the "I should have added music" or "taken the music out"; "taken up another position"; "added something" or "subtracted something"; always with an aim in view, which is to enhance the function of an activity.

It's not just scoring 'Brownie points': "I've done 'hours and hours and hours' of exercises and I'm a better person." Yes, to be sure, I hope so, but that is not what it's all about—one cannot judge it on that basis. It's qualitative and not quantitative.

Remembering situations when I might have said something is valuable, providing one is allowing for human fallibility, and providing that the situation you might have been in with me is not used as an excuse for stupidity, laziness or lack of thought.

# YAD KARDAN

Everybody says "perish the thought" but this is a factor because people tend to remember things out of context. "I remember once that Agha said "I hate meat" therefore "we all hate meat" or "we should all be vegetarians" or something. The context might have been that I might have already had lunch, and somebody with the best will in the world brought me a large steak, which made me react in that fashion.

The factor becomes even more complex when it gets into the area of "Somebody says that someone said that ..." — this is already the soup of the soup. Your memory or recall of a context with me, or when you remember what I might have said, should always be, when practising this rule, taking place in the first person—that is "I remember when..." — so that you can replay it.

You don't necessarily have to quote it to yourself in the form of "chapter and verse" — but at least capture the approximate situation, or recreate the circumstance or quality— and see under what conditions any particular thing might have been said, or some particular aspect of it dwelt upon.

The time factor is all-important. Within the context of a group, when I am talking, for instance, to more than one person: there are some things which are general in the sense that they apply to everybody, in all groups, at almost any time.

There are also some specifics, which, to put it mildly, become confusing when taken out of context. This does not cause permanent damage, but I do equate confusion with loss of time and loss of energy. If somebody spends five minutes trying to work out why I do something—or what it means that somebody told somebody who told somebody else that I said such-and-such—as far as I'm concerned, that is a wasted five minutes, and I begrudge that sort of situation.

So therefore to ask: "He said such and such a thing to me—what should I have replied?"—The answer is usually simply what you feel you want to reply. If you become obsessed with what you 'ought to be' replying, you are looking at it in only one way, which means that you are limited in your response or your reaction.

He said "Good morning" so therefore I should have, and in fact I did, say "Good morning" in reply. That is a polite conversational gambit, and it is perfectly normal. If I say "Good morning" and somebody replies "Good evening," we both have to look at our watches to see who is wrong. How one should have acted, how one should have responded, how one did respond, did react—taken in the context—is the important thing.

"I could have done this, that and the other thing" or "I should have done this that and the other thing"— well, the question is not a searching one in the sense that one is trying to prove oneself to have been in error. What one is trying to look at—for instance, in the context of a meeting with me and other friends—is the energy inherent in that situation, in various qualities and in various quantities—how best does one react?

Quite simply, one sits down and feels as harmonious as possible with the other people, one expresses to oneself a positive intent and one flows with the situation. One doesn't have to be constantly tense as to "What should I be doing?" One should be as much as possible in a situation of alertness, so that any signal which comes from within oneself about what one should do should not necessarily be obeyed as an impulse, but should be considered, looked at, measured according to the circumstance, and reacted to accordingly.

It's not as complicated as it possibly sounds because at

an everyday level people do this all the time. They assimilate impacts, and they scan, feel, hear, think, and then they react on a reasonable level.

There is no need to have any great esoteric skill in reacting to anything I do or say. Any method of communication, telepathy or telekinesis, or whatever, which is going on—if it is going on—is not something I will make a song and dance out of. If I'm doing it, I'm doing it, I may be doing it, I may not be doing it, I may be capable of it, I may not be capable of it. This is not the question which should be even at the back of anybody's mind, because I will communicate what is necessary to be communicated, in terms of explanation, energy, terms of reference or anything else.

So by attention and by alertness, the whole concentration of a person should be focused on what he or she is doing in the context of the Tradition at the time they are doing it. For instance, if one is sewing something in a fairly meticulous fashion, it is a perfectly normal thing for one's whole attention at that time to be concentrated on a very small area.

It is quite possible and achievable to bring certain aspects of one's faculties of inner being to focus onto certain aspects of the rest of one's being, and to relate to certain aspects of the Tradition so that they lock together. After all, they are harmonious, they are of the same nature, and it is not by any means an impossible or mechanical task to put them together. Like attracts like.

If one is in a state of receptivity and alertness, and if there is energy, if there are signals, if there are impacts—a person will receive them according to whether (a) they can use them at the moment, (b) store them for use later, or c) store them to pass onto somebody else. In itself, this is a very intricate system of change, exchange, counter-exchange and use of energy, but it should not be a preoccupying factor: "Am I doing this or that?" In such a situation, one is as a passive or active recipient.

But the human capacity for clouding the issue is infinite. Again we are going back to conditioning: nobody in their right mind—which of course absolves everybody present—will freely take upon themselves, by their own volition, a train of thought which is going to lead them into confusion. They just say "I don't want to know" and they're absolutely right, because their instinct is telling them that whatever it is, it is going to be confusing—however people do manufacture and disseminate clouds of confusion as a result of all sorts of aspects of conditioning. One understands this and allows for it.

If I then quote Churchill who first said it, and scream: "Up with this one does not put!" you can either have no reaction at all, or else you can say "You have to excuse him because he's mad." If he is mad, that's unfortunate, then one tucks him away somewhere nicely and they look after him. If he is assuming the garb of madness in order to avoid responsibility towards himself or others, then one shakes him out of it, either violently or gently.

This can apply to something of a philosophical, geographical or economic nature: if a person is reading something which has certain terms of reference or a certain direction—while they are reading this work, assuming they are literate, they are understanding or assimilating it while reading, they are obviously not just working through the alphabet— they are reading the words, understanding them, seeing the explanation coming out, and reacting, on whatever level applies——i.e. "This is illiterate" or "the spelling is wrong" or "the use of that phrase is wrong" or "I don't understand this" or "what is he getting at?"——so there is an ingestion taking place.

Then there is also 'filtering through' in the sense of "Who

was this bloody "communist/socialist/Tory" or whatever is writing this "obvious propaganda"—or else "this is irreligious" or "sanctimonious" or whatever. What this means is that such an assimilation of a reading or conversation always passes through filters.

The initial filter it passes through, which is very basic, is the sound filter: "This noise, music, voice or whatever; is it dangerous? Is it on a harmonic which signals danger?" If it isn't, the person will listen to it.

If this person is a professional musician, he or she will listen to it with professional interest: how interestingly that particular instrument is used, or how it comes in and complements the other one and so forth, and they use terms of reference. Now these terms of reference can sometimes be a result of deep conditioning.

They thus absorb through all these filters—if these filters can inhibit one, for instance by saying "By definition, this is written by so-and-so and we all know he is "mad", "red" or whatever"—the person is already reading it with a certain amount of bad intention. They are trying to pick holes in it in order to be able to say "You see, I knew it was going to be rubbish" etc.

So how does one avoid this? How does one sort out the gold from the dross? By being alert to the harmonics of a person, a text, a music, an ambiance, a situation.

Again, I repeat this because it is necessary to do so— paying attention and being open or alert does not mean being vulnerable, because we are not talking about that type of absorption. What I am depicting here is the way one is talking and relating to a series of functions within oneself which are in a receiving mode at any particular time. All of them are not receiving at the same time, they are not exchanging or transmitting, they can cut off at will, and they are doing it in a harmonious fashion.

This concept of remembering or recollecting of *Yad Kardan* is not a random exercise, a haphazard reeling back of the memory tapes in order to pick out things which one thinks were interesting or which might have provoked thought or energy in the past—it means specifically remembering and recollecting situations of a positive value and nature.

Recollecting is not just remembering a particular circumstance or situation, it is remembering it in its relationship with the teaching, at that particular time.

It is not random in the sense that "I remember such and such a thing once upon a time" or "I was in such and such a place." This is normal memory and recollection, which can be nostalgic and informative and, indeed, quite usable as a teaching in one's normal everyday life. In ordinary life this faculty is called "using one's experience." I don't like applying the word "mechanical" or "automatic" to it, because it implies a certain robot-like quality, but it is in fact something which normally becomes part of one.

When you go down every morning to drive your car, you don't have to learn how to drive a car all over again. The experience is already there—you know how to change gear and how to steer and operate the vehicle because it is already in your memory. When you get into the car, you switch on that part of the memory which relates to the experience you are undergoing, i.e. driving a car. Hopefully, you won't engage another area in the memory at the same time which might be "How to ride a bicycle" because if you operate a car the way you drive a bicycle, the results are discordant.

# YAD KARDAN

But if you say "It's not working" to some people, they can be too busy pedalling to stop and think about what they are actually doing. They get over-involved in an activity which seems to be productive because they are pedalling. On a bicycle, you pedal to go forward, in a car you pedal only under certain circumstances as when you are accelerating, changing gear or braking—you don't pedal all the time. So by definition, pedalling does not always correspond to a useful forward movement, nor is it a movement to be used all the time.

This is all plain common sense: unfortunately, people do not always use it to the utmost, so as you will have noticed, the rules are here to steer you back on course in most circumstances which apply—certainly in aspects of the Tradition, where the Tradition should apply.

Again, everybody should know that they don't pedal under all circumstances. They know "I am in a car, I will behave as if I am in a car. If I am on a bicycle, I will behave like that. I am on a horse, I will do it like that." This is part of the memory, and the person switches on only that part of the memory which relates—it is not an effort in the sense that one reaches in and switches from here to there in the body in order to go through it all, and work out the relevant arm and leg movements—an autonomic factor comes in.

By the same token, it is possible, useful and necessary to be able to recollect, to remember certain positive circumstances where one has done or tried something, when a circumstance has been fulfilling, useful, valuable and positive.

In a selective memory—the memory is selective in the sense that one doesn't always want to remember some unpleasant things. However, even an average memory remembers everything, and one doesn't have to be a genius for this to take place. Every little sound, sight, touch, feeling,

149

and even every thought, is stored in the memory somewhere.

Certain memories and certain levels of memory become receptive under certain circumstances. The average three or four top or surface layers of memory are the ones one might call nonessential memories. They function like the "magic slate" one used to be able to buy for children: you write on it and the writing adheres, and then you move a bar and wipe it out. That is how the front-line cells function: they hold onto the memories which you need for the moment.

Another example: I know perfectly well that I have this teacup in my hand, so in order to drink from it, I have to sit forward, reach out, and bring it to my lips. I don't have to remember that fact forever, for the obvious reason that either it won't be there or I myself won't be here tomorrow, so it is shunted off onto a siding. If I think tomorrow "Where was the teacup at such and such a time?": the memory will still be there, but I can wash that out very easily by putting in the picture of wherever the teacup is tomorrow. So the instantaneous memory which one needs to use at any given time is taken on and sorted very swiftly. And if it is more valuable or more useful, it goes deeper—it's marked, or typed, or coloured, into the memory, and then filed.

The average human memory is a very fascinating thing and cannot be created, or even made in the form of a computer.

The memory has one faculty which can never be reproduced by data processing—it has a selective and a protective capacity. It protect itself by filtering impacts such as sound, music, thought, somebody's voice or whatever, and it checks them and allows them through as they are tested and found to be useful, positive, non-hostile or non-alien in the sense that they might be dangerous.

# YAD KARDAN

The memory will also take a concept, a thought, a piece of music, a situation—and remember it and put it to one side without filing it, because it is not quite sure how and where it applies.

The memory will do that and keep it there for the person, but the person does not become inhibited by this presence because the person's being will sort it out. It therefore doesn't have to become a sort of indigestible thing to be worked over, i.e., a problem or a thought in the sense of "What should I do with it?" This is not a random faculty that enables it to fit in, because if the memory holds it as being something valuable, it will 'tag' the thought or concept with a question mark—in other words, it will test it.

The being of the person will then either receive it or find it wanting, and therefore reject it, and it will then be put out and forgotten. There's no great struggle involved in this process of rejection and pushing out: it's an autonomic and ongoing process. No computer can do such a thing, because no computer has a being—no computer lives in the sense that it can measure. It can only measure according to the way it's been programmed.

Now you may say "Aha, but you hold that we're all programmed"——Yes, you are, but part of the function of remembering is to remember circumstances and then, without any debate, aggression or collision, to compare an experience or a circumstance with some value, point of view, or experience, which has a conditioned quality about it.

For instance, I was brought up to believe that eggs are good for you. Let's take a perfectly healthy concept which applies to Britain: "Bovril is good for you" (Bovril being meat extract and bones boiled down with hooves and horns and things, and I'm sure it's very good—personally I prefer Marmite, but that's a matter of choice).

# RULES OR SECRETS OF THE NAQSHBANDI ORDER

One can say: "We were all brought up or conditioned with certain catchphrases like "Bovril is good for you"—shall I therefore call Bovril into question? — Not automatically.

There was a time I remember with great fondness, when I was in Paris several years ago now, where everything was quote "put back into question" unquote—which was perfectly healthy and interesting if you were sitting all day in the Coupole or other places of great learning and esotericism.

Nevertheless, there are certain obvious measures, values and terms of reference which one has taken on or inherited and which are perfectly valid and do not necessarily, by definition, have to be examined microscopically.

One has an area of conditioning, from whatever source: be it social, genetic, political or whatever, and then when another aspect comes along, it is normal and reasonable to compare the two. They won't always be at complete variance with each other in the sense of black or white, it can simply be a different aspect, a different point of view, or a different way of looking at whatever you are dealing with.

One should be careful about using terms of reference so that you don't overuse them. Using is useful, measuring is useful, overusing, over-measuring, over-stressing can become a form of neurosis.

Let us assume that I am looking at a bottle of mineral water. I look at the cap, at the label, at the weight of the bottle, at the colour of the glass, I count the number of bubbles in it, I measure its height and everything else—does that do anything for the taste? It can confirm to me that it has no bacteria in it, it has no aluminium in it, it has no eggs in it, it has nothing in it: it is just water. And anybody who has tasted distilled water, which has had everything taken out of it, knows that it tastes awful.

# YAD KARDAN

Now you don't have to examine water beyond a certain point. Is it wet? Well, yes. Are you thirsty? Yes. Do you want to drink it? Yes. Does it slake your thirst? Yes. All right, finish.

You can examine the molecular structure of it at your leisure if it happens to relate to you or if you need to know about it, for instance if you're a physicist or chemist or something like that. This is perfectly reasonable. But there are degrees of investigation, terms of reference which you do not need to use.

Okay, in the nineteen sixties and so forth, this was called "intellectual laziness" because one was supposed to "re-evaluate everything and put it to the test" and so forth. As I say, this could easily become a preoccupation for some people, and it did, for many.

What has this got to do with remembering? The answer is absolutely nothing, but it is a description of the way that people's thoughts wander off onto a sideline. They say "I am in a particular situation, I want to remember something useful or a positive circumstance, situation or impact." That's all right, so you reel back the memory. What you want is a value, a quality, a bit of energy from a situation which relates to the situation you're in now, or one of the same nature.

It's no good saying "The situation I am working out is how to write a letter to somebody: I would like to relate to a positive situation so I can communicate something positive through this letter."

So you think of a successful situation: "When I passed my driving test." You evoke the satisfaction, the happiness, the situation that was positive and useful—yes, it is a positive recollection, but it doesn't help you to write the letter.

You might say "Doesn't getting that sort of happy glow of passing the driving test communicate through and enable me to write a better letter?"

The answer is no, because the quality of happiness is not enough. In a situation like that, you want to write a letter which has to convey a certain amount of energy or a certain charge. You have to think of a similar circumstance. You may not need to limit this to letter-writing. Letter-writing is communication, right. So reel back, think of a circumstance when you were able to communicate by voice, by touch, by telephone or some other means: a communication circumstance.

This is a similar quality of push or energy or recollection: "How did it work then, how did I set the situation up, how did I then carry it out in a positive way?"

So when you are doing the *Yad Kardan* or *Recollecting*, the text beneath the rule specifically indicates *"Remembering positive situations in the past which one could have used more positively."*

That doesn't mean to say that you remember circumstances which might have been positive or useful, and then use them to criticize yourself by hindsight, because *Remembering* does not mean putting yourself under a spotlight in a critical sense, but seeing how it could have been done better, so that in a similar circumstance, which will undoubtedly offer itself in the future, you will be able to react in a more positive way.

No circumstance in the future is exactly the same as a circumstance in the past, for the simple reason that the time factor changes, yet the mechanics of doing a thing remain similar. You have a piece of paper, a pen, and you are going to write a letter: the mechanics of that action are always the same. However if you have learned from recollection how best to write a letter to that particular person or that particular office or department, your shallow memory serves you well enough to do the job. You say "The last time I wrote to the Inland Revenue, I wrote 'You damned swine, if you think you're going to get any money out of me, you're wrong' and the next morning the bailiffs were on the doorstep." Now that didn't work. Right. That is not a very fundamental memory, but you learn. So if anybody later says to you "Write down 'Dear Swine, I'm not going to '..'" you say to them: "Oh no, I tried that once." That is what is called experience and learning.

So you take an old piece of paper you've torn off an old newspaper hoarding or something, and a stub of a pencil to show how poor you are, and you write the most abject letter, asking for pity, time, release from bondage, and anything else you can think of—that too is called experience.

So *Remembering* is also experience: after all, if you have been through a situation which is bad and you have suffered as a result of your own mistake or miscalculation, when you get out of that situation you don't remember the degree of hurt or suffering, otherwise as I said in the case of the dentist, anyone who remembered it to the same degree as when it happened would never go to a dentist again. Fortunately, time dims the memory. This is where the memory, again, is selective.

But what you do remember is that a certain thing worked.

You then try and go into the deeper memory and try and think how you could maximize on a situation, the context, the contact, by being more receptive to positive impacts or more insensitive to negative ones.

Again, the defence is selective—one does not adopt the withdrawn defensive, because that is turning inwards. Remembering situations which worked out positively and usefully, recollecting how one felt, what one thought, and then taking them out and adding them to a present circumstance, situation, tactic or effort—is how one pushes them forward like that.

If you've had a lesson which has been painful, you have paid for that lesson, so use it. This is where the memory comes in—you should have contact with your memory—not running it through all the time, but keeping the maximum contact with your memory so that at any given moment, without fixating yourself, one can bring to surface a positive recollection which will stimulate an action, a thought, a word or a movement which can then improve a situation.

It is not merely a chewing-gum type of action of turning the memories over—after all, there are childhood memories which are full of nostalgia. Nobody is saying "forget them" or "That's a lot of useless clutter"— they exist in areas of the memory where it is perfectly normal, reasonable, and natural for them to be there. You cannot expunge or wipe them out, because you don't need to—they are not occupying what is called valuable space.

There is adequate space in the memory for everything you could ever learn, and more space becomes available as the person learns how to use the memory in a useful way. Brains don't get any bigger, but they become more usefully exploited.

At the present level of human existence, the brain is under-used, because the method of teaching how to use the brain is limited. People who are supposedly teaching one how to use the brain don't know how the brain works. This is a great handicap, but they go on regardless.

3.11.88

# REMEMBERING AND FORGETTING ONESELF

Much emphasis is placed in the Sufi Tradition on remembering oneself, and also, simultaneously, a seeming contradiction is the same emphasis on forgetting oneself.

These two things are not really as contradictory as they might appear, because remembering oneself is one of the Naqshbandi rules. It comes about by the examination of oneself under different circumstances, i.e. the calm and balanced examination of one's thoughts, one's feelings and one's intentions.

Forgetting oneself comes into the picture when it is one's intention to forget or not use certain aspects of one's thinking, or a certain conditioning which one has, and which one has unconsciously or consciously assimilated. In our terms, one wants to forget, or rather lose, that type of conditioning.

What you are expected to do—and using the Naqshbandi rules is one of the means by which you see how to do it—is to watch and examine yourself in a balanced, harmonious and friendly way, using the rules as measuring points in one's behaviour, and seeing in what way any particular aspect of your life or behaviour could be improved by increasing your association with the Naqshbandi rules—hence deepening your relationship to the energy which comes from following them.

When you are using one or other of the rules, you are linking into a source of wisdom or energy which will give you an extra impetus in exercising those rules.

# RULES OR SECRETS OF THE NAQSHBANDI ORDER

Living in the world, earning a living and being subjected to all the impacts, dramas, tension and hurry that this implies, very often obscures from oneself that one is getting further away from a balanced behaviour, further away from some things which feel extremely good to oneself, and getting into an artificial mould in which neither one's time, one's thoughts or one's behaviour is one's own. One is, in fact, conforming to what society demands us to be.

In a western society, it is neither possible nor advisable to completely distance oneself from everybody or every situation. This would be a life of a hermit, which is something we neither encourage nor approve of in the Tradition. A person can be subjected to the tensions, hurry and problems of everyday life and still remain the master of his own soul—but it still requires a conscious and unconscious effort to defend that soul, and also to enhance its knowledge, its feeling and its capacity.

Conforming totally to every conditioning one carries means that there is little time and energy left over to enter into a communion with one's own soul, and it leaves little time for a spiritual energy to be built up.

In observing oneself and using one of the rules, or else in observing oneself through, or together with, one of the rules, one can find a pattern of thought or behaviour which inhibits the full benefit of this particular rule being used.

It may be through a lack of patience or a lack of disciplined thinking that one says "Yes, I'm following this rule and I don't feel it functioning or working." You do not judge in this way—following a rule is not like putting on a coat of paint, in the sense that when you put a coating of paint on a surface, you can physically see and touch that paint, and hence know you have painted that particular area.

# *REMEMBERING* AND FORGETTING ONESELF

In using one of the rules, you do not judge as you go along. While using the rule, you do not try and measure to what degree you are using it, how efficient this rule is for you at the time or whether it is the right rule to be using under the circumstances.

There is never a wrong rule to use. Some rules apply better to some circumstances, and other rules apply better to others. The only measure you have of how much, how efficiently or how positively or usefully you used a rule is a feeling which you get—a feeling of harmony with that rule.

This harmony may produce any number of sensations: it may be tranquility or quiet, a person may feel safer or more encouraged, and, depending on their background or personality, they will manifest it to themselves as a result.

However the investment of time and/or energy while using one or other of the rules does not imply that you will get a tangible result at the end of a certain time. Using the rules, observing oneself, improving one's harmony with the rules and with the Tradition, are all, as it were, stocking up energy to your credit, which you use in an hour, a day, a week, or a month later.

This energy you stock up is an energy you cannot waste by any misjudgment of your actions. For instance, supposing you have successfully achieved certain positive things, and acted in a way which is satisfactory to yourself and harmonious to your activities—you may feel a quiet satisfaction with it, and that may be the only time you feel the buildup of energy, until such a time as the situation is right and the energy itself dictates to you that you should use it under a particular circumstance.

This is of course one of the benefits of latching onto and tuning into this type of energy. Knowing the human person, if one could monitor and measure the amount of positive energy one has at a particular time, the individual would constantly be monitoring: "How much energy have I got? How can I use it? When do I use it?" This can become a preoccupation, and it would be disturbing rather than helpful.

Therefore in order that they not be disturbed by a buildup of positive energy, by the same token, people cannot use that energy in a wrong way. This energy is valuable. It is built up with effort and is of a quality which can transform or convert a situation into a positive one—even if it is a negative one on the surface—assuming that it is allowed to manifest itself under the right circumstances.

Now the forgetting of oneself is not the forgetting of everything which one has learnt or of every experience which one has had. It is putting certain circumstances or situations which were painful into the past, having extracted the lesson from them, and forgetting them to the extent that they no longer come up in a negative way or dominate your thinking under these circumstances where there may be an opportunity for the negative to come in and operate.

As I have said before, don't forget that the only function of the negative is to disturb, disrupt or impede the manufacture and generation of energy—it has no other function. In the average person, the negative energy is perhaps between 10 and 15%, and it seeks the opportunity to distract you and disturb your thinking, especially if there is anything you are thinking about or doing in a positive way. Its function is to disturb—its function cannot be to control.

It sometimes manifests itself in certain circumstances where a person is not fully balanced in regards to what they will do. The negative will very often give them a further push toward the negative, and because of lack of discipline, lack of thought, laziness or imprecision, they will continue onwards in a negative direction until the positive wakes up to the fact that there is a negative impulse operating, and puts the brake on.

Many theories about people's personality and their inner being have been spread around, especially in the West. A favourite one is the theory that the individual is divided into two 'good' and 'bad' parts, or the positive and the negative. The implication here is that the person is divided equally, and you therefore have a lifetime battle between the two sides to see which will conquer and dominate the individual.

This is completely and utterly untrue and a complete fabrication. Short of some distinct mental aberration of an organic nature, the average person is between 10 and 15 per cent negative, or even less.

The positive is less ingenious and less alert, so that if a person is influenced momentarily by a negative impulse or is involved in a negative situation for a time and goes that way, it takes time for the positive side to get into action in order to feed more than the negative into the person, overcome it, cancel it out and bring the person back. The positive always does this, but it sometimes can take longer—and it also depends on the person's strength of belief and how efficient their thinking is. To an extent, it also depends on the conditioning they have which has influenced them into giving more prominence to the negative.

Society in general will help you magnify certain negative things, and you can quite easily do so, but it is up to the individual to limit the influence of the negative by flooding the inner being with the positive, to use that positive frequently enough so that the reaction of the positive to a negative situation will be almost instantaneous. This is better than allowing the situation to first become negative, and only then becoming alerted enough to activate the positive into bringing the person back to step one.

If you have a stop/go situation like that, in which a person is subject to negative influences—either from where they work or with the society they live in—the more one has to be on guard against the negative.

The negative is not a menace, and one should not be afraid of it—because being afraid of it encourages the tendency to give it greater importance that it actually has. One must be aware of the confusions and problems that negative actions and thinking produce, but that does not mean generating a neurosis within oneself about it, or a constant hesitation in case one is falling into a negative pattern of thinking or activity.

Of course one can most certainly act on impulse and only find out after the mistake has been made, and it's too late, that a certain pattern of thinking was of a negative nature—and then pull oneself out of it. This can be repeated, because there are human weaknesses and failings, and one cannot always be aware of the consequences of one's actions until, sometimes, the action has already taken place. This means that one can then take advantage of it if it's good—or repair it if it is dangerous or has caused damage—but again, without magnifying it.

One has to believe that the positive is there. This has to be a strong and firm belief, not one that varies according to mood. The energy of the Tradition has been and is still established for the use of people in the Tradition. The key to that energy is their activity within the Tradition—the Tradition does not reach out and touch them at random.

People seek the Tradition—and when they find it, however lightly it may have touched them, and however mildly they may have been in contact, they never lose that contact. They can only improve and enhance it by their trust in it, and by their trust in the energy of it. This has to be a tangible thing which they can feel in different ways. Even if they can't actually touch it, they can see it acting for and with them under varied circumstances.

Remembering oneself is also remembering how, in certain circumstances, one has achieved contact of a deeper and more spiritual nature, and then seeking not only to repeat the experience, but to put it into one's deeper consciousness—on the assumption, which is true, that it will manifest itself in a positive way when the need arises.

There is no such thing as a 'hit or miss' use of the energy. This is why a person has no control over its use. It comes out of a person when it is attracted by a need or by a positive circumstance which requires a little more boost, and the way it manifests itself is as function.

This should be an encouragement because it is not an abstract connotation. It is not luck, it is something a person works for and achieves, and as such, one earns the right to benefit from the energy. People benefit from the energy which they produce themselves, from the energy which is produced by the group, from the energy of all the groups acting together, and from the energy implicit in the Tradition itself.

Another promise implicit in the Tradition is one I have already mentioned—it doesn't promise you heaven and it doesn't threaten you with hell. What it does is make available to you a path and a way in which the spiritual dimension can be enhanced, and which will reflect, in turn, upon the person's everyday life.

The path is a long one. It is full of hard work, but it is an investment of one's energy and feeling. It is an investment and a sample of a person's trust, one's own confidence that it can be achieved.

Nothing the Tradition promises is beyond the reach of an average person with more than average dedication and discipline.

It needs discipline, confidence, trust, and it needs a feeling for oneself—because what ever else it may be, it is a path which is being trodden by the persons themselves, so that he or she has every reason to enhance their own being. Yes, it is a selfish requirement, but it is the person who is benefiting, and by implication, as the spiritual development is reflected outside, so this benefits and influences one's family, one's circle, one's friends and one's society.

It is a person's own responsibility and freedom of choice which makes him or her enter into the Tradition—they must therefore abide by the discipline of the Tradition and the requirements it imposes on them. They must be honest with themselves, and not merely in order to say: "Yes, yes, that's all right, that's what I'm doing."

No, they must be conscious of doing it, and do it with determination, not as an neurotic impulse of "Time is passing, I've got to get something done now!"

There is always time to do what is necessary. It is choosing the right thing to do at the right time which is part of the function which the Tradition offers.

So get yourselves closer to the Naqshbandi rules. Apply them in whatever circumstance you feel. Familiarize yourself with them. Have them as a part of, if you like, your reactive mechanism.

# *REMEMBERING* AND FORGETTING ONESELF

Don't go through them every time you reach a situation, because this is time-consuming. They should manifest themselves to you in a certain circumstance, or you can choose one which seems to apply particularly to a certain circumstance, and then apply it—but do it correctly.

But do it with full confidence. Do it with a belief that the energy that goes with that intention can carry it through.

28.01.93

## 8. BAAZ GASHT
### or *Restraint*

*"Restraint" is the imposition of self-discipline upon oneself in various ways. It should reflect in one's everyday activity and in one's activity in the Tradition. One restraint that one imposes is patience.*

Now the next one is *Restraint*. *Restraint* does not imply the imposing of automatic forms of limitation on oneself: within the context of the Tradition, *Restraint* means avoiding ill-thought impulse—reaction, as distinct from action as a result of some stimulus.

People say "Oh I'm impulsive." It's perfectly all right—if one is an impulsive shopper, one goes into a place and buys all sorts of things by impulse—as long as one has an understanding bank manager, this, I suppose, is possible. It can be detrimental.

But in the context of the Tradition, things should not be impulsive in the sense that they are millisecond reactions. "I suppose I should do... that's what!"—and if that particular thing doesn't work, then one tries something else—and once again, you get into the usual pattern of "I tried it, and it didn't work" and "I am a fool" or "He is a fool" or something like that.

So *Restraint* does not imply restraint in the sense of: "Don't do anything in case it'll be wrong." Use your own experience as a restraint.

21.11.85

# BAAZ GASHT

To the foregoing, I would add that one is patient with oneself and also patient with other people. Again, patience is not an excuse, not another word for laziness. People say "Patience is a virtue"—yes, patience is a virtue, a quality, and also a very useful tool.

Knowing when to use patience and when to be inactive are two different things. Being inactive means disengaging one's thoughts or one's actions and just dreaming, if there is no particular reason to do anything at a particular time.

Being patient is imposing a form of restraint upon oneself—but again, not in a conditioned way: "If you are not patient, this that and the other will happen."

This is the carrot and the stick—"If you don't, you will suffer"—no. If you don't exercise a faculty of patience which you are capable of exercising, you lose out on a lot of things.

"What things?"

All sorts of things.

"Can you be more specific?"

No.

"Will I lose this and that?"

Probably.

Again, one does not exercise patience by gritting the teeth, gazing into the distance and thinking about oneself: "Oh goodness, I wish this or that would go away." This is a tactic, not a technique.

If wishes were horses, beggars would ride.

One can indeed wish this or that would go away—and it does happen under certain circumstances—but it is more fulfilling to do something positive in order either to attract something, to keep something away, or to keep something from influencing one in a negative way.

The restraint factor is because *Restraint* imposed by oneself upon oneself prevents what one calls the immediate reaction— either the hostile, or the involuntary reaction of "gimme now" or "explain it to me immediately."

As I have said before, there are no doubt many circumstances where involuntary and instantaneous action is necessary and laudable. If there is a charging elephant, you do not reflect upon the virtues of restraint and patience: you shimmy up a tree—preferably big—as quickly as possible. Nobody will say "Poor fellow, he did exercise the most extraordinary patience with that elephant." They will look at the patch of strawberry jam on the ground and say: "Bloody fool, why didn't he run?"

Patience is a virtue under circumstances where it can be used as such. The use of patience towards oneself should be more limited than your use of patience toward other people. Why? Because you are or should be more open to yourself, you are more vulnerable to yourself than other people are to you.

If you are open, fair, honest and direct with yourself, you can criticize yourself in a kindly way, you are not your own worst enemy or worst inquisitor. One should not get into the "negative side of me undermining the positive" and all that sort of thing.

It is perfectly possible to say to oneself "Yes, I did mess that up" or "I did do that" or "this worked." This is fine and good: you can be happy with yourself, and you can also be sad about yourself.

But in addition to this, you should have a communication, a conversation with yourself—without seeming to do so in public, because it attracts attention. But one can use *Restraint* with oneself to have a conversation or contact with oneself without obviously doing so and being carried off to the nuthouse.

By definition, *Restraint* does not always mean "the stopping of," or restraining in the sense of "to restrain" or "to prevent." It means the patient use of a faculty that one develops in certain circumstances.

There is patience, patience and patience—one can wait. There is no time limit to patience in the sense of "I'll be patient for a minute" or "for today" or "for a week": because what happens then? Do I then go mad? Not necessarily. When playing solitaire, you have a card game called "Patience" in which you can wait patiently for the opportunity to win. If you're playing chess, by definition you have to be patient.

Exercising patience does not imply being slow: patience does not mean laziness, it means just that—restraining yourself until you understand the situation and can do something. Restraining yourself until you have built up enough energy to use in a circumstance, or restraining yourself from doing something you are not sure of, is not to be mixed up with a "hit or miss" sort of hesitation.

*Restraint* is an adult activity insofar as it is a thoughtful and self-imposed condition in the sense of "I will do what I can do" and "what I know I can do" and "I will try all the time to do it a little bit better." You're not challenging yourself to do something, you're not setting yourself an impossible goal, so that every time you fall short you say "You see, I knew I could never make it" and flagellate yourself.

By definition, patience is waiting for the moment or opportunity to use tactics, techniques, faculties, or energy of which you must be, on some level, conscious. On the conscious level, if it is an ability, a dexterity or something you have learned, you know perfectly well how capable you are of doing that particular thing: so you try and push it a little bit further.

You are patient with yourself insofar as you don't push yourself, you don't 'make haste.' You also don't use that as an excuse for hesitation in the sense of "Oh, I might not be able to"—"Oh, shall I do it?"—"Oh, is the time right?": because this becomes an excuse for doing nothing.

"I tried that once and didn't like it." Right, examine it again using *Recollection*: "Did I use enough patience at a particular time, did somebody else show patience?" — because don't forget that with patience, using it is one thing, identifying in another person is another.

"Did they use it? Didn't they use it? Could I have encouraged them to use it? Could they have encouraged me to use it" and so forth. I mean, this is not a one-way street—none of these things are.

Patience is also looking at oneself, and errors are mentioned here: *One is patient with one's errors and one learns from them.* This does not mean that one excuses one's errors— the word used here is "patient with"—i.e., patient with them to the degree that one understands why, what the basis of it was, and then one tries to do something about it.

"This error was because I wasn't patient enough with somebody, with myself, with the circumstance ..."

# BAAZ GASHT

"Had I been patient, I would have ..."

Right, that's with the benefit of hindsight.

As far as one can, keep all these rules in mind.

Keep them circulating—not to the exclusion of anything else—because they should be constantly percolating through and operating on different levels.

You do not stand at the bus stop, hail a taxi, or do your shopping according to *Yad Kardan, Baaz Gasht* or anything else like that. You have worked them into yourself so that they have become a part of you. When they can be operative, they should be attracted out by the situation itself.

You should perhaps first feel a situation and think "Right, I will use it." You don't say "When I finish breakfast I will pass the whole day in *Yad Kardan*"—there may be circumstances where it doesn't apply, there may be circumstances where two or three of the rules apply at a precise time—and then don't apply again for the next week, ten days or the next month or year.

That doesn't mean to say that they move in cycles in the sense that "Aha, today is *Yad Kardan* day!"—Otherwise I would have circulated a sort of calendar marked red, green and blue and so forth.

At which point some people would look at it and say "To hell with it, I'm not getting up today." This is certainly possible, some people find it difficult to get up whatever day it is, but this will be a result of a conditioning: "I never get up on Ash Wednesday" or something. This is an artificial restraint.

The opposite of an imposed restraint is a self-imposed

restraint due to the fact that one has decided it has a value: it has a use, it has a place, and it's a tactic which one employs— but not to the exclusion of ordinary general life.

One uses these rules not in competition with each other, but together with each other—one or two or three. Time changes during the day, during the week, and sometimes some situations seem to attract, demand, provoke or produce a reaction which can come under one or a permutation of these rules.

As I say, you do not decide beforehand that "the entire day" or "the entire week will be according to whichever rule." What you can do—and this is something which is always within your capabilities and grasp—is to maybe think about a situation, a meeting or a context before it takes place. Think what the situation could be: "It's going to go like this" or "it's going to go like that" and then—assuming the rules can be applied—"How might I use one or more of the rules in this forthcoming context?"

You do not say to yourself "I will apply such and such a rule, willy-nilly, whatever happens." Maybe the appropriate tactic or technique for the particular circumstance should be one in which one should be slightly hostile, say, or even aggressive, for professional or social reasons.

If this is required professionally, or socially, or antisocially or whatever, one might consider that it would immediately come into conflict with one of the rules, because one would say "Oh, I shouldn't do that." Now if the other person is playing by the same rules, okay: there should not be the head-on clash. But if they're not playing by the same rules in a professional or other situation, you can't say: "Hey, I was using that one" because they'll just say "Ha, ha, tough luck." If they don't share the same terms of reference, you can't expect them to.

What you can and should expect yourself to do is to be able to call up, and use, one or other, or a permutation of several of these rules, plus the energy from the Tradition.

They are there to be used and they are functional. They cover all aspects of almost every situation. If one doesn't take advantage of their qualities, if one doesn't put them together with the energy, which is available, and fashion them into something which is functional, well, nobody is going to force you to do it. I'm not going to tap you on the shoulder and write your name in a black book, since I am not in that sort of business.

But what it comes down to is that, having read and learned the rules, one doesn't just say "Right, what's next?"

What comes next is the constant application of them.

Not in the form of a preoccupation : "Oh, I had lunch and I didn't use such-and-such a rule"—because, hopefully, in order to eat, you use a knife and fork. Your digestive capacity is not dependant upon your knowledge of the rules.

Therefore you do not try and bend the rules to fit your convenience. You try and mould your lives as much as possible around the rules.

3.11.88

## 9. UKUFI ZAMANI
### or *The Time-Halt*

*This is the halting of intellect and conditioned thinking. This is not a halt of thought. You put yourself into a situation where your so-called educational background, terms of reference, conditioning and brainwashing are put to one side. You basically suspend judgement based on your social conditioning. You put aside preconceived attitudes. Your concern may be the exterior function of your being, but you put the decision in the hands of your Master.*

Number 9 is the *Time-Halt* and it is defined as halting all intellect and emotion. Now that's a pretty big order. It is a form—a slightly more refined form—of detachment.

One is trying gently—not with great tension—to stop the mental processes. Some people have said, you know, you close your eyes and lie back and relax and "think of nothing."

Well, to all intents and purposes, this is impossible to do. It would be a somewhat sad reflection on your mental processes if you could, as a matter of fact, because, unless you were anaesthetized so that you think of nothing unconsciously, you don't recall it in order not to react to pain.

You might say "Anaesthesia is the best form of relaxation because the senses are all dulled."

True, the senses are indeed dulled to the extremes of pain,

174

but even under anaesthesia the system perceives and suffers from pain. Otherwise you wouldn't have what is called postoperative shock.

The system has felt the pain; okay, it doesn't come to the surface so it's not terrible, but the senses are not cut off. What is called the locomotor centre is still recording the fact that this has happened. So when the *Time-Halt* says you're halting intellect and emotion; it means that in effect you're not using them. You are not pulling a fuse—you are detaching as far from them as is necessary for a useful circumstance.

21.11.85

The last three rules all involve the aspect of halt or stop. In the Tradition the word *"pif"* or *stop* implies a halt.

By definition a halt does not necessarily mean a stop of any fixed duration : it can be milliseconds, seconds, minutes, days, hours or weeks.

A halt means a stage between two points: going forwards or going backwards.

Now if we look at the text following the rule, what is this *"decision"* that you *"put in the hands of your Master?"*

The decision as to what form this halt or pause is taking.

Basically, it is the halting, pausing, and the using of certain terms of reference in certain situations and in certain conditions within oneself. The catch-all question in this particular rule is that you put the decision in the hands of your Master.

Does that mean that at any given moment, when you feel the necessity or need of halting the so-called intellectualizing or conditioned thinking, you have to ask? The answer is no,

175

because there are, again, situations where physically and for various other reasons, it is not possible to ask the question directly. There are situations where it would not be possible to interrupt a conversation or a meeting to telephone or something like that.

As in the other rules which we try to apply, you have this *Time-Halt* present in your memory. In asking your master which halt you are using, how does that apply?

The asking takes several forms—there is direct asking: "Excuse me, do I apply this, that and the other thing?"; "Should I apply this or that?" or "In such and such a time in the future, I may be faced with x, y, or z—should I apply it?"

There is another way of asking, which is one of the reasons why I am dealing with all three of these *"time"* rules together, because they match each other in the time area. You can ask by making a contact which does not necessarily have to be of a telephonic or even of a telepathic nature—it can be in the nature of "feeling in contact with."

It is not necessarily a "visualization" exercise. If in a given situation a person feels or thinks to be in contact with me, then the contact is made. At that point the contact really exists.

The visualization aspect of it is something which one has to be a little bit careful of. As a result of some phobia, fear, hallucination—maybe because of something they have eaten or because of a nightmare—some friends among you might visualize me for reasons of this type. This has been known to happen, and it is a perfectly natural, and more or less undesirable, phenomenon.

One has to be a bit careful of it not so much because one doesn't want to get into the 'cult of personality' area, but simply because one is trying to maximise one's energy and attention. If a certain amount of one's attention is used for a visualization, it is better that this visualization should take the form of a shape, a form or a colour, rather than a person.

There are very practical reasons for this.

Putting a clear and indelible visual picture of a person or the image of a place into one's mind and keeping it there and relating to it can be useful—and there's no reason why one would not do this—but if a person is sensing a colour, a particular geometric shape or visualizing a place and all it implies on different levels, there is more communication than with just a flat shape.

So if one is in a situation where one wishes to use the *Time-Halt*, your use of it should be thoughtful.

You're not stopping time, as such, for whatever reason—maybe because you feel timidity or doubt—so you say: "I don't want to go into this because of 'this, that and the other thing,' so I will indefinitely postpone it." This is not particularly useful, it is treading water or just passing time.

There are situations where one wants to look at one's own self or at circumstances around oneself in a perceptive and deep way. Therefore, by halting the use of conditioned thinking, one is focusing one's deeper consciousness on the fact, that is, on the factor or the situation in hand.

On one level, one is putting all one's concentration, attention and intent upon a particular situation existing at that time, and one is therefore effectively stopping time as far as indulging in conditioned thoughts or in reactions that are coming out are concerned.

# RULES OR SECRETS OF THE NAQSHBANDI ORDER

The way you involve me in it is simply by remembering as far as possible what I have said about this *Time-Halt*, and using it. You are then putting me in the picture as well, making the connection and link, and using me as a touchstone.

You shouldn't either consciously or subconsciously be trying to get my approval before doing it. You should rather be thinking about whether your intention of using this particular rule accords with what I have said about it.

That is where I come in. It's not a matter of ringing me up and saying "Is this the time or not?" but being in tune with what I have said and seeing whether it really and honestly does accord, and not "It would appear that such-and-such, so I hope"— yes, one can always hope, but don't try and bend a rule to fit the circumstance. It either fits and applies, or it doesn't.

If it doesn't apply, let go—because, as in any of these rules, one might pick one and try and apply it to a situation, circumstance or train of thought where it doesn't apply.

It may flow with the circumstance or thought, or it may decay in the sense that it can apply at the beginning or during the course of a situation, and then dip out of sight. It isn't then lost or destroyed. It may have fulfilled a function and another rule may now apply at the same time.

So when you use the *Time-Halt*, as it says in the text: *"It is the halt of the conditioning, it is not the pause or halt in thought."*

You can always try and do what people are allegedly told to do by some schools of meditation: "Make your mind a blank." Now some of your minds may already be blank and it's not my problem, but I can assure you that it is psychologically and physiologically impossible to make one's mind a total blank.

# UKUFI ZAMANI

If you close your eyes and "make your mind a blank"; you would also have to stuff your ears with wax, stop any sound coming in, insulate yourself from any tactile sense, cover your body with insulation to prevent it sensing any change of temperature, and prevent any movement so that you're not disturbed—so what would you do then?

I am told that in the United States some people go and lie in tubs of salt water brine, covering their eyes with eyepatches in order to provoke a sort of return to the womb situation—it is very expensive and whether it does anything or not, I don't know, but at the best of times, it will be an artificial thing. It is much better to use a tactic and technique one can use without going to the extreme expense of making and getting into subterranean brine tubs.

One already has all the ability and capacity needed to follow and use all these rules—within the reasonable context of one's life, profession and other things. Any detachment required is, again, covered by the rules.

To what degree do you detach from a situation? How do you detach? Are there techniques? Are there ways of breathing, ways of positioning, contexts in which one should?

The answer to all of these questions is yes, and you find them, not just by slavishly following a number of rules but by understanding yourself and your reactions: "How do I, me, Joe Soap, Mr. Average, react to certain situations?"

"My tendency is X, Y or Z"——If it is beneficial and positive, follow that. If it is not, try and let this tendency, weakness, fault or whatever be diluted by a positive in the situation, so that you can say "Ah, in certain given circumstances, my tendency is to do such-and-such a thing."

If one then says "This is not useful or positive so I will avoid all such circumstances"—that's all very well and good— but supposing these circumstances are part of one's everyday life or job, how does one then avoid them? Change one's job? Change one's friends? Change the circumstances or the country one lives in?

All these things are possible solutions, but how do you live with a situation which is difficult, whether professionally, socially or otherwise?

If you say: "In a given situation, I tend to do this or that and it produces negativity or tension": to a degree, you can fight it—you can stand up against it without making it into a great crisis and without tearing yourself to pieces.

You can also do another thing. You can say, "Right, in certain given circumstances, in a given context, my tendency is to react in such-and-such a way." Add to that: "When I react in that such-and-such a way, it will also be my intention to introduce into that situation something from the Tradition as well."

"After all, whether it's tension, weakness, hesitation, anger or fear that I am bringing into this situation, I am introducing it as a result of some conditioning, so I am not going to fight against it with a 'stand or fall' or 'make or break' attitude."

You simply say: "By the same token, I will introduce something from the Tradition more and more into the situation" and balance out the negative, the tension, the fear, the anguish or whatever.

After all, a person who is twenty, thirty or forty years old has twenty, thirty or forty years of conditioning. You are not expected to overcome it at one go and you do not do so, but you can lessen its effect by using these techniques of detaching yourself and introducing aspects of the Tradition into circumstances where you feel there is a negativity.

The *Halt* factor here is that suspension—not of thought, but of conditioned reaction—and, at that same moment, the introduction of some specific element from the Tradition during that halt period.

The *Halt* period is not just halting to think, although it certainly can be that, but halting with the purpose of doing something—using that halt for some specific purpose.

9.03.89

## 10. UKUFI ADADI
### or *The Number-Halt*

*These are interior exercises carried out with numbers. They are based on the Abjad system and you divide the parts of your body into segments. Different segments can be put into operation at different times, under different circumstances. Your Master will tell you which, and with which parts of the body you can or should operate at a given time. Again, from the conditioned point of view, do not ask why or how: do it.*

And at number 10 you have the *Number-Halt*. That is when the interior exercise is carried out in numbers. Now this is interesting, perhaps because it sounds rather like an army thing—hup, one, two, three—it isn't that actually.

What it actually means is that the rule is carried out *to* numbers. It should be more felicitously phrased as being carried out to a particular rhythm.

21.11.85

The word *Abjad* means the numerological significance of letters in the Arabic language. Each letter has a value, and certain numbers make certain letters and vice-versa. The application of the numbers or letters also represent sounds and colours, and the whole thing interrelates in that way.

The body is basically divided up into different segments, and these segments are referred to in the *Abjad* or numerological code by certain numbers. The application of the numbers does

# UKUFI ADADI

not mean that one is conditioning oneself or learning to say "I am operating number 61, which is my right thumb" or something like that.

This technique for the value and use of numbers has unfortunately been scrambled over the years, and was used widely in certain pseudo-Sufi studies with the numbers equated to certain movements, rhythms and dances.

That is the result of misunderstood and unlearned factors, and we needn't go into that—but briefly, the idea is that, by dividing the body into certain segments—theoretically, not figuratively, in case any of you are worried—the basic idea is that just as there is a harmony in music and colours, so there is a numerological harmony based on the human body.

This is not as complicated as it sounds. All I will say about it now is that it is the equivalent of a balancing scale using weights. As you put two kilos or two pounds on one side of the scale, so you should ideally have two kilos or two pounds on the other side. That is what is called a balance or an equilibration.

It is possible to give a long explanation of why it should be so, but the clearest way to see it is to look at the currents of energy normally present and passing through the body.

As you know, in the Tradition we have various positions for doing exercises, and various positions for meditation, prayer, relaxation, and so forth, and during this process, one is optimizing the body posture on and together with the exercise or the activity.

Where there is an exercise to absorb, generate, reflect or transmit energy, the body posture can be different from that of an exercise which is to assimilate and circulate energy within the person. We're talking here about the area of magnetic currents.

If one has one's hands clasped, the definition of energy passing will be in the form of a circle. With the hands detached, the circuit is of another nature, because the circular circuit is not there.

That doesn't mean to say that if one is sitting in a detached or casual manner, as one very often does, the energy is sort of dripping off the fingertips or anything like that. It means that under certain given circumstances, adopting the best posture is maximising on the whole thought and energy system, i.e., the energy current, the positioning, and the physical comfort of the overall system.

When one gets to know the corresponding parts of the body, one can see how and why the balancing or the equilibration can be better used and better understood to be used. It is perfectly reasonable for one to explain and look at diagrams to try and understand the path or passage of energy within the human body, or even within a group, and it is a further bonus factor when one feels the activity of the passage of energy and knows that one feels it.

It is not an imaginary thing or a phenomenon which is dealt with in the abstract. It is there and palpable.

If one is in a situation where one is using, harnessing, processing and benefiting from this process and one understands how the function takes place, then one can use it, it becomes real to one. Any preconceived or conditioned notion measured against that feeling is then put in its correct place as being something preconceived or conditioned, and the sort of 'supernatural' area goes out of the window—it becomes a perfectly natural and normal phenomenon.

# UKUFI ADADI

By understanding how it is set up, one can understand how to make it function. If you have an equation, say $2 + -2 = 0$, you can see how a balanced equation can work. Let us say that you have a segment of the body which—for whatever reason—is in a depleted or minus situation, and another segment which is significantly positive, how can you then pass the positive energy on to that depleted side?

You might object to this idea, saying: "It's all within the same frame"—True, but one can implement the process by trial and error, in the sense that "Fortunately, I found that such and such a thing worked." This is perfectly good, but we're talking about areas where we don't want to have a 'hit or miss' situation.

We need to be able to say: "A person places himself or herself in a particular situation with a particular intention in a particular position in order to do an exercise, meditate, or use, receive, transmit or process energy." We want to harness every aspect, and not just ask "Why is it possible?"

You have to be able to at least try and answer some of the doubts, mostly based on one form of conditioning or another, as to whether a thing will work or not.

"Oh, I could never do that!"

Why not?

People think this way only because the idea of handling the transmission of energy, trapping and using energy, or balancing and maximising it, isn't a thing which is taught outside the physics laboratory.

9.03.89

185

# RULES OR SECRETS OF THE NAQSHBANDI ORDER

## 11. UKUFI QALBI
### *The Heart-Halt.*

*This is not the physical stopping of the heart. It means that the person uses the "Heart" concept, putting together love and duty at the same time in the same place. The heart is at the disposal of the Master, and he will do with it what is necessary.*

Then number eleven, which requires a little bit of explanation, is the *Heart-halt* or *Visualization*.

Now the *Heart-Halt*—these are direct translations, for the reason that, inevitably, since the original is written here, somebody is going to translate it and is going to say: "Oh, that doesn't mean the same as this" and "Is that this?" or "Which is what?"

The *Heart-Halt* does not mean that the heart stops. This can be produced very easily, and it can very often be a terminal experience, so one isn't trying to achieve that.

What it means is, technically, that one is, again, detached—and one is going within oneself and visualizing without being conscious of the physical side of oneself, which is the pumping of the heart.

You might say "Yes, but I'm not normally conscious of any sort of thudding, unless I've been running about and doing something physical, so it really doesn't interfere with me."

It is not a conscious effort that "I will not listen to the beating of my heart"; it is actually just a detachment between the actual physical self and the inner being.

# UKUFI QALBI

It's a technical term, so it doesn't—please—mean a sort of inducement to the coronary or anything like that.

21.11.85

It is necessary to write down *This is not the physical stopping of the heart* because there are some of our friends who with great devotion and discipline have—fortunately—been unable to physically stop the heart, much as they may have tried.

In the Tradition, the technical term or concept of *heart* or *qalb* contains other aspects. In English you can say the "heart of the matter" which means a central point, a focus.

Two concepts come together in the *Heart-Halt*, love and duty—love for, and duty within, the Tradition, duty to oneself, duty to and responsibility toward one's inner being.

The *Halt* aspect operates in a sense that one is excluding a dimension which may be of a purely sentimental nature, based on conditioning. It may be of an intrusive nature, that is, paying more attention to certain aspects than to others.

To simplify—it is allowing the inner being, with which one is trying to establish communication, to feed, and develop— while at the same time allowing it to mesh in, interleave or intermix with the concepts of love and duty.

All sorts of books, plays and films have been written about the apparent conflict between the two—everything from "My country right or wrong" down to things like "Should we fight in Vietnam?" or anywhere else. This type of question is usually posed by people who love to ask such rhetorical questions, because it is then, by definition, an invitation to expound and make comments: "Is there, and where is there, conflict between love and duty?"—"Are they the same thing?"—"Do they overlap?"—"Are they the two sides of the same picture?"

If there is an answer, it comes by looking at what one feels or what oneself knows about these two things, if indeed they are separate from each other.

In the context of the Tradition, and as far as we are concerned, love and duty are two aspects of a person, of a being, of a person's actions, of a person's responsibilities—they should not be in conflict with each other.

Again, one has the old and rather sordid question of the 'positive me' and the 'negative me,' the 'good' or 'bad' me, and the constant conflict and tug-of-war between the two. This division can be built up, and people do build it up into a full-scale war. It begins within themselves, and then it spills over to other people who are close to them, or with whom they work, and, along with various aspects of the personality showing at different times, it causes tremendous confusion to the person and to the people around that person. So define your terms of reference.

In a profession, one very often doesn't have the opportunity of behaving as one would like without attracting the displeasure, criticism, sarcasm or whatever of people with whom one works or with whom one associates.

There is therefore a certain degree of—not exactly of dissimulation—but of keeping oneself to oneself in these areas. Not that you are compromising, because if one compromises on significant values, one is compromising in an antagonistic fashion towards one's own being.

In that case, do you say "It is all right to do everything which is beneficial to oneself?"—No, because that is a recipe for selfishness, as in "Look after number one." Again, the harmonic comes into place. Taking the terms of reference as one knows them, as they are explained in these different rules—it is mostly the case that when they are applied, they are applied in a selective way. The aspects of love and duty can apply simultaneously—they can apply separately—they can apply on two different levels at the same time, on interchangeable levels.

They should not be considered to be antagonistic towards each other because by conventional understanding, they would seem to be hostile in nature. They are not hostile in the area in which, hopefully, one is working in the Tradition. One cannot and should not be hostile to anything, which, measured by one's terms of reference in the Tradition and from the point of view of the Tradition, are good, because one cannot and one certainly should not be antagonistic or hostile to oneself.

In a monolithic sense, duty can be equated to a sort of blind obedience to something or some things, to the exclusion of everything else. In this case where does love come into the picture?

Take a very simple question. One loves one's country and one does one's duty by it: if you say that or mention it as a concept, everybody will agree. "My duty is to such-and-such a thing, but I love something else"—well, where are the two factors on a collision course?

Sentimentally, politically, socially or in other areas, one can say that they could be 'thought to be' whatever—that is where the heart halts—in the sense that it is looking at a situation and taking it apart to see where the fundamental values lie within that situation.

One can apply all or any one of these rules.

# RULES OR SECRETS OF THE NAQSHBANDI ORDER

If somebody said to me: "Right, I want to live by one rule. Tell me which"—I would say choose any one and stick with it, they are all equally valid.

But none of these rules operate in a vacuum. In any given situation or context, one, two, three or several can apply, shade off, decay, and another one will apply. But all are equally valid in the sense that it would be impossible for an average human being to take one rule and follow it without encountering the others along the way: 'like attracts like.'

These rules are old, and have been practised and proved: the application of one creates a vortex, and a vortex by definition attracts other things near it, in the sense of like attracts like.

A positive action, a positive thought, will call up a train of thought which will produce an image, an experience, a feeling, which will touch on one or other of these rules.

They should be familiar to you: not occupying your mind constantly, but all of them should have a place in your mind. You go through them, you keep in touch with them, you call out one or other of any rule which applies at a given moment.

You do not decide in advance "Today I am going to operate only a specific one" because that would inhibit you. You would probably be so nervous about not remembering it that you might remember another one, reject it, and then you are getting into a conditioned "Oh dear, I shouldn't allow that!"

Why not?

It's perfectly valid. It may be trying to suggest itself.

As long as you have the rules in the front of your mind, you will attract the one that has the most affinity to a particular situation and use it. They are there to be used, not to be put in niches or hung as talismans round your neck.

They are for application, so apply them, attract them, understand them, and function with them.

They are not inhibitions: they are points of reference, points of discipline, points of guidance, and points which you need to watch.

9.03.89

# RULES OR SECRETS OF THE NAQSHBANDI ORDER

## APPROACHING THE RULES

Many of the rules I have explained to you are clear, and most of them are capable of being used in a useful way. The question here is this: how does one use them in a useful and correct way?

It's very easy to take the rules and say "I'll follow this, that or the other one" and perhaps get caught up or confused as to which particular rule one is using at which time, and which one should be used in what context.

It is important to understand that the rules should be understood when they are applied. If you just take a rule in the abstract and say "I will use this one and hope it works"; it may very well produce a positive context, with good intentions and with good and hopeful anticipation of what one is doing—but it is much better if a person says "I am using a particular rule in a particular context for a particular purpose," thus defining one's own terms of reference.

It is very easy just to say "I'll think I am using this rule for this purpose, and this purpose will lead to such-and-such a result."

It is more useful to think which rule one is using to achieve a certain particular result. One can have much enthusiasm and good conscience and use a certain rule—or two or three rules—in certain situations, and say "These rules will get me through."

It is true that the rules will help, but the question has to be "What is the intention of the person when they use the rule or rules?"

# APPROACHING THE RULES

If a person is merely saying "I am trying to do something—I think and hope I am right, and I will add the rules to this something, like some sort of magic formula which will produce a positive result": this is not always the case.

You put in the positive affirmation, the energy, and your own personal intention, and the whole scheme of things moves forward and produces something which you can feel.

If you say "I'll just try something out" this is not a question of just trying something "to see"—as if you were saying "Maybe it will work or maybe it won't." This would be some sort of magical guesswork, which is something we do not use.

The rules are there. One follows and uses the rules as far as possible, and with the help of one's own group and other groups, one pushes forward.

One's intention has to push forward in a certain area. Just to say "I'll try this out and see what happens" is not good enough, because this is chance, what one might call "luck." I've said before and I'll say again that I don't believe in luck in the sense of "Oh well, I had a bit of bad or good luck."

No, if a person works towards a certain goal, has a certain goal or achievement in mind and uses all the energy the person has—in other words the energy that comes from themselves, from the group and from the Tradition—this person can move forward in a perceptible and useful way.

If they say "We'll try, and maybe it will work out or maybe it won't"—there is a lack of precision there which leads to a weakness in a person's endeavour. In saying: "I'll try, it'll either work or it won't"—if it doesn't work, they will then ascribe it in a hundred different ways to a hundred different reasons. If it does work, they'll put it down to a hundred different other

193

things. But there is no excuse for not putting activities which one knows can work into action.

There is no excuse for saying "I already know a certain pattern of activity, of thinking, but I didn't follow it because it didn't seem to be the right time or moment"—this kind of thing can also be put down to the fact that the person is not reacting or not using the circumstance for reasons of laziness.

Very few people will admit to being lazy in their intention, because they say "My intention is there and strong, firm and clear, and I don't admit to any laziness in these areas of intention."

Unfortunately, if there is an area in which they have not succeeded in pushing themselves forward by themselves, it has to be ascribed to something. In all honesty, one can't account for it by blaming other people, and one can't deal with it by blaming the state of the world. It boils down to the fact that the person is not focusing correctly on their intention, and not using their intention in a precise enough way to produce a result.

The result is not always some extraordinary illumination or breakthrough they might be thinking about. In fact, it may just be a very slight intimation, a slight indication of something they could aspire to—and why not? If they are sitting there, thinking and hoping that an illumination of some incredible degree will descend upon them, they are then dictating the terms of reference.

Everybody hopes and waits for this illumination, but they cannot decide the terms of reference for themselves; because after all, if they are not able to receive, respond to, or use this illumination—which may or may not come—how are they placed to receive it?

# APPROACHING THE RULES

This is, in fact, greed—which is a very human stupidity: "I want it now"; "I want to know now."

If a person is able to know, they will get to know.

This is why the Tradition is long—it takes into consideration the strengths and weaknesses of the human being. It does not push or pull you, but it attracts you, it tells you, it asks you, and you must answer to that.

If you answer to that in a way which is not in harmony with the function of the Tradition, then you will find no answer. If you say "I want to understand now" and tune in without being on the same wavelength, then any signal will fall on deaf ears.

If you say "I want to understand certain things which are beyond what I think is my capacity, but tell me": the answer depends on the attitude with which one says this. If one is saying "I hope to understand, I would like to understand, to know"—then you have the basis of some sort of understanding.

With questions such as "I would like to know how"—"I can work, I would like to know what my position is" or maybe "I would like to know who I am"— from the point of view of the Tradition, all these questions are right.

But "I want to understand now" or "I want to be told now" involves a certain arrogance, and the Tradition, unfortunately, does not allow itself to be pushed in that way. If one reads enough, thinks enough, and puts enough energy into what one is trying to do, one will find that these things come in gradual measures.

As one can understand, so one does understand. There is no magic in it and no extraordinary 'flashes of light' which come from it. They come gradually, for the simple reason that if a person in a situation is flooded with points of reference they cannot use in that particular situation—what happens? They get tense, and they say "I should understand"; "I should know" or "I should use."

All this is true, because we do not provide anything for anybody which they would not be able to use, understand or comprehend—otherwise it is not a service to them. It is no charity to load people with too much—so that they feel that they are somehow lacking in some understanding, and are therefore stupid, hopeless, useless, or lost.

A lot of people can be, and are, stupid, and this is due to their terms of reference or to the way they think. But lost? No. Loose terms such as these which are used in the West are exaggerated. Nobody is lost if they can think and feel once.

Nobody is lost if they feel and carry on. Nobody is lost if they hold out their hand and that hand is taken. They can consider themselves lost—this is their privilege—but it is also their weakness or their stupidity.

"I don't know what I am supposed to do."

Think and do.

"How should I do?"

Do what is right.

"What is right?"

What one thinks.

After all, in the Tradition we go back a long way. For instance, if you take the sayings, behaviour or teachings of

# APPROACHING THE RULES

Bahaudin Naqshband, you will find that these teachings and sayings are as applicable today as they were in his time.

The skill—and it is a skill inherent in the Naqshbandi Tradition from the time of its establishment—is to be able to apply these values, secrets or knowledge, no matter what the circumstances.

You don't say "That belonged to that time." What belongs to that time belongs equally to this time if it is as important as it was then, which it is. For us, the teaching is as important.

This has been partially changed over generations, because of social, political and other circumstances, but it is still valid.

So we will hold through it, stick with it and go with it, and you will find that if you follow it, there is no error. The error may be within yourself, but the error on the greater margin, the greater Tradition, is not there. The error is nonexistent. The truth is ever existent.

24.10.92

# RULES OR SECRETS OF THE NAQSHBANDI ORDER

## NAQSHBANDI RULES AND PERSONAL FILTERS

In order to make the rules function usefully for you, and to help you remember them better, I suggest that you try and examine situations in which you have already tried to use either one, another, or else a simultaneous permutation of the various rules—or again, that you initiate situations where it would be appropriate to do so.

When I suggest things, I don't just toss ideas out in the hope that they will be understood, remembered or acted upon. The suggestions I make are just that—suggestions. They have some merit, they are of some use and they have a function.

I hope and expect them to be remembered for a useful reason, and I do monitor if they have been actually implemented, that is, whether these suggestions have been followed up or not. I monitor it simply because the degree to which the Naqshbandi rules are implemented—in this case the degree to which suggestions of mine are used—does produce a feedback.

This feedback is not only produced in terms of an individual. These suggestions also produce a feedback in terms of the group. If I can measure either one or both of those factors, I can get a pretty good idea of how much—in the sense of how successfully—these ideas or rules have been implemented. And here I really mean "how successfully," I do not mean "how much" and I'll tell you why:

When I say I measure "how much" movement, success or progress has been made by using these rules, I am not just measuring how often an individual person has tried them, or how often the group, as a group, has tried them, because all you would then get is a volume measurement in terms of "eight thousand" or "eight hundred" times, or whatever—which is not good enough.

Of course, that would already be a useful measure in itself, because it would give a rough idea of how regularly or with what intensity members of a group remember to remember either themselves or something useful. It gives you the number of initiations or ignition points—when a person has thought "I might do this" or "I should think like that" or "I should connect myself better with my intention" say fifteen times over a certain period, you have what I'm calling initiation or ignition points.

But what really counts is if they have been successful in carrying through the activity, meeting, conversation or whatever they are doing and have brought it to a reasonably successful conclusion—that factor is what obviously interests me more.

Of course, you can't have one without the other.

You can't have 500 ignition points and 10,000 achievement points unless each ignition point is 'striking outwards'—it can happen, but we're getting into a very convoluted area here, and it usually doesn't.

I would therefore rather see a reasonable carry-through—that is, the two figures roughly proportionate to each other.

It should be quite obvious that the number of occasions, situations and contexts in which one remembers one or other of the Naqshbandi rules are not limitless. That is to say, you do not and should not necessarily measure every single thing you do by one or other of the Naqshbandi rules.

# RULES OR SECRETS OF THE NAQSHBANDI ORDER

The Naqshbandi rules suggest certain terms of reference, certain ways of looking at things in a better and deeper way, and in a way which helps you to enhance your perception.

They do not tell you about the reasonably average, normal and mundane things which are part of the everyday pattern of life, which may be boring, repetitive, and which, of course, should be carried out with proper care, skill and attention—but not necessarily with reference to one or other of the rules.

One's taste-buds are not enhanced by the use of the Naqshbandi rules, any more than a cup of coffee tastes better if one is remembering oneself when one is drinking it. This is overkill, and some people do it. Some people will even do this kind of thing in a very dedicated way, and it can produce an almost hypnotic fascination of association: "I was thinking of such-and-such a rule when I drank that cup of coffee."

This leads one into either: "It tasted better so therefore it's fine," or else again: "I don't remember whether it tasted better or not, what's wrong with me?"; or again, any number of permutations you want to add to that.

So in simple words: in a circumstance, a situation, a meeting, an occasion or whatever it may be: if you have the opportunity, and you decide or think or feel that the use of one or other of the rules could be appropriate in a particular circumstance, then most certainly, use it—but do not feel obliged to make the rules fit your every second, or every passing minute of the day, any more than your every second or every day need fit one or other of the rules, because you can have a situation which is called "over-adherence to"; i.e., "I'll take a bath while in the state of *Khilwat dar Anjuman.*"

Well, there is nothing really to be said for or against such a thing, as long as the function of the bath, which usually is either to wash you or relax you, is not altered—assuming you have time to lie in the water and play with rubber ducks and that sort of thing. If that is the case, well and good. If you can profit from that period to let yourself relax to the degree that you can pick out one of the rules at random and think about it, fine. But it should not be considered as an esoteric bath-salt.

People can work on things in this way and feel themselves particularly unfulfilled because they can't recall whether they "associated themselves with such-and-such"; and this leads them into a labyrinth of their own making. They are then chasing their own tails, and are becoming dissatisfied, disillusioned, desperate, questioning and so forth, rather than using the rules in a sort of "pepper and salt" situation, in other words, adding as required.

When an opportunity or circumstance proposes itself or seems to apply, then by all means apply them, but the inflexible attitude of "I will not do it without having such-and-such" produces a rigidity. This is strange, but true. It produces a rigidity of thought rather than a flexibility of thought.

Furthermore, if the person has gone through the whole list of rules and hasn't found one which applied, the time has either passed when they could have applied one, or else the person feels "I have failed" or "the rules have failed me" and there is insecurity or something like that. In fact, in terms of the actual situation at that time, they have simply lost touch with the reality of the moment.

The skill of using any tactics, techniques or instruments of the Tradition lies in provoking situations or either making or finding time for situations in which one can use them best or use them better. Or again, to provoke times, situations and moments when you can exercise them and show to yourself that you have assimilated a reasonable ability to use them.

# RULES OR SECRETS OF THE NAQSHBANDI ORDER

Balance and reason are basic to the above process.

You don't stop a passer-by in the street and say: "Did you notice how well I crossed the road?" because you either get a punch in the eye, or they call the police, or else they didn't notice you and you hate them for not noticing. Or else again, you cross the road next time carrying a banner saying "Watch me as I cross the road!" which means you've attracted attention and done little else.

But if you were doing it while thinking about something useful, you don't necessarily have to get the approval, disapproval or attention of anybody other than yourself at that time.

In fact, you do have to know that you're doing it, because by doing it, the intention itself is transmitted through the action which you are taking vis-à-vis the situation, the circumstance, the person, or whatever. This means that the circuit is filled, and the equation is then complete.

Of course the equation is itself part of a series of equations. It's not like a self-contained block standing alone: there is a continuity.

People very often get into situations where they say, either to me, to themselves, or to others, that there is such and such a "problem."

At the expense of our French friends, I often joke that every conversation I had for years in France was prefaced by "Agha, j'ai un problème. Est-ce que je peux vous poser une question?" But remember, when I joke about French friends here, it means I'm joking about you when I'm there, so the honours are even.

Okay, even though there is a certain amount of fun to be

had in pointing out certain preoccupations that various groups tend to enhance or work on, one thing that eludes most people is what they categorize as being a "problem."

Now most things in life, from the mundane, superfluous and boring, to the interesting, fascinating, embarrassing or something, are situations.

Going to lunch with three people is a situation. It can become a problem, depending on the topic of conversation, whether people get drunk, whether there's harmony or not, etc., but if one is exercised about a problem and one wants advice about it, or to work on it, one has to be sure that it really is a problem that needs attention and energy focused upon it.

Otherwise one would lump all situations and all questions together into problems. You then have a buildup of "my problems"—i.e., this great black cloud hanging over one—composed of everything in that area from "I forgot to post the letter" to "My house is going to be bulldozed away."

The moment you mention the word "problem" either to yourself or to other people, this already prepares fertile ground for a sort of "So and so has got a problem" syndrome.

When you tell someone "I have a problem"—you know the old story "a problem shared is a problem halved"?— this is not true. A problem shared is a problem doubled, because you've got two people worrying about it instead of one. With the best will in the world, those two people go and discuss so-and-so's problem, meaning that four people are worrying about it—which may indeed be a problem.

If it really is a problem, let's look at it, examine it and see what might or should be done, now or later, i.e., assess its degree.

Also, check that it really is a problem—is it just an inconvenience? Is it just a happening or an event? Is it an aberration, or what? Analyse it—what does it merit? How much attention, exhaustive soul-searching, seeking, looking, finding and looking it up does it need?

Take things in reality: let us assume somebody is researching something in the real world, say a palaeontologist who goes to a quarry and finds a fossil.

If he is a professional, he doesn't worry about it. He doesn't go about the place saying "I have this problem, I have found a fossil" because the first normally sane palaeontologist he sees—there are a few—will say: "What sort of a fossil is it?" and he will have to reply "Brontosaurus Rex" or whatever, and the fellow will then say "There's a book about it by so-and-so." This is what is called normal research or analysis.

Before you decide to put the "red sticker" on a situation saying "Here is a problem"; decide whether it really is one: what its nature is, what its content and context is, and how much energy, attention, concern, fear and dread is actually initiated by it? Is it a question, a doubt? What is its classification? What is its nature?

You assess what in military terms is called "the degree of threat"—threat being everything ranging from extinction to annoyance. You assess it, and usually see what steps should be taken. If one looks at all situations from the point of view of a true and reasonable analysis before you put them into the category of "Problem" with a capital P, you analyse whenever analysis is indicated, or when you have the time and ability to analyse it.

As I said before, you do not spend a quarter of an hour deciding on which bus to get for Chalk Farm or something like that. You can make it hard for yourself, and work your way through all the bus routes, or you can make it easier, but the question of how to get from Hyde Park to Dulwich is not really a problem as such, it's a situation.

What is the degree of threat here?

The degree of threat is low-threshold.

How does one solve it?

One finds somebody, a timetable, a policeman or a tube station, and one takes the requisite first steps. In a case like this, one does not normally panic instantaneously.

If one does panic or get ruffled, disturbed, despondent or anything like that, it is usually because one has not taken advantage of one's own inherent common sense; the common and basic contact everybody has with objective reality.

This objective reality, i.e., this capacity to analyse and look at things objectively, is a capacity which can be developed, and part of the activities in the Tradition are to enhance such a clarity of vision or clarity of thought.

Unfortunately, even the simplest and most pedestrian common sense can be obscured by simply saying: "I don't have it. I'm just stupid."

Firstly, this is not true.

Secondly, what is happening here is that people are placing an artificial limit on themselves. In doing so, they are by no means doing themselves justice.

If the solution to a problem, or a step along the path of development can be smoothed or helped by an instrument or a tactic within the Tradition; then this tactic, instrument or gambit can and should be used—but it should not be used in the abstract sense, in other words, that it is by implication 'alien' to the person. It is not a tin-opener they borrowed to open a can and which they must then give back—which brings them back to being without a tin-opener all over again.

Enhancement or development is exactly that: an enhancement or development of something which is already there. By definition, you cannot develop or enhance something in an abstract sense. You cannot enhance or develop something which was not there to start with.

You therefore do not look upon or use the Tradition to open cans of sardines more swiftly or with more panache, because this would be gilding the lily—any more than people would use a Fabergé tin-opener—which, for all I know, may exist—to get at their sardines. But the function is there: you can use a battered old army knife to get at the contents—if you're hungry or desperate enough, you'll use your teeth.

So what are you imposing as strictures or limitations on yourself, when performing tasks of whatever nature that are, in fact, within your competence? How much are you doing on your own before you bring in the heavy guns or artillery, which in this case might be further energy or contact from the Tradition?

A person or a group can do an awful lot of groundwork among themselves, and with themselves, before they judge— or before it is judged for them—that the time is right to feed in a degree or degrees of energy from the Tradition.

I repeat, a person does not become dependent upon the supply of energy, because this would inhibit, to a degree, their own spontaneous ability to act in a responsible way.

# NAQSHBANDI RULES AND PERSONAL FILTERS

The type of spontaneity I mean is becoming aware of an unfolding situation, and then playing it in order to propel it forward. In other words, to use the medium, the situation and the energy which already exists, feeding in more as one feels it necessary, doing what is necessary to keep the thing moving and the momentum going. The reliance factor—"Oh everything will turn out all right, I'll just sit down and wait for it to happen"—is not correct.

The energy of the contact with the Tradition does not work in this fashion, because if it did work like this, everybody would sit down and do nothing, and just wait for the bus to come along. When you get the reliance factor, you also get the Pavlovian dog factor.

In the Tradition, we have interdependence insofar as the Tradition does not function on this planet except through people. People function with the energy and contact of the Tradition, therefore you have interdependence.

Total reliance of one person on another produces a dependency culture, which in turn produces an attitude of: "Well, if I am doing right, it will show" and "If I'm not doing right, I'll just get to know somehow, I suppose."

This is not a useful or practical way of doing things. In everyday life it doesn't work, so why should one consider—if anyone does, and there are many who do—that if you just "sign on" as it were, you'll get carried forward to some sort of New Jerusalem on a wave of enthusiasm and energy.

For them as thinks like that, I can assure you that this is not how it works.

All the backup is already there in the form of the energy, opportunity, emphasis and boost from the Tradition, but individuals and groups have to take the ball and run.

You cannot get any form of enhancement—be it professional or in a deeper, more profound area—without working on it, without being conscious of the fact that it is there and then exercising it. Whatever the stratagem or technique: if it has the quality of enhancement, it must, by definition, be exercised.

"Practice makes perfect" is a wise old saying, and everybody says "Yes, yes, we know all about that. What about all the goodies?"

Practice makes perfect. One exercises one's craft, one's capacity, which all people have in one way or another, and they must then let themselves feel drawn along on a current—not as if participating in some magic carpet—but rather through something they are a part of, by their own effort, by developing, using, absorbing, working on, and therefore enhancing.

"There is no such thing as a free lunch." Equally, there are no free rides in the Tradition. Anybody can get a ticket, but the whole function of the ride is to participate in the journey or voyage. Otherwise one can quite happily remain at the bus-stop, watching the buses go by and rejoicing for those who got on the buses, or else cursing them because one missed the bus oneself. One then laments and blames everybody, including oneself.

Why not reasonably analyse situations which have a worry factor, and in the case of important situations, analyse them at greater depth, and then overcome this worry by natural talent and common sense?

Having got to a certain degree of either overcoming problems or seeing one's way through them—or else plotting a course and maybe feeling a little bit lost or lacking in impetus or something like that—at that point and at that time, one can and should quite logically connect with, or plug into, the reservoir of energy from the Tradition, in order to make use of it rather than just being carried by it.

The energy is palpably there to be used. But its function is to be used, not to use.

After all, why should it manifest itself through the pathetic floundering people do in the name of activity?

"Why can't it just sit where it is, comfortable in the fact that it is?"

Because its function is to work through people, to enhance capacities they already have, however much they may disregard, denigrate or abandon them without using them. Nobody can honestly lay claim to being so dumb, inactive, stupid or unimaginative that there is no way in which they can fit in, express themselves, work actively, be useful or become a coherent member of a community.

Anybody who says such a thing is not focusing on one of the Tradition's central features: in the Tradition we are most certainly interested in enhancing and deepening the perception of the individual—but no man is an island. If this enhancement or development takes place, it must inevitably have an effect and therefore influence the people in contact with this person, thus drawing them along and influencing them positively and usefully: i.e., the oil-spot technique.

One works on oneself, a group works on itself, and different groups relate with each other and complement each other, because whatever is singularly, individually, or collectively experienced by different groups all over becomes part of the accepted knowledge of the whole, and one is therefore tapping into the useful knowledge of each member of any of the disparate groups.

This is not some sort of esoteric telephone exchange in which you say "Just a minute, I'll focus on Buenos Aires today to find out what the temperature is." This might be conceivably useful, but it would be unnecessary.

What happens is similar to any normal social situation; if a member of such a grouping is asked to leave the group because of some activity or activities that are detrimental to the unity of the group, this person would not be welcome in other groups.

Now why do I say this?

Because the same thing applies in the Tradition. Wherever a person gets a reputation for doing something seriously stupid, by that knowledge—not by gossip, but by knowledge—the other groups should be aware that this person is of a negative character. Such a person is not exactly any sort of threat—because that's putting his importance too high—nor is he any sort of worry to other groups, because that knowledge will have spread: "So-and-so is a bit off."

The same thing applies in terms of energy and its use, assimilation and its absorption. One person's or a single group's experience is not a sort of breakthrough or something, but a movement or a situation that goes into a common memory. And that itself is the result of cause and effect; it is the outcome of the knowledge which becomes available to individuals and groups wherever they may be.

There is nothing weird or supernatural about this. One can call it an "experience update," a "situation update" or

# NAQSHBANDI RULES AND PERSONAL FILTERS

something like that, just as, as I say, on a very simple and mundane level, when the theory and practice of a particular therapeutic action has been deemed to be useful by some clinical group, say in Mexico, they normally pass such information onto other people for everybody else to use.

Now this happens on that level, and it's very useful. It also happens on other levels as well, but unless a person makes a conscious effort to push themselves and hold themselves up, while at the same time making a connection with the energy in order to be able to use it in a more and more useful, skilful, tangible and familiar fashion; then the equation doesn't quite work.

At that point it still becomes abstract, or slightly: "Oh, should I, can I?"; "How?"; "Do I dare?"; "Have I the right?" and all these other kinds of questions which can be produced.

The answer to all such questions is yes—because the decision to make an effort in a particular direction is well-judged, thought-out, thoughtful and analytic. One can then make contact with the energy and use it as a fuel, a guidance system or a map: but not as a cushion against reality, because that is the last thing it should be considered to be.

People are all the time interposing different filters, colours and meshes between themselves and reality, in order to allow less and less or more and more through.

Furthermore, they are so busy about doing this that they get out of touch with the reality of their own person and being, and also the reality of their own purpose. "Oh, I'm way off in the clouds"—it could conceivably be exciting, but what is the reality?

If one is living in an abstract way, or in a clam-like situation

211

or something like that: how can one then use the energy of the Tradition? Inside one's clam shell? In order to lacquer the outside of one's shell? To float on bigger and bigger and nicer and more brightly-coloured clouds? Softer and softer? Higher and higher? Flatter and flatter?

I mean, there are two points here: the abstract—which can sometimes be very interesting—and the actual reality of a person's development, their capacity and capability, which are in fact then going in completely opposite directions.

You focus either on one, or else on the other, or again, you bring them both into focus and find the meeting point between them, and then enhance that meeting point and steer them both in a proper direction.

I do commend that you at least consider that there is such a thing as objective reality.

Objective reality is not always simplest, kindest, nicest or best. Sometimes choices have to be made which seemingly run contrary to what one might call "ethereal values."

Well, there is nothing really ethereal about good solid effort in a particular direction—the direction in which one knows one has the relevant capacity, capability, ability, knowledge, balance and ambition.

Focusing on things does not necessarily mean narrowing down one's area of vision in the sense that "You don't see this or that"—because by definition, focusing means "bringing into focus" which should allow and encourage one to look more clearly at oneself and others, at situations and incidents.

Learn from some, forget some and enhance others—these are the tactical moves which should be made.

# NAQSHBANDI RULES AND PERSONAL FILTERS

Where, when and in which situation one uses which rule depends on how skilful you are at understanding the rules and using them.

You don't use them all the time, and you don't get worried about them "in case I make a mistake." It is marginally better to overuse rather than to underuse.

After all, not everything benefits from the rules, any more than everything wishes to or needs to be energized. But when you have decided that something does merit energizing, then do it.

Do it properly and do it well. Do it stubbornly and slowly, or at whatever speed you can achieve.

4.05.89

# RULES OR SECRETS OF THE NAQSHBANDI ORDER

## SELF-ACCOMPANIMENT

It may appear to be a slightly curious phrase, but when one commits oneself to a journey, a path or anything which hopefully leads to an enhancement of one's consciousness, abilities or talents, one should "take oneself along with one."

This represents something real, because there is a familiar situation which affects a lot of people, which is that one can, on occasion "go ahead of oneself."

Going ahead of oneself can sometimes be exciting, because one is seemingly achieving things or planning them out, and there is a degree of abstract in it. But then, if one stops, maybe that initial amount of achievement hasn't been achieved because one has left oneself behind.

One may have left oneself behind in a technical way, a physical way, a social way or in any number of ways.

One hasn't caught up. Possibly one hasn't really practised this technique or gambit well enough—or else the putting together with the energy hasn't become familiar enough to become, again, not automatic, but part of one's normal activities in a perfectly usual way.

If one is harnessing one's person, one's abilities, one's knowledge, one's activities, with everything else in a useful way; this will undoubtedly attract a positive according to the law of "Like attracts like"—but remember, the positive which is attracted has an independent character of its own.

# SELF-ACCOMPANIMENT

It doesn't take over the person's activity and come out as something which is all neatly packaged. It takes on the colouring, character and nature of the product a person is aiming for: the end achievement.

A person can quite clearly and proudly claim: "I did it." There are some situations where they get backup, and there are some situations where they don't. They may sense that they got backup or not. In either case one can often claim: "I did it myself, I can do it, therefore I can repeat it."

So as individuals or as a group, don't be forever writing yourselves escape clauses: "I will do this, but subject to that" or "I think I could do this, but if I don't, never mind" etc.

This is not a healthy, useful or real occupation. Having made the connection to a real situation, enhance that.

This is a simple theory, and I assure you, it's a very practical one. It may often not be very exciting. Some things may be deadly dull. Pouring concrete is not the most exciting thing in the world, but you cannot really construct buildings without a foundation. Somebody has to lay the bricks, saw the wood and cut the trees.

Everybody would like to stand back and look at the completed masterpiece, but if everybody is standing back to look at it—or for that matter, everybody is busy cutting wood or pouring concrete—to put it mildly, you will have overlapping activities; and at worst, complete chaos. Chaos I don't like, because it goes against any sort of constructive programming.

To the extent of my ability, I am in the business of being several guesses ahead of a lot of events. Not all of them— I wouldn't want to, in any case, even if I could.

215

# RULES OR SECRETS OF THE NAQSHBANDI ORDER

If one is trying to make order from a number of events, one can take on or allow for a certain amount or degree of chaos—because if one handles chaos with one hand, one should be able to do the planting or planning with the other.

Nevertheless, if a time comes or a stage is reached when one is using more time in sorting out chaos and less time in planning, the sorting-out of the chaos is slowing down the forward planning. This is just as true in individuals as it is in groups. It applies to the relation between one group and another and to relations between various groups.

Don't forget that the key word is enhancement: the enhancement of whatever qualities, capacities, abilities or knowledge existing within a person, within a group, and which are available to different groups. Deepening and enhancing are the two basic factors, and neither of them can be accomplished in isolation. Neither can be done in an atmosphere of, or with any considerable degree of, chaos, whether in thought or action.

So don't allow chaotic patterns to develop. If they do develop or are forced upon you—and goodness knows I'm not saying that everyday life does not produce enough chaos on its own—I am not advocating monastic retreats or nunneries or anything like that. One handles these situations; one gives them as much care and consideration as is justified, either by dismissing them or by tackling them head-on, or again, by avoiding or sidestepping them, or else by using any degree of native cunning one might have to protect one's capacity and ability to maintain one's momentum.

As I've said so many times before, in order to start a thing spinning you need a big push, and then it takes a little effort to keep it going and maintain that momentum, but under no circumstances should it be allowed to decay.

4.05.89

# OVERCOMING PICK 'N MIX

Tonight I would like to talk about two related subjects which concern what one might call the future of the Tradition in the West.

It involves two points: one is that the transmission of the teaching in the East is a natural and progressive thing which people encounter during their childhood, because if any member of their family is associated with the Sufi Tradition, say a father, an uncle, a cousin or a brother or something, they will then in turn introduce, influence or make information about the Tradition available to a younger person, who can then take it on quite naturally as they grow to learn more about it and understand it.

The second point is that in the West it is a more difficult problem, because there are certain terms of reference and measurements which have become common, as well as various irrelevant philosophical, literary, and other values by which people judge themselves and other people, and by which they judge a teaching.

This is not to say that there is an absence of philosophical or spiritual teaching in the West. As I have had occasion to say, it happens because what is generally called the esoteric aspect of such teachings has been either left out or deliberately cut out, or else again because nobody has written about it in such a way as to make it applicable to a person's everyday life in a practical way.

This means that it has gone more and more into the realm

of heretical views. In other words, there was no encouragement for the average person to follow a natural philosophy, a philosophy leading to a form of self-understanding or self-development, because nobody was permitted or even given the opportunity to explain to people that a positive philosophy can be lived as well as read about.

So it was difficult for them to project this idea. And even when they could project it, they had limited success, because the formal and fundamental Church said that their own teaching was in itself enough to follow for a person to "aspire to everlasting life" and other similar promises.

Now what I am doing here is using the comparison of bringing a teaching to the West and teaching it, displaying it, following it up and guiding it, just as, in the same way, the teaching is taught to children or members of the younger generation.

Those friends in the various groups who have children of different ages, can and do make use of familiar things like the Nasrudin stories to interest the children in the Tradition; but this is a difficult and uphill task which is very delicate and which has to be handled with a great deal of care.

This is because, as you all know, if a child is told something at school, that is "The Law" and they have to believe it. A child will come home and say: "Teacher says such-and-such"—this is absolute fact, it's the absolute truth, and they have to believe it.

If you correct them and say "No, I don't think so," they will go to school next day and say to the teacher "My daddy or mummy says you are wrong" or whatever—and who gets caught in the middle? The child. The teacher may then take a venomous dislike to this child or a virulent dislike to the parents as a result of being criticised, and the parents may equally object to certain things that a child is being taught.

Why this is such a delicate area is because a child wants and needs to learn from a teacher, and therefore needs to develop some rapport with that teacher in order to be taught. They also want the love and affection of the parents.

So putting them in a position where they don't know whether they should read one thing or another, for instance where daddy says: "What you're reading in school is silly"— or else they take a book from home into school and the teacher says "That's a silly book"—they get caught between two fires and don't know what to do.

So at one point you are faced with a person who in many ways is not yet conditioned socially, politically and otherwise— which is beneficial. On the other hand, if you suggest certain points of reference or certain ways of thinking to that child which might be at variance with the thoughts, ideas or beliefs of the teacher, and which they might also bring out at school or in public, you have a problem.

You therefore have a beneficial situation—access to the child—but you also have the danger that this child will be marked out by schoolmates or teachers as being 'different' and therefore, according to their way of thinking, hostile—and we all know what happens to children who are different. Other children can be very cruel and mean, and this doesn't even take into account the attitude of the teacher.

So regarding the comparison between bringing the teaching to the West and teaching a young child, there are similarities.

The similarities, however, end with the following

question: how much of it is actually teaching the child to understand something and use it, and how much of it is doing a sort of counter-conditioning?

An average person has a certain number of years of conditioning. It is possible to de-condition them in areas where such a de-conditioning is valuable or necessary for them to better understand and function in the Tradition.

You do not completely re-condition a person because they must maintain a certain normal, reasonable status and behaviour which is 85% of the time imposed upon them by the strictures, strains, and problems of living in the world, earning a living and holding down an ordinary job.

Nevertheless you must allow them and teach them how to use a philosophy for when they are within themselves, in order to be able to understand themselves and to be able to benefit from the Tradition.

They do that by an educated choice, an educated guess or a feeling. Many people have the feeling they need a teaching. They look for it, even search for it, find echoes of it in books and in various schools of philosophy; and if they search long enough they will almost certainly find one which will satisfy them, and to which they can relate.

With a child, this process is more difficult because they can make the choice based on a purely emotional attachment to the parent or teacher. It then becomes a form of conditioning. Therefore where and how do you start?

This is a partial answer to the many questions I have received about introducing children to the teaching—it is that you start as soon as possible in the form of, say, using Nasrudin stories and other materials, and being very careful not to suggest to the child that this is "a way of thinking" or "philosophy" because they don't know what these terms of reference mean.

You don't explain to an eight year-old old child what a point of view or an attitude is, because they will go through many points of view and they will develop many different attitudes as they grow older. You limit yourself to providing them with the contact. You make the books and various other things of the teaching available to them, and you explain that it is something you are interested in.

The answer is therefore to make it available, just as it is available to children in eastern countries who live in a village, town or city where the Tradition operates on a much larger scale.

The whole function of a person being in the Tradition is to make their contact available to other people. That doesn't mean they go out and sign everybody on, or do things like handing out leaflets. Nevertheless, if they do feel that another person, be it a friend or someone in their own family, would benefit from a discipline such as the Tradition, then they are encouraged, not to proselytize, but maybe to give somebody a book to make the contact.

With the person—in this case a friend, a neighbour or somebody in the family—(the situation also applies to a child)—having made the contact; once it is there, that contact will remain, and it can be followed up. It can be followed up by an individual or maybe by a child who asks more about it, but I repeat that in the case of children, one has to be very careful that nothing which one tells them or gives them to read runs counter to what they are studying or how they are behaving at school, because you then put them into an intolerable situation. It should be made available to them, no more.

# RULES OR SECRETS OF THE NAQSHBANDI ORDER

Certainly as they get older and hopefully wiser, as they learn more about the Tradition they can and do ask more questions, and they may wish to be more involved in it—in which case one can involve them more by giving them other things to read, by talking to them, by explaining to them—within the limits of one's own understanding.

Another important factor in this area is something I mention again because it has to be treated with considerable precision, and which is especially relevant if one is talking about young people.

From their teens upward, young people have all sorts of interests. They are young and keen, their minds are not stuffed full of the trash and rubbish and other things which accumulate later through life; so they experiment with different philosophies, with different ideas, with different political or social ideas and things like that, which is perfectly normal.

A very familiar thing which happens not only to children but to adults as well is what I call—it's an American expression used for selling candy—"pick 'n mix."

Let us say a person is looking for a philosophy they can hopefully understand and which hopefully accords to the rules by which they can live. They may be attracted to some aspects of one philosophy, and some aspects of another, and some aspects of yet a third. In this way they may come under the influence of astrology, astronomy, tarot-reading, table-moving, crystal-gazing or any number of things which are supposed to be sources of knowledge.

One occasionally meets people who have sort of nailed or cobbled together a philosophy for themselves out of various bits and pieces. You will then find they are perhaps reciting a Buddhist mantra, reading to Sufi music dressed in a garment

222

belonging to some other philosophy, and following a diet based on something else again.

I know of such people and I'm sure you all do as well, they are not rare. Some of them are dilettantes who, shall we say, take the Benedictine vows but don't like the harshness of Benedictine life, so they call themselves "sort of Benedictines" and for two days in Lent once every ten years, if it's Tuesday, they don't eat fish or dessert, and they convince themselves that this has satisfied certain aspects of a Benedictine code. In other words, they take the things they like, put them together themselves, and think about them and do them. They may be very sincere about what they are doing. They may also be completely mad, as some people are, and this will most certainly make them madder.

Not to put too fine a point on it, one cannot take significant techniques or aspects of one philosophical teaching and try and match it with another, and heaven prevent one from taking a philosophical teaching, which may be the Tradition—it may be Buddhism, Taoism, or a number of other philosophical systems—to which they add some sort of spooky thing like stars, the Tarot, omens, or various different superstitions.

This leads to complete confusion.

If there was merit in what they were doing when they started off, whether it took the form of following a vegetarian diet or reciting a particular mantra—any merit they may attain or achieve through following this pattern can be diluted and diminished by what is, in effect, a very often fixative attitude towards one of these semi-mystical Tarot-reading, stargazing or crystal-gazing phenomena.

This refers also to younger people, because grownups do not have the monopoly of stupidity by any means.

# RULES OR SECRETS OF THE NAQSHBANDI ORDER

A younger person may be attracted to various aspects of different philosophies. They may read widely—and why not?—about different philosophies, and consider that one activity from, shall we say, a Buddhist way of thinking, can be put together with a Naqshbandi, Chisti or Suhrawardi music while the moon is in Libra or whatever, and that this is an "extra-special ingredient."

Well, whether or not I believe in astrology is beside the point, but what matters to me is what enhances people's capability or quality—in other words, what enhances their being.

You can go back to the twelfth century and you'll find books in all the european and oriental languages telling you that the curative value of a particular herb is greater when it's plucked under the full moon, or when the moon is in Sagittarius, or Jupiter is in Capricorn or goodness knows what, and then you go through the whole ritual of "Boil and bubble, toil and trouble"—it probably doesn't do you any harm, but it certainly doesn't define a discipline to you in any clear way.

If one is to be able to achieve something dependant upon particular solar or planetary aspects, this in itself is a full-time job. There are ways of doing it, and there are indeed very devoted people who cast astrological charts: people have done it right from the beginning of time. I mean Hitler did it, and look what happened to him.

So these things are by no means infallible, and to consider that a particular planetary aspect influences a particular parson at a particular time shows either gross ignorance or immense self-importance. Certain aspects of stars and planetary arrangements do influence certain things, this is for sure, but those people who want to be guided by these things, who read in the papers that "today isn't a good day for you" so they don't go out, are better suited to think of a philosophy which will allow them to do what they already want to do.

The Tradition is not such a philosophy. The Tradition lays down certain rules, makes certain demands on a person, and requires a person to follow certain disciplines which are harmonious with that person by freedom of choice. Nobody is told "You must do this, otherwise you will perish"—this is an Old Moore's Almanac type of prophecy which really doesn't mean anything and certainly doesn't help anything.

If a person says "I have every intention of benefiting myself by following a certain discipline, in a certain way, under certain specific and precise orders" they then have every reason to hope that they can harmonize with a discipline and achieve something.

If they say "I am subject to all of the whims of nature, I am just a leaf borne on the wind" and "If Saturn happens to be my birth sign on a given day, I won't go out"—well, they are not really paying enough attention to what they can do. There is a quotation from Shakespeare I can't remember, which says something about that, but certainly, cosmological phenomena do cause influence. Certain geodetic and geomorphic phenomena have cause and effect in them, but to imagine that a person can go through life putting together a philosophy by which they can live, and do this while ignoring certain valid philosophies is, as I say, either very stupid or very arrogant.

One is not saying that all philosophies except the Tradition are negative or useless. All we say is that the least one can offer to people is a programmed path and the existence of teachers and certain extra energies which come from certain specific activities. To what extent a person benefits is up to them. "It's just poor little me"—well, if one wants to think that way, one can, but there's nothing constructive in that. "It was written in my stars, I was born under Uranus" or something—how may times has one heard people saying this kind of thing?

The real question boils down to something simple: if a person understands something, they can use it. If they use it properly, and they themselves, harmonizing with that, become more and more able to use it and can feel the use actually happening, they can feel themselves using that aspect or thing they have learnt upon themselves.

Again, with a child or with a younger person, this is very difficult, because since the whole of life lies before them, there are so many things to be done and so many things which attract their attention that it's very difficult for them to have to discipline themselves in certain ways. Nevertheless, it is not difficult if they can understand that the fundamental basis of the Tradition is, after all, to back a person up and to give them the qualities and the possibilities to develop those qualities and possibilities they already have within themselves, and to be able to know how and when to use them, and at what time, and to what degree.

Different activities have different times, and emphasis is put on different activities at different times. That doesn't mean to say, again, that one is saying "Between twelve and one o'clock today is going to be better than at twelve o'clock at the same time next week"—no, there is no point in thinking this way. Nevertheless, an individual can craft or put together a certain valuable time for themselves.

What does "valuable time" mean in this context? It means a period during a twenty-four hour period, say ten or fifteen minutes when people can sit down, lie down, be at home, be somewhere calm and quiet, and think about themselves, think about what they're doing, think about what they'd like to do, think about what they can do, and see how they can harmonize with the Tradition.

A bit of this is valuable time. It's not a random thing, like running through the day's events—one does that automatically—but putting time aside to feel and think about oneself produces a valuable time, whether it's nine o'clock in the morning, nine o'clock at night, ten o'clock or seven o'clock at night, so that there's no sort of, shall we say, "fixed" valuable time.

A number of people can come together in a place and meet to do an exercise or else talk about something—that time or period which they have given over to this activity is, again, a valuable time, individually and as a group. So there is time, there is different time and there is valuable time.

Unless one starts to feel harmonious towards the discipline, there is always a danger, which I've mentioned before, of a person imagining or thinking even subconsciously that this is some sort of really alien teaching, something which doesn't quite mesh in with themselves as western Europeans or Americans or South Americans. Such questions should not be of any geographical consequence, because wherever there is a human being, that human being is a being. From the point of view of nationality, colour or background, their identity may be completely different, but in every person there is a being which needs to be nourished, and can be.

With a child, there is a being which equally requires nourishment, but this really comes in at a bit of a later stage, as a teaching. But however young the age, once the contact is there, the contact will last. But as far as actually working on the activity is concerned, unless they precisely understand what they are doing, then it is not necessary for them to make a commitment until such time as they really feel they understand what they are doing and can harmonize with it properly.

# RULES OR SECRETS OF THE NAQSHBANDI ORDER

Growing up in an atmosphere of the Tradition is obviously much easier. A child growing up in a family related to the Tradition is given an earlier introduction and has the benefit of an earlier contact: this is an advantage. In comparison, the average westerner is disadvantaged in the sense that he or she has so much more conditioning to replace.

But again, the balance does have to be quite delicate. In your job, you can't go up to your boss and say "I can't work like this: I have too much work and in any case I am a Sufi" because the man will say "There is the door, use it."

In your professional life, it doesn't help you to make such a claim. Equally, a child who says "I don't believe this and that which you tell us because my daddy or my mummy says otherwise" won't have their prospects enhanced in school.

There are advantages in one way and there are disadvantages in the other way. As long as the contact is made available to the children at some juncture in their lives, they will either be able to follow it up or else find it again at a later stage—but it is valuable to note the fact that there is this temptation, both by adults and children, to add in the mysterious and the supernatural in order to explain certain aspects of the teaching.

Certain aspects of the teaching are not explained in so many words, since they are meant to be felt and then used—not necessarily understood in the sense of the printed word, because it is not necessary to do so. Therefore a person will sometimes find what they imagine to be a gap or a lack of explanation about a particular phenomena, and will fill it in with some superstitious idea or metaphysical explanation which actually distances them from the reality of the Tradition; since every time they find something they can't quite understand or which they find to be missing, they may then

OVERCOMING PICK 'N MIX

fill it with some sort of superstitious metaphysical rubbish. By each of these steps, each time they do it, the actual practical reality of the Tradition is being insulated.

It's as if somebody once told them that "unless it's Friday" or "the such-and-such day in the month" or "unless the moon is in such-and-such", "unless somebody is wearing this and doing that and listening to that other thing"—nothing will happen. The result of this is that they are waiting for all these factors to come into operation before they think they can function. But a person can function within the Tradition with a zikr, with an exercise, in a bus, a taxi, a train or in an aeroplane. You don't have to say "No, I can't take the train that day because I should be doing a zikr".

All these things are to be done while one is in the world—so do not allow these extraneous superstitions, other ideas, or bits and pieces from other philosophies to get attached to the Tradition. And especially, as I say, because children growing up will tend to put things together arbitrarily and say "Well, there's no harm."

There's no actual harm: the only harm is that it can lead to confusion. What is actually the impact of a piece of music in the Sufi Tradition? I can tell you what the impact of a piece of music from the Tradition is, but I can't tell you what the impact of a piece of Buddhist music will be upon you while you are doing an exercise from the Sufi Tradition.

I know that one will harmonize with the other. The other, I don't know. It may harmonize on one level, it may disturb on another. So those are two subjects I have lightly touched upon today but they are ones which are a result of people's questions that are put to me, and I do try and answer questions when I can.

2.04.92

229

# REASON

There is a word much used in the West and in other cultures both as a word and a concept; it can mean as much or as little as people like it to mean. In many ways it is abused and also used as an excuse or a rationalization for a lot of attitudes or errors people commit.

This word, which is also a verb, is "reason."

For instance, people say that the difference between animals and us or between people of greater or lesser intellect is in their power to reason. If this were really true, then the people who use it as a justification for their actions could indeed be proud. Unfortunately there are marginally philosophical schools of intellect that use "reason" or "being reasonable" as their main term of reference.

In the Tradition, we have certain books, terms of reference and ways of thinking which are reason to us in themselves. That is to say that if we examine a thing, use an argument or want to explain something to ourselves or to other people in the Tradition, we use a form of reason inherent to the Tradition.

This may be in the form of certain terms of reference. If you say something to somebody in the Tradition, you may use a particular technical phrase, and if you explain whatever it is to them using that phrase, point of view, or term of reference, you can hopefully be pretty sure that they will understand the feelings you express when you refer to that. You are thus not just establishing common terms of reference but also certain common feelings, a sort of common ground or basis of exchange.

# REASON

You're not being unreasonable here, insofar as, if you are talking about an activity in the Tradition, you are not implying extraneous or alien examinations or terms of reference.

Admittedly, for some people who are so-called, self-styled or genetically "intellectually minded", this can impose certain limits on their study or research. They say "When looking at Rumi, Hafiz, Jami, Saadi or one of the activities within the Tradition, couldn't we look at it from the point of view of Schopenhauer, Jung, Marx, Engels or Harold Wilson"?

No, you can only use like with like.

When dealing with something of this nature, it therefore imposes a severe limitation on certain intellectual schools, because they say something like "We want to get to the bottom of this"; or again, if you're talking about energy, harmony, influence, or feeling, they will say something along the lines of "We want to pin it down", which is tantamount to saying "examine it, weigh it, measure it, label it, pigeonhole it, and eventually use it to our own advantage."

"Using it to their advantage" here means to hold forth interminably about various intellectual nuances within it. I challenge anybody to take any one of the texts which we have, and assuming they quote it correctly, use it to produce as much gibberish as is produced by so-called intellectual writers in the West.

This is not just one of my favourite tirades against the intellectual West. I know a lot of people in the West and I even have friends there, so I don't damn all of them. Just selectively.

For instance, if I have been critical in commenting on a book they wrote or something they are doing, people will say: "Oh don't be unreasonable"; and I say "I am the soul of reason.

I am the most reasonable, happy, charming, laughing, nice person I know"—but only within limits. Once my limits are reached, I become a little less reasonable. When such limits are transgressed, I certainly do become unreasonable from their point of view. To my own satisfaction, I may be absolutely reasonable, which is all I care about, as long as I stick to the main line.

The use of reason implies thought processes, in other words how one thinks, how one puts experience together with feeling to dictate to oneself what one should or could do, what one might aspire to, what limits one imposes on oneself and how one examines these limits—for instance whether they're real or not. If these things are all looked at, and if real and deep reason is used, we can hope that reason might certainly be useful to us.

Following this, if people examine themselves, their problems, their situations or their future, and constantly come up with either mildly or highly critical and tension-making results; it is an easy and quick way of getting into a depressive state of: "I can't do anything, I can't achieve anything, I tried it and it didn't work" and then the whole process repeats itself.

As I have said *ad nauseam*, and I will go on repeating this idea: like attracts like.

If one uses the basic reasoning capacities one already has, based on experience, feeling, and clear and reasonable mental processes, one will find that this should be of a helpful nature.

Using the useful nature of the reasoning process means that it is encouraging, illuminating and explanatory to oneself. Surely this rhythm of using reason, enhanced by contact with the Tradition, should produce a more effective reasoning?

# REASON

Why I'm talking about it is because it is based on one's own thought processes, one's own experience, but also on another factor, which we can call the random factor in the equation—and this can be where professional intellectuals trained in the Café de La Coupole school of philosophy fall out with me. This other factor which appears is the "feeling factor" which comes from within the person, i.e., how one feels about a situation or an activity so that one can enhance it, so that one can improve it.

If people in the Tradition are really aiming at a form of higher consciousness—and if they are able to experience it as a result of doing something, reading something or as a result of a contact—they should indeed be able to use their ability to improve on that experience in order to enhance it.

We are not proposing to aim for a level of permanent consciousness which makes the person unaware of everything else going on, because, after all, one is required to pursue an activity, perform a job in the working world, and thus be normally concerned with worldly activities. One doesn't detach oneself and float on a cloud.

The so-called professional reasoners will say "Yes but I mean, this 'X factor' or feeling: define it."

Well, if you can define "reason" to me, I will define that feeling to you.

So you then say "I will reason as a result of the 'cognitive goodness-knows-what' and whatever, using big words I don't understand, and I have no intention of trying to understand them at my time of life.

Let's begin again. What is reason?

# RULES OR SECRETS OF THE NAQSHBANDI ORDER

You can either have subjective reason or objective reason, but it is much better to have a certain quantity and quality of objective reasoning, the idea here being to make it into simple terms of reference to which one can relate.

One very good term of reference which one constantly uses in order to get correct signals back from oneself (although sometimes one doesn't) is to ask oneself: "What is the signal coming back from me?"

People do this all the time. If they go into a shop to buy a cake, and they see one with violet and green icing and yellow blobs, they react by thinking "Yuck", but there is some sort of reasoning there. If they say "Yuck" it is because they don't like that combination of colours.

You could say "This is instinctive, so what should I do? Go around looking for discord so that I can react?" Of course not, but in the same way that one senses this automatically, so one should feel a feedback from oneself: it is the same as the very familiar feeling one has when one reads something or visits a place and then feels something coming back from it.

You already know the feeling and you know that a feeling has been engendered or produced, but you don't need to define how you know it. You don't even need to call it the "X" or "Y" feeling or anything like that; you just know it is a feeling associated with something positive, useful and developmental.

Why I say the word "reason" or the verb "to reason" is so often abused, is because when doing something, you often hear people say "I reasoned this out" or "I reasoned that such-and-such ...", and sometimes I will react to this by saying "You didn't really reason it. There was no reason in what you did." It was, in fact, a reaction to circumstances in the form of an impulsion.

# REASON

But one must not mess around with words here—I know I'm a semanticist, I can argue all day about the finer points of a word's meaning—but it is also true that people take things on too easily, and it's not a point which is so important that one should fight about it all the time.

In the same way, you don't fight with yourself either. What you do is examine something calmly. You use the reasoning you already have, because you need understanding and reason just to read a sentence. It's part of the thought process, which is to put a phrase together. Having done that, you then add the deeper reasoning from within yourself.

"What does that place, activity, thing I am reading or piece of music produce in me, what does it evoke?"

That way, it also becomes a means of reasoning a thing out or examining something; feeling that it is either working or not. It's right or it's wrong.

Subjective reasoning certainly does come into it, but if one is using certain distinct terms of reference from the Tradition, the tendency will be not to steer you towards a sort of autopilot in which you become zombified in your thinking or reaction, but towards the feeling that you are in tune, in line or in harmony with the activities.

When reason is used and abused in the sense of "The reason I did this or that is ..."—the falsity of using reason to this end is partly due to sloppy speech, and also partly because somebody will say to themselves, "The reason I did this or that was .." when this so-called reason is, in fact, a rationalization, an attempt to explain away why they did something stupid, why they made a fool of themselves, or else why they didn't do their utmost, or why they didn't take advantage of other things that were available to bring something to a successful conclusion.

They'll say something like "Oh well, the reason was ..." and quickly manufacture something, either for the satisfaction of the person they are talking to, or worse, for their own satisfaction. Because one can always produce enough reason and justification for doing something unproductive, stupid, destructive, silly or negative—it happens. And if one does produce enough of this kind of justification to satisfy oneself, one has a problem. But the word "reason" should never be associated with such a process.

Whether it's used as an excuse, an apology, a half-apology or something like that, it's too easy to gloss it over this way, and people should not do it to themselves.

For instance, you come in late for a job or do something slipshod and quickly manufacture an excuse: as long as you know that this excuse was manufactured and you're just trying to avoid punishment or being shouted at or something of that nature, it's all right, but only as long as you know that.

If you start to manufacture it, and then 'sell' it to yourself and then you begin believing it in the name of "The reason that..."—there's no reason behind it at all. It's just a manufactured excuse.

So in yourselves and in your activities, and certainly within the group, watch out wherever and whenever the words "to reason", "reasoning", "reasonable" or "the reason why" are used.

If you look through the Naqshbandi rules, you will find that some of them apply to this 'reasoning factor', whether it's *'examining oneself'*; *'looking within oneself,'* or looking at one's relations with activities.

Avoid getting into areas where the so-called 'reason' is a

coverall simplification, as in "Know thyself."

The point of view of what is considered correct western intellectual or even what they call 'metaphysical' reasoning is what I would mildly call unreasonable; because they want to quantify certain things or arguments in the form of a formula: "A + B - C = D" which appears to be nice and tidy. Mind you, probably only they and a very chosen few others will ever be able to understand what that equation means. Nevertheless, they are satisfied because there is an equation representing it.

But the real question involved is: "Can we use it? Can we understand it? How does it function?"

"Never mind, just hang it around your neck."

Well, that's not good enough.

Or else again, they will write a treatise on reason and the reason for it. And by the time you've read your way through all of that, if you can, you probably can be converted to it. But you still cannot effectively use it.

You might say to yourself: "Maybe it was a stumbling-block, I don't quite understand the reason, but since I have read "Humperdink on Reason", it means that I must understand it, mustn't I?" and everybody says "Yes, of course."

You are doing yourselves no favour in thinking this way. The reason to be listened to in terms of the Tradition is the reasoning of reason itself, and the reason for the Tradition.

All theses things are inextricably linked. You cannot divide one from another. You can't say "I reserve the right to hold onto or to be able to reason out something in the Tradition which is at variance to something which may appear in Rumi, Hafiz,

# RULES OR SECRETS OF THE NAQSHBANDI ORDER

Saadi or Jami.

I wouldn't welcome such an attitude, because, in my experience, if a person has said "I can reason my way through this" or "I can reason my way out of it", it's usually another way of saying "I can weasel my way out of it."

Reason is therefore a thing which is very useful and in fact, quite essential, providing its formulation, and the way it is produced, is sound.

As I have said, you can take aspects of the Tradition and look at them from a chemical, sociological, political, economic, ethnic or demographic point of view and find that there is no way they can be applied: but if these different aspects are put together in the context of the Tradition, they all work together and enhance each other.

If they are separated out into separate viewpoints from the point of view of Western reasoning, if you like, they have no particular function because they don't fit in. But in fact, we are not concerned about whether they do fit in or not. I'm not at all worried about whether I am approved of by Oxford, Cambridge, Stevenage or Watford North.

If I was worried about that sort of thing I'd already be more insane than I am. But I am not.

All I am interested in is instructing people in the most efficient use of the texts, instruments, music, and activities we have available. In the context of the Tradition, I will only operate with people who are prepared to use the Tradition's reasoning and terms of reference, and who are prepared not to use measurements or terms of reference which are not only external but even hostile to it.

# REASON

If you take this tasbee into a pawnshop and put it on the counter: the fellow will say "I don't know, two pounds fifty" or something like that. To him, it's worth two pounds fifty, to me it's worth quite a lot more.

But if I say to him "You are a fool, this is worth X"—who is the fool? He doesn't want to know and I don't have the time to tell him. So therefore, the twain don't meet. He 'll say: "What is it? It's a stone innit, I mean it's sort of greenish, Hmmm."

If you say to him, "Actually it's *chamaksu*, it's one of the oldest *chamaksu* in existence" he'll say something like "Where is that—up Liverpool way or something?"

Then you say "Ah, the fool".

No, no way.

He is using his own terms of reasoning and I am using reason in an entirely fruitless and useless way. If I'm so clever, I shouldn't be in the pawnshop trying to flog it anyway.

So the whole of that thinking process is beside the point.

What it means is that you have to watch out for reason. Watch out for how you reason.

Go back to the Naqshbandi rules.

See the production of a thought or the feeling of a situation, and gauge it and measure it reasonably.

Measure it within the terms of reference of the Tradition.

30.05.91

# SELF-HYPNOSIS

With almost anything, especially if there is a repetitive element, there is a tendency for a state of sort of auto-hypnosis to occur; and on occasions this auto-hypnosis can take the form of literal sleep. A person can go to sleep to all intents and purposes, and according to their own measurement, they are possibly "floating" or "drifting"—in fact they can physically be asleep.

Another situation is that they get so profoundly into a state of auto-hypnosis that everything goes completely blank. They have no sensation of floating or movement or anything, it's just complete blankness. Both these states; that is, the complete auto-hypnosis and blankness and sleep, are, in their own way, unproductive.

The sleep state, although it entails the benefit of sleeping and relaxation, is unproductive because it's not really producing anything.

A complete auto-hypnosis and blankness can be counterproductive in a much more negative way. If it occurs, part of the person's consciousness or attention can be conscious of the fact that one is sort of going into a blank, and a part of the consciousness can be pushing against this, or rejecting it and feeling that it is unproductive, which means you've got a tussle or tug-of-war going on. One portion of the consciousness is going into complete relaxation and inertia, and another portion is trying to pull it back, so you've got that conflict going on.

The state of concentration in an exercise is one in which

the attention or concentration is what we call "elevated" in the sense that a person, as a result of practice—because it doesn't come about immediately—the person should try and achieve a state where they almost detach themselves from their body.

Now there's a lot of guff, jargon, superstition and all sorts of doubtful things connected with this state. It's been called "going into the astro-area" and things like that. One doesn't necessarily need to define what sort of state it is, so long as that particular state is fairly well defined as far as one is concerned for oneself. That is to say, when I say you don't have to define it, it means you don't have to define it to other people, you don't have to explain it, as long as you can define it to yourself— and it is a tangible state—you can call it "my state" or "my elevated state of being" or "my moments" or whatever you like, as long as you yourself know what it is. So long as it is tangible and palpable for you, then it won't get into the airy-fairy, wandering-about, uncoordinated and uncontrolled area.

It is a state which one creates oneself, in tune with harmonious activities. Having achieved that state, subsequent exercises go towards improving the consciousness within the state when one is in it, and when the subsequent aim is an improvement of that state, following either the word or phrase which one begins, or the music or whatever—and as you go along with it, viewing it from within that state, which means that there is a correspondence and communication between oneself in that state. Also, in terms of the music of an exercise, the contact with the other people or the ambience, the communication and rapport is enhanced by one's state.

The different levels of communication are enhanced, they are increased; to put it in simple terms, things which one might hear or the place where one is, somehow mean more to one because of the enhanced character of that state.

23.01.86

241

# RULES OR SECRETS OF THE NAQSHBANDI ORDER

## THE RULES AND GROUP ACTIVITIES

I would like to point out certain facts to you. Because of geographical and other factors, there is sometimes an interruption in the transmission of energy between groups. Because of geographical, climatic or other situations, there can also be a difference in the rhythm or momentum a group builds up and sustains.

I have already used the analogy of individuals in a group or groups acting as links in a chain. Once it is made, the chain must necessarily act together, and it is not necessary to associate the word "chain" with being "held" or "closed." The analogy of a chain or link is used in the sense of interlinking circles, with energy traversing the circle and corresponding to the next link, with the chain in itself forming a larger link containing energy within it.

By definition, a chain is only as strong as its weakest link: in the question of transmission of effort or energy, every link must be equally efficient.

Any factors which disturb the communication of a chain should be examined, but there is a point beyond which examination or re-examination becomes an activity in itself. If this type of activity is carried on in any group, it becomes necessary to examine one's terms of reference and intention.

Any group which experiences any form of dysfunction has to examine itself with the question: "Are we in fact a group? What do we share in terms of intention? What amount of energy are we prepared to invest in this activity?"

# THE RULES AND GROUP ACTIVITIES

One should also define the priorities of a group: just as a group should occasionally examine its function in a reasonable manner, so I must in turn examine each group, and I must also decide from my point of view whether it is a coherent group or a bunch of individuals.

Of course a group is composed of individual people with their own professions, activities and hobbies. Becoming a member of a group does not mean one loses one's own identity. Nothing is lost in terms of a person's personality because the individual personality should not be too prominent or visible in the context of a group.

The only element that should be important and prominent is the energy put into the group which then reflects the amount of energy which comes out of the group situation.

I am basically in favour of group situations and group activities for the simple reason that participation in such activity enhances a person's energy output, but if this becomes some sort of unhappy fellowship then it is not for me or for anybody to force this together.

I regularly scan and check on the functioning of everything in a group, and I ask questions in regard to each of them. How is the group benefiting the Tradition and how is the Tradition benefiting the group?

The relationship between a group and the Tradition is not a one-way street: the Tradition exists among people and within people. As elsewhere, in the Tradition such a relationship can also exist between individuals. It is usually more beneficial and more functionally useful to have a group rather than a scattering of individuals, but speaking as a professional, it is not within my authority to force a group situation.

# RULES OR SECRETS OF THE NAQSHBANDI ORDER

I can appreciate that under certain circumstances, whether in Munich or Spain or anywhere, people of differing character or nature are put together. This putting together can of itself produce certain situations: you notice I use the word "situation" and not "problem." All problems are situations but not all situations are problems. Usually the root or basis of a problem exists within the group: it is not some external influence or impact which has caused it.

The majority of circumstances, which may be complex and difficult, should normally be resolved within the group itself: the terms of reference and techniques are available and present. If they are used selectively and correctly, they can identify and compensate for a negative situation.

If a negative situation is sustained for any length of time, one has to ask oneself whether this is ignorance or error.

The mechanics of examination or identification within a group are identical to the mechanics of examining oneself, one's own person. If you apply one or other or a combination of the Naqshbandi rules on a personal basis or on a group basis, the *travelling within oneself* or this similar 'travelling within a group' should identify certain factors.

Human beings often try to hide aspects of reality from themselves—people make excuses and explain to themselves why they thought of something or why they did something, and if the excuse is honest and logical, it will shed increasing light on the composition of their being.

If they hide things from themselves or deny the existence of certain things within themselves, they are not approaching an understanding of their own being.

If they ignore or disguise a factor, they will they will find that this factor will raise its head at the worst possible moment, and the person will then be surprised, worried, distraught or anxious at the appearance of this hostile element.

A deep knowledge of oneself produces a situation of familiarity and it should also produce a balance. If one has not tried to get an adequate picture of one's being, one is laying oneself open to a series of surprises, and unfortunately, these surprises can be unpleasant, or a shock.

As in an individual, so in a group.

15.05.89

# RULES OR SECRETS OF THE NAQSHBANDI ORDER

## THE RULES AS GROUP ASSESSMENT TOOLS

The Naqshbandi rules have been translated and have been made available to you. They are a set of technical rules that govern measurement and assessment. You do not just read and learn them in order to put them on your bookshelf, you apply them consciously. If you follow them and use them in a spirit of investigation, and not in an inquisitorial way, they will become a part of your thought and behaviour pattern.

It is not an application of a hostile or alien set of rules. You refer to them as you would refer to the advice of a friend. You seek to use them and you seek opportunities of using them. You do not wake up in the morning and decide "I am going to follow a particular rule during the day" because perhaps there may be occasions when the strict application of a particular rule may not apply throughout the day. If they are all present in your consciousness, you can apply one or another or a combination of them, in a given circumstance.

They are there, they are useful and efficient—the question is how you apply them. Do you apply them emotionally, objectively or scientifically?

As you familiarize yourself with their use, you should find more and more opportunities to produce circumstances when you can actually use them. The rules are not used in isolation: they have been distributed at a time when certain aspects of fundamental learning have been given. You are all capable of using them, so my question is "Why are they not being used more frequently among you?"

# THE RULES AS GROUP ASSESSMENT TOOLS

It comes down to the intention of the person and the joint intention of the group. Like all groups, you have to decide whether you wish to remain as a group and take on your share of the responsibilities as individuals in a group; or whether you wish to maintain an up-and-down motion without moving forward in a coherent way.

I assure you that I am not preoccupied with the idea of forcing individuals together: what does interest me is guiding, supervising and pushing forward a united activity. You will find from me or from any text in the Tradition that the path is clearly laid out. The degree to which you identify with that path is up to you individually.

So examine situations: examine your situation.

Decide whether you are a group and decide whether you want to be one. With goodwill, you can identify and solve the different situations, problems or concerns which come up. If various elements of confusion or competition continue to disturb, then the group will remain in a state of chasing its own tail.

I am not threatening you with doom, nor am I giving you an ultimatum. I would say—and I have said—to many groups: "Take a sensible look at yourselves as a group."

No gathering of individuals or group lacks reasonable sense and intelligence, but what any group or number of individuals can do is introduce random factors which deflect the actual direction of the activity by dissipating and diluting it.

Try and observe your actions and reactions, and measure them against the Naqshbandi Rules.

15.05.89

## USE AND MISUSE OF ENHANCEMENT

What I would like to commend to your attention within the discipline of the Naqshbandi Rules, is to reflect regularly on at least one aspect of what you are doing or trying to do.

Take it one aspect at a time. Other aspects will be attracted by your train of thought, but keep to a main train of thought.

In the Tradition, one is trying to build up, develop, and enhance certain faculties. The best word to describe this is "enhance" which means to improve and develop a deep and abiding consciousness within oneself, to which one refers under certain circumstances, and with which one relates in the various circumstances of readings, zikrs, exercises or other contexts.

Enhancing means elevating, refining, purifying one's essential or inner being. Now if one is enhancing things which are capable of being enhanced, it means that they should have some nature or quality, or at least some definition to start with.

You do not have to aim at enhancing every aspect of your behaviour, life and activity in the same way or at the same pace. In our terms of reference, within the Tradition, you do not enhance your coffee drinking, cigarette smoking, bus catching or shopping, in terms of, or in relation to, the Tradition. One might enhance one's lifestyle or behaviour, or even enhance one's terms of reference, and doing so might influence one's behavioural patterns: at that point one dilute spin-off might be how one prepares one's coffee, or does one's shopping, orcarries out certain mundane tasks.

# USE AND MISUSE OF ENHANCEMENT

Enhancing one's terms of reference, clarifying one's thought processes and patterns should hopefully and inevitably lead to what one might call a tidiness of mind, an efficient thinking, and in turn, that might be reflected in one's daily activities.

One might say "All right, today I have this, that, and the other thing to do, how can I best plan my day? Geographically, I do the things which are nearest, first when I'm fresh, or if they are not very important tasks, I do them on my way home, because they require less thought, effort or energy, so they can be left to the last."

You work out your pattern of behaviour based on certain assumptions: you assume that it will be an average day, that one won't be interfered with more than usual by other people, things, or events, so that, based on the things one can reasonably predict such as where one has to go during the day, how one is feeling, what the weather is like, one feeds in certain predictable factors and one goes through the day on the basis of these, modified by changes of weather, temperature, peoples' availability or otherwise.

Okay, we'll call that reasonably planning one's day. You try and reserve a certain amount of mental or physical energy for certain situations which predictably will require them.

You don't say: "I am going to go and do the week's shopping. I will reserve an "X" amount of special, refined or intellectual energy or intelligence for doing it." It is a fairly well disciplined and mundane task. One does the shopping based on experience: "Which fish fingers or hamburgers taste better or are cheaper?" or whatever. One uses basic terms of reference which one has developed by experience.

You do not "enhance" your shopping, as in: "What shall

# RULES OR SECRETS OF THE NAQSHBANDI ORDER

I do in relation to the Tradition when I am shopping?" This factor does not come into it. If, as I say, your behavioural and thought patterns, your efficiency, has been enhanced by your contact with the Tradition, there will be a spin-off and hopefully you will do your various things a little bit better or more efficiently.

You are not shopping 'as a Naqshbandi.' You are not driving a car as a dervish. Both of these things are implicit in a person, but I mean, does a dervish drive on the right or the left? Does his beard get tangled up with the gear shift? Is he wearing a robe or not wearing a robe, does he ignore traffic lights because he is a dervish? Does he get out of jail by the same token? No.

So one normally engages certain faculties, and terms of reference in world situations, apparently without a thought. Right.

You do not over-apply physical or mental activity in situations where this excess is wasteful, unnecessary or uncalled for. You don't have to use a volume of the Encyclopaedia Britannica to squash a fly, when a rolled up newspaper is more efficient and gives you the same end result.

So one does not overuse a tactic or an ability just because it "probably might help." It is not only called "gilding the lily"; it is in fact also selling the activity short. Why? Because you are saying "Right, I will use the energy I have built up with exercises in the Tradition," or "I will lock onto the Tradition" at a very low level of activity. You are in effect trying to use a very refined, pure and rare element of energy in a very banal way.

If a person does this, that person is using a precious material, which is difficult to obtain and generate, in a very stupid way. This is a pity, because of the amount of effort which goes into generating and manufacturing a certain quality of energy.

As I have said before, if this energy is received or manufactured, it cannot be wasted or dissipated in a negative way. So if one says "I will use all the energy of the Tradition to post this letter," the energy which one uses in that mundane task, which only really involves getting onto one's feet, walking to the corner, making sure that there is a postbox and posting it, the amount of energy or intellect needed to do this simply does not involve the Tradition.

You don't waste energy. What you are doing here is in fact bringing your use of the energy of the Tradition, and therefore the Tradition itself, down to a very low level.

If you bring it down to such a low level, several familiar things happen: firstly, instead of involving a selective use or a selective thought, it becomes an almost superstitious correlation of factors. "Unless I post the letter within the context of the Tradition it will a) bring me bad luck, b) it won't get there, c) something dreadful will happen, d) I'd better get out my rabbit's foot and touch wood"—and all the other things which go with it. What you then get is, technically, a degeneration into a superstitious practice, just as you have the whole panoply of "touching wood."

Now as a matter of interest, what does "touching wood" mean? It is a superstitious act. It had and still does have a basis of fact, but people don't relate to it.

This and lots of other things have gone into the realm of superstition. I will not—and neither will anybody who has any degree of responsibility in the Tradition—permit the Tradition to get into the realm of superstition or the folk-tale type of area, whether it be in terms of a tactic, the theory, or techniques.

# RULES OR SECRETS OF THE NAQSHBANDI ORDER

We have all seen too many valid religions, philosophies and terms of reference become diluted out of sight, to the point that they have just become useless to the people who continue on with a so-called ritual without knowing the meaning of it. They are miming activities. They are a shadow, a reflection of a shadow.

As we say, it becomes just like passing water from hand to hand. It is true that something is passing, but it is diminishing and evaporating. Its function has been lost because it has taken on a ritualistic aspect.

This is why I don't countenance or encourage the practice of thinking about every last thing from the point of view of the Tradition. Again I repeat, not because a person might waste the energy—there is a protection against that happening—but because it gets them into a frame of mind where you have some cause and effect, and people say "Well I did it and it didn't work, so it's my fault"; "it's the technique"; "it's the Tradition"; "it's Agha" or somebody else; "its the evil eye"; or "it was a cat that ran across my path" and goodness knows what else—the actual reality of what happened is diluted. The intention might have been there, but the execution of it was ineffectually carried out, there was no carry-through. I don't want to see a fruit or blossom wither on the branch—its function is not to do that.

Now, quite apart from the area of the dilution or degeneration of a religion or philosophy into folk-tale, superstition, or the "secrets" of the extraordinary, unbelievable, unimaginable—(and therefore un-understandable, unusable, un-contactable)—this thinking process can easily lead a person, a people or a nation to take refuge in time-consuming ritualistic forms which seem to bear some relation to something.

Now there may be some substance there—I mean, a

shadow is cast by something—therefore somewhere, as I say, there is an original shape or form. A reflection in a looking glass, in a stream or in a bowl of water is a reflection of something, so it is true to say that something must be there. Right.

But we should be concerned with what has cast the shadow, what light has caused the shadow, or what image has caused the reflection in that looking glass, stream or bowl of water. If we continue—as some philosophers have—to concern ourselves with the nature of the shadow or the reflection, rather than looking at what caused or gave its nature to the shadow, then we divert ourselves away from the mainstream activity.

I have said this all before, and I have already carried on about it for hours. It is a factor which disturbs me, since I see it happening with great regularity in various groups from time to time, showing its head in different guises and forms.

What is involved here is a type of formalised superstition either based on: "Oh everything will be all right," or "Agha will look after us, touch wood, cross myself, feel my crystal, pass my rabbit's paw over my left shoulder, don't spill the salt, don't walk under ladders, watch out for black cats, and cross my fingers." One then follows it by saying: "With a little bit of luck, everything will be all right."

Now what does that have to do with God? All these manifestations of touching wood, rabbit's feet, and black cats are possibly elements of the creation and the cosmic structure, but they are created by an entity, and the basic entity which is central to all our activities within the Tradition, is God.

If, as part of our activities, we wish to try and work out, hazard a guess or estimate how or where we stand in relation to God and to the rest of creation, what then is our function? What is our mandate? What are our terms of reference?

# RULES OR SECRETS OF THE NAQSHBANDI ORDER

How can we function in a way which might hopefully attract the approval of the Creator?

Different races and civilisations have had their own ideas and have put their own interpretations on how best to please the Creator, or the particular One or bunch which was esteemed at that particular time.

Through burnt offerings and human and animal sacrifices, through all manner of manifestations, aimed basically at offering something to God, whether in the form of a direct or indirect offering, or a bribe—whatever form it took—this was a sort of basic intention.

Now it would be logical to consider that God created the Universe, the cosmos, the galaxy, the whole lot, for a purpose. Defining exactly the actual purpose and so forth has consumed a lot of people's time, a lot of books have been written about it, and I don't propose to debate the rights or wrongs of any particular philosophy in this regard. I can only talk about the philosophy I know best, and our great masters are unanimous in the attitude we take, which is that one way man can aspire to achieve some degree, or varying degrees, or elevated degrees of approval from God is to benefit the creature that He has created, i.e., himself.

This is not a mandate for complete selfishness or a justification for retreating into the mountains and thinking of nothing else, because if a person does the best for himself or herself, according to our equation, they will also attract approval, as far as their internal and external being is concerned.

If their aim is right and their intention is correct, behaving in ways which are beneficial to the person internally and externally would not be a selfish, self-centred activity. It would have a ripple effect, it would influence other people around them, and it would hopefully enhance performance in various other areas.

So if you get a number of people who are engaging in activities which are not only compatible but enhance each other, then you have a buildup of support all round the individuals, the families, the groups or the society, and benefit accrues largely.

We are not the Salvation Army. We do not go out and bang drums and do the very laudable things the Salvation Army does, because it is a tall order. In order to have a Church or army situation, you have to build up and sustain a degree of fervour which lasts only as long as the Salvation Army drum-and-fife band are there—and then the fervour drops off.

It is true that certain good works, good thoughts, harmony, friendship and so forth, do exist in, and emanate from, that Church/Army activity. "Spread the word"; "Hallelujah!"—most certainly, why not? But what one really wants is the permeation of the person, the permeation of the group, and the permeation of society in a lasting fashion.

This is a long-term aim. It has already taken generations, and it will probably take more generations for a certain structure to be built, from which those who are less, shall we say, strategically placed to have immediate contact with the Tradition, can benefit by the interaction of different groups in different places.

I repeat that this is a specific and technically advanced activity. It needs discipline in thought and action, and enhancement needs a very selective direction of the use of energy. The enhancement is analogous to a car or a truck or something which goes along, pulling a lot of other things in its wake.

# RULES OR SECRETS OF THE NAQSHBANDI ORDER

So I repeat that, as a person's behaviour, thought process and various other things are enhanced, so inevitably this must influence the incidentals, which happen to be part of life itself.

Selective direction of discipline towards a certain goal does not give one a blinkered vision in which one ignores everything else. "In the world and not of the world" means that one is working out in which way one can best relate to circumstances which are positive, and which can be injected with an even further positive, so that their status, impact and value can be enhanced, and they can function in a better way.

Somebody once said—and I think they were probably struck by lightening immediately afterwards—that when you enter the Tradition, "you stop thinking." When I heard that, I said that some people had never even started to think, but that was just a off-the-cuff reaction.

What one does is, in fact, think more—the difference being that one thinks selectively. You don't say: "I will think about philosophical matters only" because everybody knows what that leads to: the gas and electricity is cut off, and so is the telephone and everything like that—this is inefficient.

The attraction of the monastic life, or going and living on a mountain top is attractive in passing, but again it is not fulfilling a proper balance. However mean, base, stupid, idiotic or inefficient an individual may think he is, he or she still has a contribution to make. Never mind society in general, I couldn't care less about society in general—I am not supposed to save society in general, otherwise I'd be speaking in Trafalgar Square and getting mugged, or mobbed, or both. All I am concerned with is to be able to indicate things to groups, provide energy, and generally harry people in a reasonable way, in order that they should get their terms of reference fairly right, and get their alms reasonably in focus.

# USE AND MISUSE OF ENHANCEMENT

I say reasonably, because when thoughtful reason—and not intense thought—is applied, things do come into focus. One isn't constantly being focused and re-focused. Occasionally one might get nudged or pushed or that sort of thing—there's a technical correction, if you like, but a constant correction, focusing and redirecting is counterproductive, because then you get a dependance factor.

A dependance factor is not only onerous on me, but it debilitates the person because they begin to say things like: "I am incapable of making a decision" or "Should I..." or "Will I .." or "Can I .." Rather than shift the entire burden onto me, which is time-consuming to the person and unwelcome to me, everybody has abilities, capacities of rationalisation, examination, activity and working things out which can be used. By relying entirely on me, on the Tradition, or on anything else, they are selling themselves short.

If one is aiming at any form of enhancement, one should use the Tradition as a guideline, fuel, terms of reference, method, technique, tactic, all of these things—but don't weaken yourselves as individuals, or as a group, or as a group within groups. Don't weaken the activity by over-reliance in areas where you're capable of activity, and then enhanced activity.

Because it is enhancement, it's not just painting it up and making it pretty—it is a long, dogged, and very often uphill struggle. It can be a confusing and sometimes contradictory activity, but it is not one in which you say "I'm stuck with it, what am I going to do"? If you do think "I'm stuck with it, what am I going to do?" to yourself, start by examining your own motivations. See if there is still an accordance with what you are doing, and if there is, examine what might have provoked or produced this confusion or contradiction, and see if it can be reasonably explained.

Reasonably doesn't mean easily. Reasonably means "with reason." Hopefully, you do not examine a situation, an instance, a problem irrationally. Nor do you examine it unreasonably in the sense that you do it without reason or without using your analytical capacity for reasoning.

Everybody has common sense. They exercise it instinctively, intuitively, automatically, or whatever, and the results, by and large, are all right.

There are areas which touch on the deeper being of the person which can, and need to be, enhanced. So you select the areas which could, should, or might be, enhanced, and work on those. This is not to the detriment of anything else: one is using a different gear.

"Is it better that I have breakfast, or should I do an exercise?" If you're hungry, have breakfast, then do an exercise. The two are not incompatible. If you abstain from breakfast often enough you will not have the strength to do an exercise, therefore logic and reason tell you what your priorities are.

So I do commend you to discipline your thought and activity on a selective basis. Not on a basis of acceptance/rejection or positive/negative: it is better to call it useful, less useful and more useful. Putting everything up a notch, if you can.

Most activities in the outside world are geared to homogenizing thought into a grey area: "Everybody will be nice and grey and equal in thought, word and deed and everything else."

That is not so utopian as people like to label it—what it actually means is that it's removing the competitive area of life, which is part of life itself.

# USE AND MISUSE OF ENHANCEMENT

Nobody wants automatically to have people climbing on other people's shoulders, with others being downtrodden, and the "them and the us" factor. If everybody is given a reasonable equal opportunity, then there will be a certain sorting out. Some people will make more effort than others, so there will always be a certain degree of inequality: we're not trying to produce a utopian situation of equality. What we are doing is being selective.

If we are being selective in areas of contact with people, we're also being selective in the activities we're doing, as well as in the way we look at our activities within those things which we have selected.

Not on a broad front: a spade is a spade is a spade.

In the context in which it is useful, use it usefully. In other places, for instance when you have a spade and a windowbox, you have a problem because you need a trowel. The functional use of that instrument depends, not on the character of the spade, it is what you have selected to use it on, and how you then use it.

You can use a volume of the Encyclopaedia Britannica to squash a mosquito which is annoying you, and you can also knock yourself out with that volume so that you don't get annoyed by the mosquito.

You might say that the function was covered before—no it hasn't been, because you may be knocked out and then the mosquito will have a field day and it's all right, or else it subsequently collapses because it's gorged itself on you.

So you might then say: "Well, nature took its course."

No. You have just behaved in an abysmally stupid manner.

# RULES OR SECRETS OF THE NAQSHBANDI ORDER

"Oh well, never mind"

Never mind nothing. Think about it a little bit. People do this kind of thing all the time, especially when their own obvious interests are involved.

If somebody who is a smoker needs one pound fifty-eight to buy a packet of cigarettes—come hell or high water, beg, borrow, steal, ask the neighbours, he'll do something—he'll find that money.

When their own personal obvious benefit is concerned, people are queuing up to look after themselves. This is perfectly reasonable, why not?

But when a little bit of an effort is involved, in which the benefit is not an immediate return based on "I want it now"—in other words when the benefit is not immediately visible, tangible, and perceptible—people will also do it saying: "Well maybe ... I suppose I'd better go through the motions."

No. It's better not to go through the motions. If that is the attitude, if the intention is: "I'd better do it, otherwise maybe I'll get into trouble"—if that really is your motivation, just don't do it.

Examine things reasonably, sort out the wheat from the chaff, and then go for the productive things. Nothing is all bad. There are some things which are less good. But fix a line at "good" or rather "useful," and then don't examine and re-examine it over and over again from every point of view, from this that and every direction, and ask everybody's opinion. Make certain reasonable decisions based on experience, feeling, thought and intuition—and once you have made them, put them together in a coherent way, and move forward to enhance certain areas.

# USE AND MISUSE OF ENHANCEMENT

Otherwise, one is just stirring porridge and going through the motions. If you go to any museum or library with history books, you can see it laid out before you. You can look through all the civilizations, cultures and philosophies that have peaked and fallen, or which have remained stagnant, or which are completely misunderstood or not understood at all, and which churn and re-churn the same old garbage.

Once, they held valid factors, valid truths. They either fell into disrepute because of disuse, or they were so diluted by the "automatic" aspect, with people losing sight of basic aspects like "What am I doing, and why?"

One must then go through it, reaffirming one's intent, i.e., considering what one's aim is and how one hopes to achieve it.

Otherwise, as I say, one is simply going through it and stirring the porridge with ritualistic activities, all of which may be perfectly good and well-intentioned—not negative—except that they are not up to standard.

They can be brought up to standard and enhanced, but they can only be enhanced by a continuity of effort and a level of discipline. Below that level of discipline, it becomes only a treadmill, just marking time. It is true that a person is still moving, their function is there, a man standing there marking time and lifting his feet up and down is still lifting his feet up and down. But he could be doing something in a more useful way.

Of course, not everything has the same priority, and not everything is so useful from the point of view of enhancement in the Tradition. Some things are completely unrelated to activities in the Tradition but that does not mean to say they cannot be done efficiently or usefully.

# RULES OR SECRETS OF THE NAQSHBANDI ORDER

The spin-off covers everything: it should spin further and further out, to relate with other things. Not spin out to the degree where it's so thin on the ground that it just doesn't exist. After all, energy and strength ebb at a certain point.

When like attracts like, when like meets like, you have the energization factor which takes place. Once that has been locked in, a person doesn't then freewheel, but they do feel a harmonic. That harmonic or echo is like homing onto a radar signal, it tells them that this is "something." But then, you have to work on it, you have to push it, you have to maintain the discipline.

It is up to you to watch yourself—you don't push yourself in a tense way because you're not in competition with yourself. If you're in competition with anybody, it's with me, which is fine by me in the sense that I can pull a bit because I'm a little bit ahead, and can pull you along.

But when I say "make the effort" don't use that as an all-encompassing tension factor, sitting and feeling guilty because one isn't doing anything for two minutes.

25.05.89

# MAINTAINING A NORMAL LIFE

There can sometimes be a certain temptation for people in our groups to isolate themselves, in a way, from other people, such as friends and family members. By trying too hard to live within the rules of the Tradition, they turn inwards as individuals or as a group, running the risk of becoming rather introspective or inward-looking.

Using the word danger to describe this phenomenon is too strong a term, but this hazard does exist, and it is something that should be avoided—because even if a person feels happy or more at home with people in a group insofar as they share similar ideas, terms of reference or outlook, one should take care not to close oneself off from the rest of one's context, and this is what I would like to talk about.

One can perfectly well live according to the rules of the Tradition without turning inwards as a group or becoming introspective as a person. One can live both lives fully, as it were. Both harmonize with each other, and one life in fact helps the other.

In accordance with Islamic tradition, the Sufi Tradition practises no monasticism. We do not believe that it is necessary or beneficial to cut oneself off from society in order to live a life of religiously-oriented isolation, even if one practises prayer and piety all the time. The great past teachers of the Tradition taught or followed a profession at the same time as they lived and taught within the Tradition. This is a perfect balance, and it is a harmony which one should aim at.

# RULES OR SECRETS OF THE NAQSHBANDI ORDER

If you look clearly at the Naqshbandi rules one by one, or several of them at the same time, you can see that it is perfectly possible to follow them. Assuming you have first understood them and how to follow them properly, it is quite possible to follow them while carrying out a normal everyday job in an everyday life.

There are times, of course, when a person's job, social or other contacts don't come up to one's expectations, or are in some way negative. One then wishes that one sometimes had a more positive contact with people, or a more positive contact with reality. At this point, there is sometimes a feeling that a person's profession, or what might be called a normal social life, is annoying. In a way, one may feel that one is being prevented from developing oneself inwardly.

Both physically and psychologically, it is perfectly possible to allow a job, profession or social activities to prevent one from making the time to work on oneself, to look at or examine oneself and then follow the regulations of the Tradition in a correct manner—but at no time should one think that there has to be a certain number of minutes or hours per week set aside, during which time one should exclusively think about oneself, one's contact with, or the reality of the Tradition.

You can always try and estimate the amount of time you would like to devote to this, but you should always also be continuously on the lookout for opportunities of looking at yourself or at the Tradition, thinking about it, thinking of your relation with it, without, as it were, cutting yourself off from what is going on elsewhere.

As I have said before, *Khilwat dar Anjuman* or being *Alone in a Crowd* does not mean erecting a physical boundary or fence around yourself which prevents any social contact. All you are doing at that point is putting up a notice saying "Leave me

MAINTAINING A NORMAL LIFE

alone for the moment."

It is sometimes possible to be fortunate enough to be able to set aside certain fixed times in order to devote time to reading, meditating or thinking. Sometimes, if it is not possible, the very fact that it is not possible makes the person disappointed, creating tension and frustration within oneself. Goodness knows that one's everyday life, job or activity can—and in many ways does—produce confusion and frustration. One therefore does not need to try and provoke any more introspection, confusion, or questions within oneself than are already being heaped upon one by society or by the world in general.

I repeat, every one of the great masters who taught in the Tradition followed a profession, or else taught or lectured. They were completely at harmony with the activity they followed and with their position within the Tradition.

Again, a possible temptation when reading the Naqshbandi rules is to turn inwards to a degree that one is excluding certain necessary or useful impacts from outside, which means that one is not picking up certain positive or useful currents of thought, terms of reference or feelings.

Isolation is not necessarily insulation. Using some of the activities of the Tradition in order to insulate oneself from negative, disturbing or confusing impacts is perfectly all right, but this insulation should be of a nature which permits the positive or the useful to continue to be received or transmitted by the person.

After all, people don't shut themselves off when they are reading. If they are reading something meaningful from some writer in the Tradition, they don't turn off their intellect. They read it, study it, try to understand it, and more than that, try to feel it, rather than rigidly dissect it according to certain terms of reference they have been taught.

If one reads Saadi, Rumi, Hafiz, Jami or any of the other great ones, one is reading for the purpose of learning, understanding and being able to use the teaching contained in these books. Although it is possible to do so, one is not reading them from the point of view of literary criticism or poetic merit. They can be read from that point of view too, and will be found acceptable, but basically they are being read because they are books of the teaching.

They are books of behaviour, which not only contain instructions about terms of reference, but also give examples of certain situations and circumstances. That is why most of these books are broken up into a series of stories. Within the context of these stories, one inevitably sees that the subject or object of an activity is using certain ideas from or thinking along certain lines in the Tradition.

A person gradually comes to understand and identify with those individuals who, for instance, are seeking something, who may fancy themselves to be lost, who are looking for some terms of reference and a way of understanding themselves, their position or their relationship vis-à-vis reality or their relationship with God. All these stories and tales point to a series of endeavours by an individual, or a number of individuals, from different backgrounds, who are following a similar, and sometimes parallel, path.

Most of these stories—which are like medieval morality tales—have a teaching or a lesson embedded in them. They usually show the search for what one might call approximate reality, in both a graphic way as well as in the form of subconscious transmission.

There is no book which can tell one as in an A to Z type

directory, exactly what reality exists in what circumstance, because circumstances change, the person changes, impacts change, and their terms of reference as well.

People take on more terms of reference—they change— or else they learn to use these terms of reference better, or in some cases, even forget them. They can also fall into error or make mistakes, or else again, overemphasize a single aspect of their knowledge or development, which can lead to the situation becoming unbalanced.

Unbalanced in one sense also means disharmonious. Disharmony is not where a person is really trying to establish a relationship, a contact or what I would call a harmonic with another person, with a situation, or with themselves. One can then be working in a single direction, upon only one aspect of one's nature, on only a single aspect of one's character, and sometimes this means that one is ignoring another aspect which requires either equal attention or even more attention.

So disharmony implies, in certain ways, a lack of a harmonic, but it goes even further than that because a person can make a great deal of effort in a given direction, having identified to their own satisfaction a certain area within themselves which should or could be developed or improved: but having made that decision, they will sometimes strike strongly outwards with all their concentration in one particular direction, on the assumption that they are right in their evaluation of that particular aspect of themselves.

This is one of the essential requirements of the Tradition: people must use the rules to study themselves, in order, really, to find out in what areas they need to concentrate their effort, energy or attention, in order to improve those areas.

A conventional parallel to this is when people follow a

course of teaching, they may pass an examination every three or six months, or even examine themselves to see to what degree they have learned or mastered their subject in order to identify areas where they still lack knowledge. They will therefore increase their effort in those areas which are palpable and obvious to them.

If a person gets to know himself or herself, it should simply be obvious to that person what errors, faults or areas of negativity are within him or her, and which they can then recognize correctly, identify, and do something about. It is absolutely implicit to this process that a person should try and do something about any faults or weaknesses they can identify. Just to identify them and say: "Well, I'm just like that" or "Life is like that" is not really sufficient. It is avoiding responsibility by blaming the Creator or the world in general for one's state of being, at a time when the repair mechanism, if you like, already exists within that person. Having correctly identified it, the person can then see how he or she can advance in a balanced way in order to counterbalance or counteract this negative tendency or weakness.

All of these themes, disciplines and ways of examination can be followed within the context of everyday life.

Once again, it is easy enough for a person to turn inwards, or become introspective and hold everybody, everything and every circumstance to blame for every problem, because some of these problems originate in themselves, and others can come from external circumstances. But to deal with them, it is necessary for a person to begin by opening themselves to the energy of the Tradition, and then use the techniques of the Tradition to first try and overcome and then eradicate faults or weaknesses.

# MAINTAINING A NORMAL LIFE

This can all take place without having to abandon one's profession or all other activities to concentrate on just one area in oneself; i.e., on the single factor in one's behaviour which attracts one's attention as being of a negative potential.

As I say, this has been the reason behind the many monastic orders which have said that people must spend their lives in a monastery or in a cave, totally absorbed in bettering themselves or in overcoming their problems.

This is not recommended in the Tradition because we hold that every person fulfils some useful and valuable function toward themselves, their society or their family, and they cannot leave that responsibility to go away and sit in a mountain cave just to try and think about themselves and their own improvement.

Our view is that it would be selfish to act this way, perhaps because such people have nothing very much to worry about in the cave. They have their bread and water and don't have to worry about the telephone, electricity, taxes, whatever they should be wearing or anything like that; meaning, of course, that they can devote their entire attention and activity towards improving themselves.

This may be very laudable, and I'm not claiming that it is wrong to do this. What I'm saying is that within the process and context of the Tradition, it is not considered necessary to do so, because it is considered that the right activity done at the right time is equal to a long time of sitting in a cave.

Therefore, assuming that one is open to the energy, and assuming that one is continually looking at oneself, monitoring one's own thoughts, feelings and reactions—not with tension but in a relaxed way—and then seeing in which way these can be clarified to oneself if they do cause confusion—one can then also see how these areas can be improved, if areas of weakness do exist.

A lot of people ask me questions about various subjects which cause them confusion, but it is always better to begin by trying to solve a problem oneself than by asking somebody else to help you solve it.

This is very easy to say and difficult to do, because it is a natural tendency to ask people's advice about things. But in terms of the questions and answers concerning one's inner development, if the questions are valid, a person should search around with such amount of knowledge of themselves as they do have, in order to find an answer. If one can't find an answer, one should look a bit further away than just at oneself, because everybody is part of a pattern, whether it is as a family, a society, a company or whatever.

There may indeed be impacts or influences of a negative nature which are producing this confusion within the person. If there is no way that the person can find an answer on their own, and the confusion persists, then, of course, one can ask.

Being confused does not necessarily imply that the confusion comes from within the person. Just as it does not necessarily mean that it comes from somewhere outside. Nevertheless it does come from somewhere: if it is imaginary or a result of some misapprehension, i.e., something which is not correctly understood, one can go back and clarify it to oneself in order to find the source of a misunderstanding.

Regarding any misunderstandings which arise from outside impacts: people should then try and understand to what degree these impacts influence them (or have influenced or impacted upon them in the past). They can then consider to what degree they can then get rid of it, if it is a real negative impact.

# MAINTAINING A NORMAL LIFE

So, briefly, regarding the search within oneself—the search for oneself in the sense of deepening one's knowledge of oneself starts with oneself, and remains a chief feature of one's activity; but not to the degree of introspection, and not to the degree of confusion following upon confusion.

The situation can be that one says "Right, I must find the answer to this myself" and no matter how hard one tries, one can still fail to do so. This may cause anguish and confusion, but there is a way out. As I say, if one cannot find it out for oneself, it's always possible to ask.

But an old trick which is used by psychologists is to backtrack a reasonable amount, in order to find out which impacts caused that particular confusion. Don't backtrack too far—we are not going into this postnatal or prenatal influence type of business, because that is a whole new ball game. But it is possible that certain semiconscious, subconscious, subconsciously felt or heard impacts have left behind a negative influence which is out of all proportion to the actual situation. If such an influence goes unidentified, this may be a source of confusion.

This examination not only starts with oneself, it remains with oneself for good, because it is a lifetime's work. But it's also possible to share the energy of a group, the energy of an activity and the energy of the Tradition in order to help oneself solve certain complex questions, confusions or areas in which one finds oneself either confused or negatively disposed.

But do not work on the assumption that one can do all this on one's own without an awful lot of effort.

It is possible to do it on one's own, but the reason why the Tradition has been organized as it is, i.e., based on the individual as a participant in a group, with the group as a participant in a larger group within a still larger chain of activities, is because it enables the individuals to share the energy.

They are not supposed to work everything out for themselves, and they are equally not supposed to ask everybody's opinion about everything. There is a balanced way between the two. The energy comes from the Tradition. The techniques and contact are there, so a person is not expected to work on alone on oneself.

People work within certain constraints, within a certain context, with a certain precision, with precise tools and precise terms of reference, but without a hermit mentality—avoiding introspection and turning inwards and just sitting there saying "I am as I am."

Everybody who comes voluntarily into the Tradition comes in for the purpose of trying to open and develop themselves, and this is done in order to develop, take on and make use of certain new terms of reference and values, which are, in fact, the old values.

The idea is to use these new and/or old terms of reference and values continuously and practically, with a view to understanding them. But not using them to the exclusion of everything else—using them in a selective fashion.

9.07.92

# ENABLING PEOPLE TO FIND THEIR OWN ANSWERS

There are many areas in the Tradition which encourage a certain amount of speculation in respect to esoteric or extraterrestrial and other phenomena. They encourage this in the sense that they either welcome such thinking or they ask you to think about such things.

This is because if there is no convenient explanation or convenient way of measuring particular phenomena, whether it's because of western culture or just because they are human beings, people will tend to "fill in the blanks" with things which are either more exciting or more attention-getting than maybe such things actually are.

What I am talking about here is not the area of speculation or the exercise of trying to fill in certain gaps which may really exist, since this is not necessarily a bad or destructive thing—but what very often happens is that it can cause a certain amount of confusion to people, insofar as one says that there is a train or pattern of thought in a particular writing or book—say from a particular teacher—which "tends to suggest that..." or which "leads us to the point of..." and then, it is followed by "Are we to?" or "Should we?" or "Do we then take off from there?"—in other words, filling in the blanks ourselves with our own imaginations—or are we just supposed to be left in a state of suspended animation?

If one has read a text or a teaching in a useful way, there should be no sensation of being 'left up in the air.' If it's been read, digested or understood properly, the explanation of each parameter, point of view or experience is already contained in the text itself.

The idea is not to wind people up, as it were, to the point that they are "impelled" by some sort of "force", and then left to fly on their own or fall down. The idea behind all texts and all documents, is to produce an awareness, a consciousness, based on the person's own experience which then becomes self-explanatory.

It is self-explanatory in the sense that if the person reads, digests and understands it, and then puts in their own feeling, own understanding and own reaction to circumstances, a person will produce a meaning for a particular thing. Whereas if a text is read in isolation, without adding any experience or feeling of one's own, all these documents or texts in the Tradition can be either incomprehensible or else produce a sort of 'trip', a sort of 'high.'

I have said before that any sort of 'high'—assuming it is achieved—should be sustained by the effort or understanding of the person or group. It's not an 'artificial high' just to keep a person in a state of "What is going to happen now?" There is always a certain amount of questioning provoked by these things—"How does such-and-such relate to this or that?"—because there is always a certain degree, area, element or margin of speculation and thought, relating to those various things.

But this should not take place in the sense of increasing the expectation and adrenalin factor, with the person then being left to work it all out for themselves.

Examples and explanations of any problem or question propounded by using these texts should be inherent in every teaching or factor, otherwise the text in itself is faulty.

# ENABLING PEOPLE TO FIND THEIR OWN ANSWERS

If you have any teaching which puts an individual into the area of feeling lost or unbalanced as a result of using certain factors or things which have been offered to them, then either they have not fully understood and absorbed the teaching, or else the teaching itself is faulty. There can be no other conclusion, because by definition, anything which is developmental develops a train of thought, feeling or being, which, at the very least, enables a person to cope with the situation, and not develop any traumatic or similar type of situation as a result of something they have freely done.

If you have a headache, you take an aspirin on the assumption that it is going to be helpful, and you also take it as a result of a certain amount of prior experience with aspirin, perhaps due to what the aspirin suggests or promises it can do for you. If, as a result of taking aspirin, both your feet fall off, it means that there is something wrong with the theory and practice and use made of that aspirin. If you take something in an unlabelled bottle which is wholly unknown to you, thinking "I might as well have a drink of it because it might cure my headache," and your feet drop off—you are responsible, it is your problem.

Nevertheless, it is true that there will always be a problem-causing aspect inherent to any developmental teaching situation, even if it is of a useful nature—there has to be. Such a teaching situation propounds and provokes its own questions, but it also produces solutions for solving them, otherwise, to put it mildly, it would be counterproductive. It would then only be something which would be limited to producing problems, and it's easy enough just to provoke questions in people's minds.

But if there is no reasonable way in which people can be expected to find the answers to such questions, you have no right to ask them to do so. Quite simply, you can confuse people by questioning them, or by using your own greater experience, and you can leave them in the air on any level you like to think of—there is no skill in that at all. But what you can also do is provoke or produce situations in which they may involve themselves, and for instance, come up with questions about themselves and the teaching, using the Naqshbandi rules to look back and think, thus finding out, for themselves, that some aspects of the situation or the teaching which provoke the questions, also provide the answers.

So the duality must be there, otherwise provoking the questions and circumstances, without the possibility of providing answers, is incomplete. Furthermore, providing answers which people can't understand and use, is equally incomplete.

Now what is the relevance of this to people filling in the "esoteric", "subterranean" or "extraterrestrial goodness-knows-what"? It is an illogical relevance, but it is a very human way of filling in the blanks.

If there is a connection between X and B or Y and C—and if one can reasonably, logically and fairly tangibly see, work out or think out this connection—fine. If this type of connection is not worked out, there is a tendency you hear about all the time, when people say things like "I am in such-and-such a situation, but because "I am X, Y, Z," or "French, English German" or "Aries, Taurus, Gemini" or whatever—or else, again, because I have "Saturn in my eleventh House"—"and that explains everything."

Well, I don't know. I would like to think that things are that simple. I suppose it depends on how avid a reader you are of astrological columns, and I'm sure it's a great solace to large numbers of people; but if it says in the paper "All Aquarians should not venture out of the house today"—would you have one fifth of the population staying at home? I don't think so.

It either means something in the sense that they came and cut off your electricity because "closure is in the 'eleventh House'" and the fact you haven't paid the bill doesn't somehow appear at all relevant—but is the reason they are coming to get you today due to something slightly closer to home than Pluto? Sometimes, yes.

Also, in a more banal way, it is quite usual and understandable for people to say things like "We will do this, that and the other thing, and Agha will look after us." People don't say this within my hearing because I most certainly don't encourage this type of thing, insofar as we are getting into an area here which is almost of a superstitious nature.

If you haven't paid your electricity bill, I will not stand at the door to prevent the man coming in to cut you off. If you do something absolutely ridiculous, I might suggest, advise or indicate something and so forth, but one should not use either the Tradition, or me, or even Pluto, as a sort of talisman to avert evil. If you think that Jupiter being in the eleventh House means that you can go out and put five pounds on the 2.30 race and win, it doesn't quite work in that area.

Nothing compensates for, and nothing replaces, real activity, real work.

Having said that, there does exist a situation of liaison or relation, during which what might commonly be called extraterrestrial influences can and do apply—but they don't apply to your convenience.

If and when such things apply, it is because they have been attracted to a person or a situation because of that person's or that situation's potential harmony with that influence—at which time or place such an influence can then be manifested.

So it's not a case of an extraterrestrial effect influencing a person or situation willy-nilly—but like attracts like—if there is a positive potential or influence which can be used, it then becomes a useful energy—depending on the person's availability, in the sense that they can use it. Their own harmonizing enables them to use this particular energy.

The various things come together and they use it—but the persons themselves do not become extraterrestrial, or robots working on behalf of some sort of extraterrestrial influence—because if they are, they won't know it. But it is better that they have a harmony with this influence, so that things flow.

Flow is a good and useful word which is much underestimated. By definition, flow is something even or equalizing, something which carries on and involves movement.

In the Tradition, flow is exactly what you see, again and again. The word actually used is *nous* meaning flow as well as implying current—it also implies energy as well as a furtherance or development of a particular thing. Not in the form of a sort of thumping crescendo but in terms of a constant reasonable buildup.

Flow therefore implies not only movement but rhythm and movement according to certain laws, in the sense that very few rivers flow upstream against the current. If any streams do, it is because they have a particular function to do so—otherwise things flow in a particular way, establishing a particular rhythm—they do not just flow 'in the abstract.'

If there is an exchange of energy between individuals and

circumstances, between groups and individuals, or groups and circumstances, the energy or quality which passes is called the "flow" because it presupposes a cycle of natural activity. If there is this cycle or harmonic, it can be enhanced and improved, not by a gain in volume but by a gain in quality.

Once a harmonic has been established, tried and examined, if upon examination it is found to be solid, useful and capable of being transferred, then the type of message or contact can be refined to the point where the useful energy within it can be transferred.

If there is the element of the so-called "other" or "extraterrestrial" dynamic—meaning, very loosely, influences other than terrestrial—they can only happen once a contact has been established, and then further tested, in circumstances where the transmission or exchange cannot be corrupted or faulted.

The simple reason for this is that unless one is sure that a message, an impulse or an energy going from A to B will get through on the same degree of harmony, intensity and value— the message, communication or production of energy does not take place.

If there is the possibility of this message being received in an erroneous or corrupted form, and being understood as something else, then one has to err on the side of caution, and literally, not send it.

Equally, such a transmission, message, value or energy as might be contained in a book or a teaching, is concealed— but not because it is "codified" as one understands that word. It is concealed because it requires reading, rereading and rethinking—not to discover the book's "secret message"—but to enable the book to reveal its useful qualities and basic values—which can only begin to be used by oneself after the third, fifth, sixth or tenth reading.

So there is no concealment or codification in the sense of it being incomprehensible—nor is it because it is not of any use to a person in its uncodified form—in fact, there is literally an embarrassment or confusion, when such people are faced with certain things which they would perhaps like to use, or when it is indicated to them that they should be used, but which they can't use because of their degree of knowledge, expertise and appreciation.

So what then is the favour being done to them by that book? The answer is: none.

For instance, if you take any of the books we use, say a very simple work like Saadi's *Gulistan* or *The Rose Garden* which is made up of a number of stories and also contains verse. This is an entertaining book, which is a standard text in Persian, used in schools as part of the standard school syllabus there— a sort of equivalent to Macaulay or Dickens in England. Also, the language is very beautiful, it can be easily read, and it's entertaining—it contains a number of stories, moral tales and verse, things like that—and it can be read on that level, as it is, in schools.

But it can then be read again, and as I say, the more one reads it, or rather, the more aspects of it one reasonably keeps in mind while one is reading it, the more apparent it becomes. If the whole content, the whole quality of the *Gulistan* were to be written on one page, and published in that form, and given out to people, it would be so mind-boggling that people would deny it: "I'm sorry, there is no way for this to be understood."

It is therefore the telling of one story that leads in turn to the telling of another—which leads to a piece of poetry which leads on to another tale, which will then cause a person to think — but now that you have got someone to think, what do they think about?

You don't tell them exactly what to think about, because then you are just conditioning them, or else they'll just think round in circles. You encourage them to think about certain things, and when they have done this thinking about certain aspects, you encourage them to think about how to use them. Otherwise, what are you doing? Just provoking thought, and then they're going off, thinking ...

What is the product of thought? Usually, the product of thought is a certain amount of action, hopefully of a beneficial nature, leading to a beneficial conclusion—or else producing a beneficial conclusion in a circumstance for somebody else.

Again, this does not mean to say that we are a bunch of do-gooders, going around influencing a situation so that others can benefit.

If people in groups are links in a chain, what each group does should naturally and normally and usefully be beneficial in some other place at some other time, and there is nothing either superstitious, extraterrestrial, or anything like that about it. It is a very practical, clear and precise way of passing, generating, using and benefiting from energy.

So when one sees and hears people "filling in the gaps" by saying "Saadi, Hafiz, Jami" or "Rumi" said such-and-such a thing, and "I wonder if he meant such-and-such?"—if he had meant it, he would have said it.

To bring one up to the edge of something and then leave the question suspended means either that the person hasn't read the chapter or whatever went before, or else it means that one has come to a point where the answer lies together with the person himself or herself.

Not in the sense of "Who killed Cock Robin?"——"Turn to page 99"——because if you are pulling people along in a certain direction, and encouraging them—to put it mildly—to use certain feelings, terms of reference and areas of being to reach a certain indicated conclusion or truth—whether it is the specific truth that one is looking for, or expects, or wants, is a whole different ball game.

But at least it is not so intangible as something like "Pluto is in the eleventh House, what shall I do?"——not only is this a very primitive feeling that relies on people's primitive sensibilities, it is also very imprecise, and we do not deal with imprecision.

What you do with the correct intention, and the tools you know about already, will produce a correct result. Whether Pluto is under your kitchen table or not may not only be an embarrassment, it is also irrelevant.

In the early sixties in Paris we had a magazine called "The"——because nobody could decide on a name and everybody was sitting around undecided, so I said: "Look, let's just call it "The", shall we?"——and that's what it was called.

In those days it was really before I had made my attitude towards astrology known, and there was a great deal of interest about things like whether the Tour Saint-Jacques was pointing North or South et tout ce que cela comporte, and there was a whole lot of mystery about this kind of thing, so I wrote a long text entitled "What if" ... and I packed into it all the so-called "occult" aspects like Neptune trines Saturn, Saturn occluded by Pluto, Pluto trines Saturn with the Moon in Venus and everything like that—and I wrote a long piece about that sort of thing. Everybody read it with great interest and avidity, and then held a meeting to decide what they should do about it—and because I was at that meeting, they were encouraged, actually, to disregard such things, unless they could actually control such phenomena—and if they couldn't, to forget about it.

Now to go back to phase one—I'm not saying disregard any possibility of extraterrestrial phenomena because certain things do, and can, manifest themselves and influence one.

You should not say "If I can't control them, I am not subject to them" or "I don't believe in them" any more than one should wander out waving a sword and clad in white samite on the twenty-first of June, expecting goodness-knows-what to happen—because the men in white coats will come and take you away, if not worse.

You neither say "If I can't control it, I don't want to know about it" nor do you say "I want to know about it, so that I can control it"——neither is the correct option.

If you know about it, you can benefit from it if you are available, and if there is any benefit.

How about that for a conundrum?

11.04.91

## COMPREHENSION, PERCOLATION & GENIUS

The practical use of techniques, information, and formats in the Tradition has to do with comprehension, which is, of course, an all-embracing term, but, as far as I am concerned, I would use this word as meaning to understand a thing really fully, and being able then to use this knowledge in a practical way and also in one's thought patterns, behaviour and attitudes.

This is, in fact, what we call the percolation factor, which means the assimilation through doing a thing, hearing something or reading something; comprehending it; and then making sure one comprehends it and then feeding it in to various levels of consciousness which produce a reaction.

Comprehension can therefore be considered here as distinct from just understanding. Understanding is already a step, but in my definition of the word, understanding is only the basis of comprehension.

Okay, all this is nothing new, but it is nevertheless something worthy of comment and study, because if somebody says: "Yes, I understand"; the next question I might ask them is: "Have you understood it fully?"—in other words, "Can you use it?" or "Can you act upon it?"—that is to say "Have you really comprehended it?"

If the answer is "I get the outline. I understand the principles"; this is simply not good enough.

The basis of a piece of information, an activity or an

exercise is to familiarize oneself with the concept, the form, and the reason why it exists. One familiarizes oneself with the way one hopes it will function, and one should then assimilate it to the degree that it is being comprehended on as many levels as it can percolate through to.

This comprehension, or to put it another way, the mechanics of comprehension, are different according to the people, according to their terms of reference, and also according to their different moods.

You cannot work out a time scale and say to yourself that three or eleven days or two months after 'Agha said something,' or after a particular exercise has been done, or a particular thing read, a certain level of 'common comprehension' will have been arrived at. You can't do this because, as I say, the operative word is percolation, in which the thing is moving through the system. At some points along the way, the comprehension factor may be slowed down. This may be a result of a mood or health factor, or it may be the result of tension and factors associated with it.

So for an actual amount of hours, days or weeks, there may be a certain blocking or stoppage of the percolation process. Nevertheless, this percolation does take place, and even if somebody might fault me scientifically by saying "By definition, percolation has to do with gravity. Water percolates through different strata drawn by gravity"—which is perfectly true, in the purest sense of the word percolation—what I am talking about here is slightly different. So the percolation or transmission of this information through different levels is nevertheless enhanced and aided by the degree of understanding and comprehension of the earlier levels.

Like anything, once an energy function is established, a base must be established on which to build, if you like, this platform. This level is enhanced by the backup and support that it gets from other levels in the Tradition in terms of energy, learning, and exercise—it is this which makes the platform solid. And on that platform which has one level, the communication between other levels takes place.

Although the transmission of the comprehension can be delayed by certain human factors, it cannot be stopped indefinitely. This happens not because it is 'overwhelming' as such, but because if it is not percolating through according to the ability or the quality of the person, there will be some sort of nudge being given to that person.

People do feel.

It is not that they feel confused, frightened, worried, guilty or anything like that, but there is something which is the degree of what we call—it doesn't translate well—a loss of taste.

There is a feeling of a "lack of something" which indicates that for some reason there is an inhibition being placed on this, and that a person is maybe not correctly tuned in, not properly harmonized or in such a state of tension or confusion that they are imposing this block or stricture.

Throughout history you have examples of people who have suddenly discovered something in the form of great breakthroughs—call it a "Eureka" factor, when a sudden discovery is made: people have called it "bursts of light" or some sort of intuitive "something" and it is usually considered a crowning achievement of genius when this extraordinarily deep and penetrating thought, idea or feeling occurs.

Well, yes and no. Yes, it can happen—but no, a person does not necessarily have to be a genius to have such an experience.

# COMPREHENSION, PERCOLATION & GENIUS

If it were so, such breakthroughs would be limited to a small number of predefined genii who would, almost predictably, discover things or make breakthroughs.

I've never experimented with this myself, but I think somebody once said that if you give a hundred typewriters to a hundred monkeys, in a thousand years or so one of them will type Shakespeare. This might possibly be true if one had to rely on genius for breakthroughs on various levels—which means that one would be inhibiting the flow of knowledge or perception by limiting it to a single category of human beings.

But there again, what is the definition of genius? If you say to almost anybody: can you think of a genius? Everybody says "Einstein" or "Leonardo" or something like that, and I'm sure it's perfectly true.

Nevertheless, if you look closely at most of the recognized geniuses, whether in mathematics, science, medicine, the arts or any other area, you'll find nine times out of ten that they did not suddenly stumble across this particular factor or great discovery, without preparation. There are occasions when this does happen, but such occasions do not happen in a haphazard fashion.

Let's take Alexander Fleming, who discovered penicillin—his whole life was spent in that area. His whole focus, attention and terms of reference were in that direction. Therefore, as a leading scientist in that field, he was automatically "honed" to make a discovery, since he was in tune with that whole area.

When he picked up a test plate on the windowsill of his hospital at St. Mary's—as a scientist and microbacteriologist, he would normally look at it before throwing it away or doing anything else.

This is an absolutely automatic reaction for a scientifically trained man. If he had just been some passer-by, he would have seen that plate, would have thought "that's the wrong place to have it, it might fall into the street" and just picked it up and thrown it away.

The right man with the right observation knew immediately that what was in that plate meant something, and he took it from there. It was therefore genius in the sense that he knew exactly where to go and what to do with that information, but it wasn't as if he was a plumber or electrician whose mind was suddenly taken over by some extraterrestrial intelligence which told him what to do. No, he was trained, he was pointed, and he was harmonized with the time, the place and the circumstance, which all came together.

I suppose that you can call this genius, but like many terms in the West, the term of genius is overused. People say: "You should use my decorator, he's a genius." No. He's probably a good decorator, but the word is being undersold and overused.

How this relates to comprehension is that, as one is building up terms of reference, energy, thought patterns, reaction patterns, while enhancing and taking notice of objective reality as well as one's own feelings—while one is putting all of these things together—they are all filtering through into different levels.

At certain points these components will come together to form a peak, and at that time, a person can experience thoughts, sensations, or a taste of something which gives them a glimpse of perception working at its best. This is usually not a result of somehow accidentally stumbling upon a 'secret' or something of that nature, because, as we all know, a lot of hard work, thought, confusion, questions and queries go into assimilating as much knowledge and information as is available in the Tradition, and using it. It is therefore reasonably and eminently predictable, although again, not in terms of hours, days, weeks, months or whatever, that a person under certain circumstances will have this feeling.

People may put it down to an intuitive feeling or they may put it down to any number of things, but it will be a sort of glimpse of whatever, of something that varies.

Now there are two functions, really, in this happening.

Firstly, this breakthrough of what one can call hyper-perception can be simulated—people have indulged in "forty days of fasting" and prayer and other activities, as a result of that, have experienced certain hallucinatory circumstances or sounds—or else, secondly, they have produced this by mechanical means, that is by means of things they have eaten, or through drugs, or other mechanical or external factors.

Right. Now if a real phenomenon of understanding occurs in the Tradition, why a) does it occur? And b) is it not perhaps a little bit cruel in the sense that you may have given a person the sight, taste, feel or sense of something to which they aspire, and then suddenly it's swept away before their face?

Well, no, because there is a well understood human desire to get what one might call feedback or results. Either between themselves or in conversation with others, people do discuss and explain things from the Tradition, or they ask questions, see how much they have understood, how much the other person has understood, or whether they can discuss it in order to enhance their understanding and perception of a thing. Also, they would like to feel, understandably, that they have made some sort of progress in perceptive understanding.

So more often than not, in a situation which is not what

one might call a 'highly-charged' or a 'high-powered' situation—if a person has an experience in a particular situation, or in a particular place; this is usually because several very powerful elemental factors have come together and provoked or produced a feeling or a circumstance. It's not just an imagined thing, it is real.

Often a person will have this impression of something which gives them a taste, a smell, a glimpse of something, in a situation which does not seem to correspond with what they are doing at the time. They might be walking, cooking, washing up, listening to the radio, watching television, or doing any sort of thing, and perhaps part of their thought is suddenly inundated or overwhelmed with an impact—colour, sound, visual, or whatever. Maybe a fleeting impression.

They cannot sensibly put that down to what they happen to be doing at the moment, in order to do more and more of it to provoke a situation—because people already do enough working, cooking, washing up, walking their dogs and looking at television, without saying: "Since it happened when I was doing such-and-such, therefore I will incessantly repeat this washing up or whatever in the hope that it will arrive again."

Under those circumstances, it won't, because it is not the circumstance which has provoked anything.

The other reason or factor in this process is that in the transmission or the percolation of the comprehension from one level to another, if there is even a slight or minute degree of excess energy, which is—I have to go into a bit of technical detail, very quickly—when a particular type of energy passes from one level of being to the other, it uses a factor as a ladder between these two levels. This factor is a form of energy, but it's a very low grade form of energy, and its function is fulfilled when the transmission or percolation takes place, so that it is then discharged or burnt off—and this can give off a momentary flash of something.

So it is a sign—it doesn't always mean that comprehension is or isn't taking place. So, if anybody sitting here is thinking "It never happened to me"; this is no cause for concern because it does not always manifest itself in this way. Also, if a person is sitting there thinking "It happens to me all the time"; it is probably their problem.

There is nothing regular in the sense of time or space. Both fill themselves, as they say, but the enhancement or transmission is based on the deepening of the comprehension and the ability to then use this comprehension.

Now as a comprehension moves into a different level it stimulates that different level to act.

It isn't just being "held there" in order to be eventually pushed up or down or whatever into another level. No, its function is to nourish and stimulate that level into action, which is the area of deeper consciousness where the terms of reference, the feeling of correctness, the feeling of harmony, is enhanced.

This means that genius in the sense of very high intellectual ability is not necessarily a credential—it is not a requirement. All development within the context of the Tradition is, and has to be, based on assimilation, and then putting what has been assimilated together with energy and activities, and then the using of that—not just amassing it for the purpose of amassing it.

You have the unity of energy on the different levels. You are basically nourishing, polishing up, replenishing and putting different levels into better and better function. As I have said before, just as a tree owes it's life and it's function to the roots, and the roots are necessary for the leaves, and vice versa—as their capacity is enhanced and as they are put more and more into function, these levels must and do harmonize with each other. They do not operate independently in the sense that one might have an overdevelopment of one level to the detriment of others, or in the sense that one level might be withholding the information and not allowing it to percolate through, because an equilibrated percolation, assimilation and use of knowledge is balanced.

You have a very good example, again, in a cosmological sense: a planet has satellites of different shapes and forms, within their contexts. They relate to each other in respect to their trajectory, their magnetic fields, and so forth.

Just as events of the earth not only relate to the sun and moon, the earth also needs them according to a harmonious degree. Nobody wants a hundred degrees temperature and 98.9 percent humidity all year round. Only some parts of the world get it, need it, want it, and in that area, it's desirable. There is a reasonable balance.

You can say that the sun and the moon influence the earth—so does the earth influence other planets, and so do all bodies in the cosmos influence each other one way or another. They do not trespass on each other's path or on each other's function. They all obey the laws of magnetism and follow particular paths, harmonizing with, and benefiting, each other.

Therefore within the human system, there is no pushing for power, or rather there should be no pushing for power. It is fortunate that a person does not have an immediate personal control or access to the different levels of their own consciousness, for the reason that if people could have this control they would try and exercise it. They would interfere, and they would dominate, and then bring out the "seventh me on the left", and "that's the tenth me", and here is the "twelfth me", and all that garbage. We have enough of that game on the intellectual level.

However, what happens is that when and as different levels of perfection are enhanced, and a person familiarizes themselves with the state of being when those levels are operating, those levels come to work at the time and under circumstances at which they harmonize.

They are not jockeying for position. A person only does that themselves: "Which side of my personality will I show in such and such a circumstance?" And they can dictate it—it may be an interview and therefore one wants to show certain positive sides of oneself. It may be an interview at the bank, where one wants to show one's craven and slavish attitude towards one's bank manager. It depends. A person can always change the facets of personality they show to the outside world, but they shouldn't try the same trick with themselves, because that is really asking for trouble.

This being said, the facet or the aspect of a person's deeper being comes to the surface and modifies, moulds, directs and guides their thoughts and action to a degree that it doesn't take them over, but it influences them to a degree that they have, say if they have a choice to make, if they will look and if they have time to be objective, they will find that their choice, in fact, narrows down to a degree where, if they are really harmonized, they will have this state which is called absence of choice.

Not lack of choice. I mean a choice is everything you can think of, but I am talking about the right thing at the right time, as a result of this "nudge" which a person is getting in a particular direction.

One can in fact establish a closer contact with certain levels of one's being by using zikrs or exercises.

That is not to say that one is provoking a particular aspect of one's inner being in a particular circumstance because, again, you cannot force it out or tempt it out.

If it is there, it is there for your benefit, and therefore if it is the wrong time, the wrong circumstance or the wrong moment, it will not come out, any more than you can force it out.

It is quite a normal and usual thing in the Tradition to do this—if one is doing something or wants to do something, one can tell oneself what one's intention is, what we call to "clear" your intention to yourself and ascertaining that one's intention is, as far as one can see, reasonably and objectively and in a balanced way, correct. One can then use a zikr or another word to further push forward one's intention in the hope that it is correct, and one will then find that this part or parts of the being will flow naturally into the context.

You don't wait for some sort of amazing result. That is not to say that it doesn't come or that it never comes. Things come very often by coincidence.

Now also, mark and remember the part of the rules entitled: *Remembering*—the remembering of coincidences. Remembering situations in which things 'clicked in'; 'went okay'; 'moved.'

How? Why? What circumstances prevailed?

You ask yourself these questions not necessarily to recreate those exact circumstances, because one circumstance, of course, that you cannot recreate is time.

# COMPREHENSION, PERCOLATION & GENIUS

But you can recreate the ambience, the situation and various other things, as far as one remembered them, in order to recreate in one's mind the feeling or the sensation.

"Things came together. Things harmonized, coincidentally" or whatever, it doesn't really matter in what terms you put it as long as you don't allow it to go into the realm of superstition. "Oh, it went right because I had the rabbit's foot" or goodness knows what. No, with or without the rabbit's foot, it would have happened.

So an intention, clearly expressed, tunes one in and harnesses the level or levels of one's inner being, and gives the energy the chance to function, and it also propels you in a way which is inexorable—not in the sense that you can't stop it, because then the person would become a sort of marionette.

It is that the direction and the focus is so clear that one is acting with the circumstances actively, not just like a leaf is blown in the wind or something like that. The function of the person is coinciding with the function of the activity, in a harmonious way, and therefore the whole wheel is turning.

29.06.89

# RULES OR SECRETS OF THE NAQSHBANDI ORDER

## THE TRADITION AS A PRACTICAL PHILOSOPHY

Many times before now you heard me refer to the Tradition as a way of life and a way of behaviour, and also as a practical philosophy.

One has to be a little bit careful when one gets into the area of what is conventionally and known in the West as philosophy, because there are certain schools of philosophy which are eastern and which we would call the surrendering, tranquil, almost inactive type of philosophy, such as Buddhism.

The Tradition is an active philosophy in the sense that it has its rules, books and textbooks, going right back to the beginning—and those textbooks are eminently available and have been translated and have continued to be used until today.

In all these textbooks, whether it be from Ibn Arabi, Hafiz, Jami, Saadi or anyone else, you will find that the active principle is being stressed—and along with the activity principle being stressed, you have stories or examples both of what to think and how to think.

As I have said, this is not exchanging one conditioning for another, because it is only after having measured the value of the terms of reference in the Tradition that one makes the attempt to change from the terms of reference which one may have been brought up with, or been educated into, in those areas which are sensitive to your own philosophical or internal development. Why I say you have to be careful is that very often the word philosophy itself raises that idea of old, thick and difficult books, with very complex thought patterns and explanations.

# THE TRADITION AS A PRACTICAL PHILOSOPHY

At that point, ideas which seem to be valid cannot be fed into the active area of one's thought or life, but are better suited to academic discussions or among more meditative forms of philosophy.

We use, of course, meditation in the Tradition. It is one of the activities—activity, not 'dis-activity.' It is recommended as an activity, which along with other exercises and activities, form the whole corpus of what we mean by a philosophy.

Certain other philosophies we see, both in the East and the West, are very often exercises in hairsplitting. From my point of view, they do not give one sufficient nourishment for oneself, and they are not active enough to carry a person along to some form of true understanding or realization of themselves or of their place in the universe.

We claim—and with reason—that the Tradition contains an energy, and the activities of people create energy as well. This energy is used by groups and individuals, in order to help them and stimulate the activities and their thought patterns in a way which helps them to explain certain things which they are looking for.

No philosophy—and by that I include also the Tradition—will explain to you categorically and exactly, in a simple manner, what one's relation with God, or what one's place in the Cosmos is to be. This is because the individual being heightens the knowledge, the understanding, through activities—which differ according to their way of thinking, the speed with which they can change their way of thinking or behaviour, the degree to which they benefit from contact with the Tradition and the energy, as well as their own intention and their own harmony within themselves.

The Tradition offers a path, a teaching, a formulation by

# RULES OR SECRETS OF THE NAQSHBANDI ORDER

which a person is encouraged to look at themselves, perhaps to understand a little more about themselves, to understand what their motivation is, in order possibly to understand what they can hope to achieve through this greater understanding of themselves, and how they can use this understanding to build some form of development.

All the books of the Tradition are, without doubt, textbooks which can be used within the context of present-day thinking and present day life. As I said the other week, they do not require a person to retire into a monastery and isolate themselves. On the contrary.

This knowledge, this energy contained within the Tradition, that is within its books and in its places, can be fed into a person's activity, with themselves, within the context of a proper active learning scheme in the Tradition.

But philosophies—some of a eastern nature such as Buddhism and Taoism, as far as we in the Tradition are concerned, rely too much upon the meditative side and less on the active side. Certainly, as I said before, there's everything to be said in favour of meditation, but it should be done in a balanced way and it should be a meditation directed towards a purpose, towards achieving a tangible goal, i.e., a goal which one can say that one feels that one has either achieved, or at least got sight of—in order to navigate, if you like, through the philosophy, and find which areas are areas of harmony on which one can depend, and which areas are areas which contain some, perhaps, hostile element—that is, an element which is hostile possibly because it is built up of conditioning of a different nature.

A person may therefore find it difficult to overcome this and replace it with something which is functioning more usefully.

298

# THE TRADITION AS A PRACTICAL PHILOSOPHY

In all areas where one is expected to function in the Tradition, the important point is the intention that one puts into doing what one is doing. If it is a matter of merely following certain terms of reference and hoping that they will work, this is an insufficient intention. Their intention has to be that the person is aiming, not necessarily at making a quantum leap, but towards making some distinct advances in the areas of their inner consciousness with which they can harmonize and which they can actually feel.

Many times I have said that a person may try to judge the degree to which they have developed themselves or developed some aspects of their character, and it is very difficult to do so. This is because, firstly, it requires a very considerable knowledge of oneself and one's reactions to measure any change. Secondly, and in a useful way, it prevents a person from indulging in the temptation of examining themselves all the time, rather than examining themselves and seeing in which way they imagine that they might develop.

That is not a conundrum—it sounds like the opposite, but it isn't—because a habit which can be easily developed in a person, based on conditioning from the time one is at school, is that of examination of achievements. As I say, this is a habit which is instilled into a person, and they are, in fact, encouraged to feel that their knowledge has increased in certain fields of education. This is perfectly reasonable and rational.

However, if they were able to measure what I might call their internal dimension of their development, the danger is that either self-satisfaction might set in, or in some areas, a feeling of hopelessness could set in if a person has measured that particular area and found it to be active. So, to avoid the pitfalls of excessive satisfaction or bewilderment or confusion, the only time when one feels a breakthrough, if you like, is under certain circumstances, when perhaps one is reading something, listening to something, or visiting a place where the harmonic comes to surface briefly and is established, which gives the person a hint of the fact that something is actually happening.

It's only a brief instance, a brief sort of glimpse in the mirror of something, and it's not something which is usually capable of being held onto for any length of time. It is something transitory which has an autonomous existence, and it is something which is, as it were, holding a mirror up to oneself and seeing how clear an image is in it.

The dynamism of the Tradition is such that it puts more emphasis onto the building up and using of energy and activity, and less on the subjective and meditative aspects.

There is such a thing as active meditation and such a thing as passive meditation. In every area it is stressed that proper activity, which harmonizes with the way a person feels or is feeling, is always emphasized about other things as well.

How a person is feeling, or how they might feel is, of course, dependent upon certain other factors which are outside the person's control. For instance, whether they're feeling happy or sad, or whether they're feeling fit, or ill, all influences, of course, the way in which they act, the way in which they understand, the way in which they receive the energy, and the way in which they use it.

But to digress—if they are using and following the Naqshbandi rules, then they will find that, by these rules, they will be able to measure and use this energy—through their feeling of harmony with the rules, or with a particular rule at a particular time—rather than using a subjective measurement

# THE TRADITION AS A PRACTICAL PHILOSOPHY

or an imaginary type of measurement to measure their degree of comprehension, understanding or development.

The dynamic within the Tradition is constantly being maintained, and it is up to an individual to link up with this momentum, and keep it going within themselves, and not just in a haphazard way when they meet on Thursdays or any other occasion.

After all, the Tradition has an inbuilt momentum. It can be a different momentum, depending on certain geographical and other factors, but the momentum is still there. And if a person links up with it, this momentum will carry them along to a degree—but that doesn't mean to say that they should not make the effort themselves. They should make any effort to take advantage of and use the energy which is there. Not merely absorbing it, and feeling good about having absorbed it—it has to be put into use.

Therefore every time one is examining or looking at the Tradition, or one's relationship with the Tradition, or wondering about one's place into the scheme of things, it is always useful to remember that, when dealing with these big questions like "What is the meaning of life?"; "What is my place in the scheme of things?"; "What is God?"—all these questions, which are very significant, are not answered by looking them up in the book.

In fact, they are not answered by the greatest of our philosophers in the Tradition. What the philosophers or teachers have done is leave books and texts to read and activities to do for us—following which, the individual for himself or herself finds a  path, a way of behaviour, in order to clarify for themselves what they may imagine, or what they really feel to be, the answers to these questions, if at all.

# RULES OR SECRETS OF THE NAQSHBANDI ORDER

In their books, anyone of the caliber of Ibn Arabi, Hafiz, Jami or Rumi, will not explain these questions nor answer them directly.

The debate here is not whether they knew the answer to those questions or not, and deliberately left them out. What we are concerned with is the use of these texts as guidebooks for a way of thought, a way of behaviour and a way of understanding which, hopefully, could conceivably point one towards finding out the answers to some of these questions. But none of the books, however deep, however profound, will answer the question a person might be asking.

Because if there is an answer—is that the answer which is satisfactory to everybody?

Perhaps. Everybody differs in their appreciation of how to develop, how much they can develop, how much they should develop, or in which way they should develop.

Perhaps you have differences in opinion regarding this, and therefore, if some of these questions were answered directly, some people might simply ignore the fact that some of these very important questions have indeed already been answered.

So it is quite deliberately that most of the thought patterns, active work and activities have to be done by the individual concerned, in order to get them used to using the textbooks to frame a feeling of harmony within themselves and for themselves, which should then encourage them to look further and deeper into themselves and into the philosophy itself.

I cannot lay too much stress on the fact that the active use of the instruments, texts and activities of the Tradition are essential in getting a balance and a harmonious state of being, which will enable a person to take a look at the questions that they ask. They take a look, and see whether they are anywhere near or nearer to getting the answer, which has to be a correct answer.

If it is a subjective answer, an answer which has been manufactured by reason of their own background or conditioning—in other words, if it is not a true answer, then somewhere along the road they will fall into error, having accepted a subjective answer rather than an objective or true one. How much subjective explanation goes on within a person is really known only to them. Sometimes people spend a great deal of time producing subjective explanations and answers to a lot of unnecessary questions. Or questions, the answers of which they do not need, concerning the state they are in.

It is no good writing down the answers to some of the most profound questions philosophers have been asking for thousands of years in textbooks unless a person, or a group, or a society, is able and ready and capable of taking on these answers, understanding them, and using them properly.

Otherwise, it's an exercise in futility to give answers to what we call 'raw' people—people who are unprepared to be able to use some particular information. It is a mistake to give it to them because it is, in fact, indigestible to them. They haven't as yet the terms of reference to be able to understand and use either the answers or the information.

It is therefore withheld from them until such a time as they, themselves, by virtue of their own efforts, dig out the answer and understand it—looking at it with a new understanding—and feed it into their conscious being, and into their behaviour patterns, in order that they should fully and properly function in the context they are using it in.

# RULES OR SECRETS OF THE NAQSHBANDI ORDER

Somebody once said somewhere that too much knowledge is a dangerous thing. Well, it depends of course on the type of knowledge. Too much knowledge can possibly be dangerous but too much knowledge can be, first of all, confusing. If a person is faced with a whole batch of knowledge, which is intended to help them to be able to develop a way of thought or a way of being which is beneficial and on a higher level, then this information, this knowledge, has to be presented to them in manageable quantities.

Too much of it confuses them—because if they are not ready to put it into function within themselves, and if they are not ready to function within the context of the Tradition with this knowledge—rather than being useful, this knowledge then becomes a burden or an embarrassment. A person feels that they have it and they should use it, but they don't find the opportunity to use it, therefore they blame themselves: "I have understood it, I think, I should therefore, be using it. If I can't use it, I'm in error, or the Tradition is in error, or my teacher is in error, or something is wrong."

So therefore, digging out the answers is very much a life's work—and not only digging them out—but having discovered them, or progressively discovering them, being also able to benefit from it, and to be able to use these answers in a way which a person finds harmonious and in a way one can use this knowledge within the context of one's own activities. Whether it is a job or another activity, people should be able to coexist in whatever activity they are doing, in whatever place they occupy in the outside world. They should be able to make interior use of the knowledge they have without disturbing the pattern of their everyday life.

The danger of too much knowledge is that the person would look it up or take it on and try to use it under certain circumstances, which by error of judgement—let us suppose—would be wrong. This would cause them more confusion than benefit. Because the correct use of a piece of information—shall we say, in a conventional learning system—is that you know when is the right time to use a particular piece of information, just as when you find yourself in a context where you are expected to speak a foreign language, you logically accept the fact that you are using or thinking in a foreign language. Therefore, it is no great gymnastic feat for which you have to change significantly.

Using a piece of knowledge interiorly is the same thing. A person is in a situation, or people find themselves in a situation, where, inevitably, a certain term of reference, a certain thought pattern, is offered to them. And they then find it right, correct, and harmonious with their individual being to follow that pattern in that circumstance or in that particular way.

The knowledge comes with understanding, and understanding only comes by familiarity with the terms of reference and the activities of the Tradition, a familiarity which causes a person to think on different planes and different ways, rather than in terms of the conventional 'how, where and when.'

These questions all have a place and a function, but it also depends on whether they are ready and able to receive an answer or answers, and whether they are able to put that knowledge to correct use within themselves.

So, positive philosophy it is. It's an ongoing philosophy, in the sense that it is constantly refuelled from the energy point of view—from which people can then partake and use this energy, which they assimilate—both to direct their thinking, and to direct their behaviour towards reasonably attainable goals.

# RULES OR SECRETS OF THE NAQSHBANDI ORDER

Not always the big question, or the second biggest, or the third biggest. But relative questions, which lead to a coherent pattern, as it were, unfolding in their thinking—so they can then say "I think I see" or "I think I'm beginning to see" or "I have seen."

But if you already have, or if you are—then continue doing it. Familiarity builds up in this way and one has the feeling that one's thinking, thought pattern, and the activity one is doing under a certain set of circumstances is right and harmonious. That is where the active factor comes in. This is where one accentuates the positive and pushes forward to a degree where one still feels comfortable.

There is no rushing, no exaggerated pushing. A breakthrough isn't in that area. One can have an image of what is there: "I will rush towards it, I will rush to capture it and hold it"—no. There is no such a thing as speed in the area of development. There is speed only in the mind, especially, in the western mind, which is that of: "I want it now." It is not always possible to have it now, and it is not always possible to use it if one has it.

One's choice of "now" can be very subjective. It is better to be objective in one's choice, and then, when a particular piece of knowledge or information is offered, to take it and use it in a way that becomes a part of one's thinking. So dynamism is always present and is always a factor. The quiescent or the inactive pattern form of development has a place, but it is not a place which is as significant as the active.

Therefore, when one is thinking about practical philosophy one has to determine the practical aspects of such a philosophy, which are built in into the activities one is trying to implement within the principles of the Tradition.

16.06.92

# FEEDING THE RULES INTO YOUR THINKING

When talking about the Naqshbandi rules over the years, I have emphasized the importance not only of following the rules and reading them regularly, but also of having one or other or a combination of them circulating at the back of your mind, and thus feeding in certain of the rules which you think do, or could, apply to your thinking, or which you want to apply in a given situation.

This means that the habit, as it should become, of consciously thinking about the use of one or other of the rules in a specific circumstance should become second nature.

People have sometimes expressed to me a mild problem they face which is quite human: they are occasionally thinking about something—say a situation, a problem, maybe something they are planning, or that has to do with their family or activity—and in such a case, they ask, how do they avoid the sort of "switch-on" situation, in the sense of "I will now think about rule number so-and-so"; and then "Click, switch that into your thinking"?

This is not necessarily a source of complaint, but people do comment on the fact that it is sometimes almost an actual physical effort to introduce one of the rules into one's line of thought at a particular time, and they find it a problem to examine all aspects of a situation while at the same time adding one or other of the rules to it.

So they often ask how they can do it without making an actual physical effort, without needing to jump outside the actuality of a situation in order to introduce what might be considered an esoteric, theoretical or even abstract aspect to it. Also, how ought one to introduce it into a situation which is actually occurring, or which may perhaps occur?

The only answer has to be that if one is sufficiently well-versed, well-practised and well-experienced in the various rules; one or other—or sometimes three or four of them—may be produced in one's mind by a given situation.

As happens in life, it may be that one creates or becomes involved a situation which is unforeseen, surprising or even confusing.

After all, one can't always choose the situation in which one might be involved, because supposing there is a discussion or negotiation to be done in your professional context with one or two other people—you cannot be answerable to the way they react to a situation or for their attitude towards it.

Say in a normal professional life, one discusses a certain aspect of what one is doing, and one has an idea of how one wishes this discussion, debate or decision to come out. One thinks about it and then one goes in with, possibly, a preconceived notion of what one wishes to achieve in that particular meeting or debate. As the discussion unfolds, you put forward your point of view, the other person or persons put forward their reactions, and there is a discussion leading to a decision which may be right according to you, or which you may reluctantly have to accept because it's been accepted by a majority.

With your argument or the points you are putting forward, you are trying to persuade other people in order to

# FEEDING THE RULES INTO YOUR THINKING

bring them round to your point of view. To do that, you can use figures, charts and logic, and you put the "package" or proposal forward. In that situation, you are responsible for the way you present your point of view, shape your arguments and put forward the proposition, and you also have to transmit the enthusiasm you yourself have for your idea to the other people.

To this situation, you add another factor. You already have your idea of how a thing should be done or how best to achieve a particular thing. You are motivated by your own enthusiasm and research, so what you do is add one or other of the rules to that motivation.

You are not expecting, nor are you expected, to transmit subliminally or in any other way, your thinking about the rule you are using to the other person. What you are doing is no more than boosting up and increasing your confidence in your idea, in yourself, and in your capacity to present yourself, your idea or your proposition more forcefully than if you were merely motivated by a desire to get that thing done or to put over that particular message.

"More forcefully" does not mean that you need to shout, pound the table or make a scene. More forcefully means that your own motivation and enthusiasm take on a different character, a different degree of strength than it would have if you had not introduced one of the rules into your thinking.

Obviously, in any debate or discussion, you cannot afford to allow your concentration to be divided, because it is inefficient and it doesn't work. You have an idea of what you want to achieve and you put all your energy into it while at the same time keeping a relevant one of the rules at the back of your mind.

# RULES OR SECRETS OF THE NAQSHBANDI ORDER

This does not mean you are expected to detach yourself from all the different aspects under discussion, in order to think about one of the rules and then come back into the discussion, as it were. The process must be simultaneous, and if a person has familiarized themselves well enough with the rules, once the decision about which rule to follow is made, the inner being of the person will not 'take over'—but it will nevertheless pick your own knowledge of the rules, or the specific rule's meaning, out of your memory, which reinforces your confidence or ability to achieve within a given situation.

So you don't have to have the rule 'circulating in front of your eyes' while discussing or negotiating something else at the same time, because it can split your attention and you don't want to do this. Once you decide which rule or rules to apply, it is rather like pressing a button to bring that specific rule to mind.

If you practise it well, you only really have to press that button once, and the rule will circulate of its own accord without you making the 'on/off' connection or having to juggle between two different concepts at the same time, because all this would do is confuse both.

It is sufficient to decide which rule or aspect of a rule one is going to use before or during a meeting, debate, confrontation or other situation. That in itself is sufficient to keep that particular rule working on you during the course of the interview or activity.

For example, touching on one's professional life, one may say "Well look, I am going into a meeting with somebody or various people, and it may be difficult, confusing, complicated or even unpleasant, but I will exercise patience. No matter what the temptation may be to get agitated, lose one's temper or feel fed up, I will grit my teeth and get this idea across by patient manipulation, patient argument or patient logic."

The same holds true if you take the rule of *Safar dar Watan (Travelling in the Homeland)* or *Watching over the Steps (Nazar ba Kadam)*. Both of these are a source of strength and guidance because if one is watching one's step during a meeting, conference or debate, the possibility of error is less.

That doesn't mean that you draw back from total involvement and say "I must watch myself" because this could lead to the person losing the initiative in a discussion or argument, insofar as they are too worried that they might 'put a foot wrong.' Since part of their mind is occupied by apprehension, this would not lead to a coherent, confident and positive attitude or presentation of whatever one is either selling or discussing.

*Travelling within Oneself (Safar Dar Watan)* is very much akin to *Watching over the Steps* or *Nazar Ba Kadam*, because within oneself, one is watching one's own performance and increasing or decreasing the emphasis one is putting on what one is talking about, according to the way one sees oneself. At a given moment one may think "Oh, oh, I'm pushing too hard" or "My argument is getting thin" or "My confidence is diminishing" and if this is so, one should take the necessary action.

In exactly the same way, it follows that one is looking at oneself, judging oneself both consciously and subconsciously, and one feels that the argument or the activity is going in the right direction. This boosts one's conscious and subconscious confidence and one continues onwards with increased confidence and harmony with oneself and with the increased motivation which comes from the feeling of performing a successful activity.

# RULES OR SECRETS OF THE NAQSHBANDI ORDER

One shouldn't always think in terms of examining oneself to "find the negative" or "watching one's step because one always makes mistakes"; because if one starts only recognizing or seeking out this negative, one can probably find, attract or even imagine a lot more of it than there actually is.

In *Travelling within Oneself (Safar Dar Watan)*, one finds both the good and the bad, the negative, the positive, the inefficient, the stupidity, the confidence, and various other aspects of one's character.

When you are travelling within yourself, you are not, as it were, shining a lamp into the 'dark corners of your mind' in the expectation that you will find something negative there.

There is a tendency in the West towards what is broadly called 'self-examination' in the form of a tendency to put oneself on trial for reasons of lack of confidence, inefficiency or stupidity. If one is constantly on the lookout for the negative aspects of one's own character, one can attract even more negativity by magnifying a minor weakness or fallibility into something bigger—and one then abandons responsibility for oneself, saying "This is too complex for me" or "I am too stupid" or "I lacked confidence" or by allowing in—it's a strange phrase but a true one—something which takes the form of a sort of 'nostalgia for blame.'

This is very much encouraged in the West by intellectuals and by the church—because if one praises oneself to oneself or, what is considered even worse, to other people—it is considered to be "showing-off" or "egotistical"; and of course, this can indeed be so.

I'm sure you know many people like this, who under certain circumstances can give way to what I might call an egotistical fantasy in which they are the central figure or most important factor in a particular situation. This clouds the vision. To be egotistical leads one into error.

But it is also true that being too humble in the sense of "Oh I can never do this"; "Oh I can't concentrate"; "Oh I can't bring myself to do it"; "Oh I'm not sure"; "I am just stupid"— clouds the vision as well.

So we have the two extremes, and I keep on repeating this fact—and I do really recommend it—to put it mildly: extremes cause confusion.

If a person is overconfident of their own abilities in a particular area, this can cause them trouble, confusion, anguish and pain.

If they are so meek and mild that they allow themselves to be weakened by what they consider to be humility—this is the other extreme which can lead to under-performance, and which inevitably leads them towards a lack of confidence in everything they do.

In turn, since they have perhaps decided "I am hopeless" in this or that area, it will certainly and without question cause them to fail or make errors in that area, and with this curious mental gymnastic, they will then be able to say "You see, I knew that I was an underachiever in this particular way, so what is the point?"

This process can gently, gradually, and almost imperceptibly erode a person's confidence in themselves. It can also dilute and erode the strength and energy they get from the Tradition—because after all, the Tradition does not produce miracles in a person overnight. It's a long hard road, some of which can be frightening, confusing and even objectionable at times, when people examine themselves and find some aspect which worries or frightens them.

So there is no sudden illumination.

Equally, if people dilute or erode their relationship or association with the Tradition or its various teachings; losing confidence in themselves or in their ability to do one thing or another will tend to make them lose confidence in the Tradition as well—either by ignorance, because they say "Well, since I can't or don't do anything, there is no point in trying anything because I'll fail"—or else because, by lack of application, concentration or lack of study, they do not apply the teachings of the Tradition correctly.

This then gives them the ready-made excuse to point out that not only are they weak, confused and stupid, but the material they are dealing with—say the activities, texts or exercises—have not produced this sudden breakthrough into actual reality.

They therefore go about throwing blame in all directions.

In the West, again, the concept of humility is not well understood—or rather not well taught or explained—either by those who should be explaining it, or else it is not well interpreted by the person who takes on the concept "lock, stock and barrel" and says "Right, I am a humble person."

The acceptance of the fact that one is a humble person has its good and bad aspects. Taken to extremes, it can mean "I don't expect anything from myself because I am so humble," i.e., "I can't ever push or be forceful; all I want is humility."

And of course, you can be so humble that everybody treads all over you, which is proof to yourself that you are nothing—but this is not a useful aspect of humility.

# FEEDING THE RULES INTO YOUR THINKING

True humility lies in the basic admission that the average person is influenced by greed, laziness, fear and confusion. True humility begins when one understands how little one knows. You can always take Rumi's Mathnavi, Hafiz, Jami, Saadi or Khayaam, and learn the texts so completely that you are able to quote any page, line or verse.

If you do that—which would be an effort in itself—it should normally increase your feeling of humility because it would show you how little you actually know, how much more there is to learn, and how important it is to put what one is learning into practice.

All the great teachers in the past (including Jalaludin Rumi) have, in one way or another, complained that they knew nothing right up to the end of their lives, regretting the fact that life had not been long enough for them to learn a little bit more.

So humility does not lie in weakness—whether of action, of decision or of function—because that undermines one's own natural, normal, logical thought-process or process of argument, or presentation, or whatever it may be.

It can be a very convenient excuse for doing nothing, because it comes very close to: "I am so modest, I won't express an opinion because it only comes from me and I know that I am just stupid."

This is why I don't like to hear the concept of humility being used as an excuse for either physical or intellectual laziness.

Certainly, from the day a person is born, they are learning from different experiences and are subject to different influences and conditionings. Some people read voraciously and remember everything—some people read little and remember little or nothing—but always, behind their thoughts and actions, should be the intention of following and consistently using one or other of the Naqshbandi rules as part of the normal thought or reactive process.

There are certainly situations in one's everyday life where the application of one or other of the rules is neither viable nor necessary, and one can needlessly complicate one's life by trying to introduce a rule where, in fact, only a normal action or reaction is required.

One can also needlessly complicate things by debating with oneself as to whether one should apply a rule or not, and then which rule and how.

If you want to go from here to Oxford Circus, you get a bus and buy a ticket—that process does not involve anything except a knowledge of bus routes and 50 p. or however much it costs to get to that stop.

If you introduce the unnecessary use of a rule into this process, you will either get on a wrong bus or you will miss the bus completely because you are standing at the bus stop debating as to whether this comes under *Travelling within the Homeland* or *Watching over the Steps*—these concepts are extraneous in the context.

Once you have caught the right bus and are on it, if you have a ten or fifteen-minute journey, you can then allow yourself the luxury of thinking about one or other of the rules in relation to what you are going to do when you get to Oxford Circus, or to the meeting, debate, or whatever it may be—because that is a five or a ten-minute period of time for your own reflection—call it, if you like, 'free-thought' time.

# FEEDING THE RULES INTO YOUR THINKING

On the bus, you can be planning what you are going to say, how you are going to react, what your position is, what your terms of reference are, and so forth, and at the same time, you can try and see, think or imagine which particular rule might apply in this oncoming circumstance.

So one or other of the rules should be omnipresent at the back of your mind most of the time—but you only bring it out and put it together in a situation.

It then backs up your determination, it backs up your enthusiasm, it backs up your motivation—but again—used with discretion.

14.10.93

## BUILDING CONFIDENCE IN THE RULES

One of the functions of the Tradition is not only to rehearse, understand and learn the rules, and have one's intention fairly well defined, but also to build up a reliance or if you like, a self-confidence in oneself based on the assumption—hopefully a solid assumption—that one has an intention, and one is guided by certain rules.

There is always the old argument that one might have with oneself, which is that a particular activity or decision may only be based on a conditioned intention—perhaps conditioned by various things outside the Tradition—or has it really been examined in terms of the values and the rules of the Tradition?

There is no simple answer to that, because as I have said many times, people are subject to all sorts of conditioning from the day they were born, so that sometimes they come to a crossroads where they say "Is my decision based on intuition, is it based on conditioning, or is it based on my intention?" And this can very often be a cause of confusion, because obviously, a person says "I would like to get it clear in my own mind."

Now given that there are certain situations where the motivation or the intention of an action is perfectly clear, or at least clear enough to be able to carry it out and not go over and over it again to understand it or make the decision, there are obviously also situations where a person says: "By what am I influenced in taking this action or making this decision?"

The answer is really quite simple: it is that if they have

318

read, understood and absorbed the teachings in the various books extant, they should be able to do what we call "bring their intention, their aim and their wish together into focus" with the rules, indications or writings we have from the teachers.

Therefore it should not be a decision of any significance, nor should it be a source or cause of any great debate within oneself. Rather it should be a comparison based on "What is my intention, what is my motivation"; and "What is the useful and positive benefit from my point of view, from the point of view of the group, from the point of view of the Tradition?"; and if those factors can be brought together and harmonized, then the answer should be quite simple.

Unfortunately, again, because here the factor of conditioning comes in, people very often don't trust what they say their deeper feeling is, what their instinct is, or what their impulse is, and they therefore hesitate in making certain significant decisions or in taking certain particularly significant steps.

That is not to say that any decision or step a person may take should involve them in stopping and saying: "I will look up something relevant to this in Hafiz, Jami, Saadi, Rumi, Ibn Arabi, and make a decision on that basis." In the long term, yes, they can do so—and having clarified the basis of the teaching and their own intention to themselves, the choice is usually quite obvious. It is harmonious with their feeling, it is harmonious with what they understand of the Tradition, and from their point of view, it is beneficial to themselves, to the group, and to the Tradition.

Decisions which are of less importance, obviously, do not necessarily have to go through such filters or comparisons, but with activities or actions which have a deeper significance or a longer effect, a person is quite right to consider their long-term effects, their long-term benefits, their long-term advantages and to spend a reasonable amount of time considering the different aspects, the different alternatives.

Now this is neither an excuse nor a recipe for indecision: "Shall I do this, shall I do that, shall I think like this, shall I think like that" and so forth, because this is an indulgence I would call an intellectual indulgence, because people will sometimes fall into the trap of saying: "Intellectually I am motivated by this, emotionally I am motivated by that, socially I am motivated by this—so where does my path lie? On what basis do I make decisions? On what basis do I function?"

Again, I must say that this is quite simple, because, given a reasonable understanding of the writings of our great masters, and a reasonable understanding of the rules, the fairly obvious social, political or other factors which might influence one can be discarded quite quickly insofar as they are really just surface impulses, surface pressures, or surface influences.

The valuable decisions a person may take and their significant decisions are what we call in the Tradition a result of a dialogue with oneself.

You might say this is a licence for interminable intellectual discussion in the sense of: "Shall I do this, shall I do that, what about this, what about that, and so forth—no, this is a ping-pong game.

Not every situation requires deep and fundamental consideration, but there are some situations which will affect or influence one's future life or activities to a degree which understandably require sifting through and a choice being made—but again, this choice is not limitless.

# BUILDING CONFIDENCE IN THE RULES

There is no great skill in looking at a decision and passing it back and forth over and over again—looking at it from the point of view of political, religious, social or whatever conditioning, and finding things "in favour" of one or "against" the other—this is an exercise in futility.

It leads to confusion. It is not an exercise in what is called intellect. It is not even an exercise of intelligence. It is esteemed to be—and there are countless western schools of thought or philosophy that encourage it—what is called "debate."

Debate is fine, I have nothing against it. But interminable debate is usually counterproductive, because the longer a debate is drawn out, the more influences, conditioning or extraneous aspects can come in. If one has a simple choice, a person—by introducing all sorts of conditionings—can make that choice no longer simple.

They can confound themselves by introducing doubt: "Well I think I'll do that, but I wonder, because 'something I heard' or 'something I think' or 'something I feel' or 'something somebody said' means that I'm not quite sure"—this is opening the door not only to confusion and hesitation, but inaction.

That is not to say that a person should examine a situation quickly and make a quick decision and do whatever occurs to them. Not necessarily.

Obviously there are situations where a quick decision based on circumstances has to be made, this is perfectly right. There are situations where more thought is necessary—but what thought? When it is Schopenhauerian, Freudian, Jungian, Adlerian, Socialist, Communist, Conservative and anything else, you are opening the door to, and inviting in, all sorts of terms of reference which seemingly apply, because, to quote, "I am an intelligent person" or "I am cultured."

Intelligence, cultural ability or mastery, is a two-edged weapon. If it is used correctly, if a decision—as I say—of any useful or positive significance is arrived at as a result of using the correct terms of reference, you're unlikely to go wrong.

If a situation occurs and a person applies either wrong or inefficient terms of reference—by definition they will make a decision which is either erroneous or confusing to themselves.

So basically: communication with oneself is something which should be enhanced in the Tradition, and it is emphasized in all the texts of the Tradition. As I say, the "dialogue with oneself" exists to arrive, not at a convenient solution, but at a correct and harmonious resolution or answer.

If one is applying the correct terms of reference, one will find, by practice, that the decision or choice one makes, or particular path one has chosen, harmonizes with one's activities. It's not a decision one is forcing upon oneself despite feeling otherwise or despite any reservations. When you say: "This must be done"—the question and operative word here really is "must."

From what point of view? Based on what terms of reference?

You don't make a decision or do something and then rationalize it afterwards, as in: "I thought it was a good idea at the time"—the question then is very often "Did you actually think?"; or was it an 'impulsive decision'? Or to take it a step further, was it an 'impulsive decision' based one of the many forms of conditioning?

So make the difference between intuitive decisions and superficial decisions very clear in your minds. Intuitive in the sense that you feel harmonious with them, and you feel they

# BUILDING CONFIDENCE IN THE RULES

are correct. Impulsive decisions may be based on how one was feeling at the time or what forces or factors were applying in that moment.

Impulsive decisions are not always wrong—but they can be. If a decision is of a fairly significant nature, a person should give that decision adequate time.

Adequate is not measured in months or years, adequate is how one defines the problem or the choice involved, and what terms of reference one brings to bear to make the decision. After all, one of the main thrusts of the Tradition is to give people not only confidence in themselves but confidence that they have the backup of the Tradition, as well as the energy of the Tradition, therefore they are to use it. There is no reason not to.

If a person hesitates because they are unsure, then give the problem or the situation adequate time, adequate thought, use the correct terms of reference and one will find that one will—perhaps not immediately, but eventually—harmonize with one's intention.

21.03.96

# RULES OR SECRETS OF THE NAQSHBANDI ORDER

## THE RULES AS CHARACTER COMPONENTS

Your time, the time which you found, the time which you use for exercise or zikr—that time is important time to you. You don't want to waste that time; I don't want you to waste that time, so therefore you must use that time to the best possible degree. You must—terrible word—maximise on that time.

We will start with some clear explanations as to things like the basic, what we call "secrets" of the Tradition: the basic ten or eleven points of the Tradition. Every activity in the Tradition comes from one of these points, therefore if one is doing an exercise, participating in a group exercise, listening to some music or somebody talking —if you know the basic rules of the Tradition, you can find how that activity applies to which rule for one very simple reason: it is a part of the human character.

If you are told to do something, a part of the person would like to know why, or "What will happen if I do it?" If they can say "Ah yes, this activity comes from this particular rule" then they don't waste time in thinking about it, they just do it.

There are occasions when a person might be asked to do something or to do an exercise which they can't relate to one of these rules. Maybe they will go through the rules again and again to find which one relates to this, or they will worry that they might have forgotten part of the rule, and blame themselves for being stupid, and me for not telling them, and the world for not being fair to them, and they will waste their time. It is better just to do it.

# THE RULES AS CHARACTER COMPONENTS

Now when you get a list and an explanation of the rules, read them and learn them: learn what is the basis, what is the spirit in that rule, i.e., not only the words but also the spirit behind it. Don't say to yourself "Ah, this comes from rule number 5" because then you're getting into numbers and not contexts.

Each rule has a name. If you remember, this is why I say "Don't say this is rule number 5" or "number 7" or "number 3"—I say that because when you associate what you're told to do with that rule, you're repeating the entirety of that rule to yourself and understanding it better each time.

So as I say, you learn these rules, and each time, without making it into any great problem, you try and relate what you're asked to do with one of these rules—and it then becomes an actual and concrete thing, not just an abstract idea.

As you probably know, in the Tradition we have a numerological system called the *Abjad*, which is that each letter of the alphabet has a numerical equivalent. Now this has a functional and a technical use, because according to a very strict framework, a whole word or a phrase or even an exercise, can be reduced to three or four numbers—and in that fashion, the whole quantity of the spirit and energy of that word or phrase can be reduced down to a very small size.

Familiarity with the rules of the Tradition is necessary, not only because you don't waste time wondering what this is about, but because each time you make the connection with the basic concept—and you are getting all the power and the energy from that concept—you are also getting as much energy and power and influence as you can use at that time.

The reason, of course, is quite obvious. If you plug in and get the full power of the energy—theoretically this is possible, but practically it's impossible—because in the practical sense, if one did plug in, a fuse would blow. In actual terms, if one gets more influence or energy than one can use, one gets a sort of philosophical indigestion. You feel full but it's uncomfortable. What are you to do with it? You should be able to use it, why can't you? Why are you so stupid? What are you doing here?—and the whole pattern starts again.

So if through an exercise or an activity, a person makes contact with a source of energy—the whole concept of that source is being used, hopefully, in that activity.

For instance: say a person wants to understand or examine their reactions to a particular situation—supposing a past situation has had a negative result.

Without automatically looking for somebody (or themselves) to blame, once they're out of the situation, they examine—and if they can, decide what went wrong. What was the cause of that error? Whether it was their error or somebody else's error—they look through the rules and find one which they could apply to control a similar situation in the future.

They may not always choose the right one, but the more familiar they become with the different rules, the more clearly they are likely to choose the right one to apply. If they choose the wrong one, nothing terrible will happen—if the intention is good and correct, even that mistake has a positive content.

One of the rules is called in Persian, *Safar dar Watan* which means *Travel in the Homeland*. *Homeland* in that context means the person themselves, that is, their physical and spiritual entity. It is called *Travel in the Homeland* because this is what it is—it is true. It is not called *'self-examination'* because there's always the possibility that this might add a critical aspect to it. *Travel in the Homeland*: if you travel in something which is familiar, you get to know it better and better. If you travel somewhere you don't know very well, you look at it carefully. You remember things about it, you make a comparison between that place and other places—you are not making a hostile or critical survey of that place.

We call it the word *Watan* or *Homeland* because it is you— it is very close to you. It should be very precious and very dear to you, because for all its faults and weaknesses, for the moment it is all you have—whether it is an embarrassment or not.

So, as a place—which is oneself, one's feelings, one's reactions, one's attitudes, one's terms of reference—become more familiar, one necessarily gets to know oneself better and better. There can be pleasant and unpleasant surprises, but at least the knowledge that one gains will help one not to be surprised.

If one identifies areas of weakness—fine. If one can do something about them, one tries to do it. If it is not possible, for the moment, to strengthen those areas, then one avoids situations in which, in such cases, one would be vulnerable.

By familiarizing oneself with oneself, one is not judging oneself forever, imposing limitations on one's ability: one examines oneself and one looks at oneself, and one says "Right, I am stupid—finish. So if I make mistakes, if I do something stupid, well it's because I am dumb."

This is usually an excuse. In any case, most people, even if they are dumb, will not admit to being dumb. It can be used as an excuse, which really means: "I am satisfied with my level of development, I don't want to make an effort."

"It would be very nice to understand such-and-such a thing, but I'm too dumb for that."

# RULES OR SECRETS OF THE NAQSHBANDI ORDER

"Well, would you like to try? Have you ever tried ?"

"No, no, I mean ask anybody, they'd just say I was dumb!"

The other end of the scale is: "I know everything about everything, and I can learn everything about everything—just tell me." There are a lot of people like that. They are intelligent, interested, active—"You know, just tell me."

So you tell them. You tell them a lot. And then they actually find out how dumb they really are. It can be a surprise to them, and very often they'll become your enemy for life, because if you have said to them "You are dumb" they don't care, because that's just your opinion—but the worst thing is if they find out for themselves that they really are dumb. For this, they'll blame you for the rest of their lives.

Usually, people are something in the middle. You have people who by background, education and personality, are more capable in certain areas. You have people who are technically-minded and people who are literary-minded. That doesn't mean that the literary-minded person has no technical ability at all, or vice-versa—it means that the technically-minded part of their personality is more in harmony with them.

In a group, in a society, this is why you have a balance between the technical and literary. They compliment each other. They are not or shouldn't be in competition, because if at some time, the literary person writes a book, he needs a technical person to print that book.

Equally, a technical person will need a literary person to write the instruction manual or teach him how to operate the technical machinery—so you have the necessary harmonic, the harmony betwcen the two aspects.

# THE RULES AS CHARACTER COMPONENTS

By getting to know oneself—familiarizing oneself with oneself more and more—a person will usually learn one lesson which can be quite surprising, and that is that at any one time, several parts of the mind or the memory are working almost in competition with each other.

Now this is not a psychiatric or psychotic situation, nor is it 'schizophrenic' or 'multiphrenic'—it is that various parts of the mind and memory are remembering tiny particles of similar experience.

Why I say it can be surprising is because it's the equivalent of one having a book with five pages, each page having a word on it. And if you look at each page, you find that each word makes up a sentence, a phrase. And that phrase, that sentence, means something.

But for whatever reasons of inefficiency or something, that sentence has not been written on one single page—it's been written on 5 available pages. The surprise can come when you take these 5 points or 5 words out of 5 different cells and put them all together—they make sense, they make a sentence—and you say "Good Heavens, I've been keeping these scattered around like this, and something makes sense." So you have got a sentence and a phrase, and four blank spare available pages—four pages which are blank and fresh and can be used for useful information or experience.

The human mind, the human memory, never forgets a sound or the word of the phrase which has a positive value.

It stores them—hundreds of millions of sounds, impacts, feelings.

One of the functions of the Tradition is bringing together these valuable experiences. Make the connection with the

Tradition and start that process functioning.

On top of the sorting-out and putting-together: if you bring out—again the analogy—the blank pages ready to be written on, these pages, if you like, have an aspect like a page and also like a photographic film. They can hold an image, a feeling, a word, a sound. The function of a zikr or an exercise is to get these out and fill them in.

During a zikr, an exercise, a meditation, there is a very brief period during which time that impact is registered.

At any moment when one wishes to examine oneself or do a positive activity, there are always three phases: the preparatory, the initial—when the person says to themselves what their intention is, what they intend to do at this time— i.e., get themselves in a physically and psychologically calm state, directing themselves in a particular direction—and after the preparatory period, the period called the clarity, the clear moment—and then the period of coming out of that state.

The most valuable pages, or images, or registered impacts, are those which are the deepest and most profound centres— and these centres are very heavily protected because they can be damaged, not in any severe way, but in a way that induces confusion if they take on or assimilate false or negative information. It is therefore understandably very difficult to get any contact or information through to those centres.

Any impact, anything a person sees or does, goes through a series of filters; and each filter is finer than the next.

So an impact, which is a social, an economic and other impact, is identified and sent to the area of the brain which is involved in that particular matter.

# THE RULES AS CHARACTER COMPONENTS

Now this is enormously sophisticated—because as you can imagine, if you're sitting in a place—say, you're talking with somebody, you're listening to what they're saying, thinking about it and replying and reacting. At the same time your ears are picking out perhaps the usual canned music, or some music in the background, your body is signalling to you all the time whether it's hot, cold, comfortable—so all these signals are coming in constantly, and the brain receives them all and reacts. And they are sorted out, and the reaction goes out instantaneously. And usually, the correct reaction will come out along the correct line.

If you're talking with somebody about a very complicated technical subject, and he says to you for instance "Can you arrange a letter of credit of one million marks?" Now that message must go in, and have an answer, a reaction along the correct lines. If the lines are crossed, you're uncomfortable and your reply to him is: "I don't know, because my bottom hurts"—this isn't useful. Normally you would say "yes" or "no" and move into a more comfortable position.

So therefore, in more sophisticated areas like the Tradition, where profound communication is going on, it is more and more important that the correct impact should be sorted out, identified, and sent to the correct centre.

Fortunately, each of the various profound centres which one is trying to develop has its own very precise examination filter. It will not accept a negative impact because it is composed, itself, of the positive—so it does an instantaneous comparison.

It is not interested in whether this impact is socially, economically, or otherwise acceptable. It is only interested in whether that impact, that energy, is of the same positive nature—and then it will accept it.

# RULES OR SECRETS OF THE NAQSHBANDI ORDER

When I say that these centres can be damaged—they can be damaged by confusion—and that confusion comes about because maybe a person accepts something they are told or that they hear, and they then try to force it to be believed and acted upon by the deep centres.

So then you have a sort of battle between the external trying to force acceptance, and the internal rejecting it.

Apart from the sort of defence mechanism and the filters which exist, everything related to the Tradition which is of a positive and useful nature, is what we call "tagged"—it's marked. It's almost like having a postal code—it doesn't appear on the surface to be any different, perhaps, from any other piece of music. It may be a place or a building or a person which has no obvious relation at all with the Tradition. But the person in the Tradition who is on the alert, that is, open—will notice, see, or feel the impact.

This is an efficient way, also, of making places—for instance, places built by the Arabs in Spain used colours, buildings, flowers and trees, in a certain relation to each other. They were not only functioning as sources of energy, but were also recognizable—not only because it was Moorish architecture so therefore it was "Moorish"—but because people who were on the alert identified it and made the connection.

So, as I say, this is one very small part of one of the rules, and all the practical and theoretical teachings come from these rules.

Obviously it is up to the teacher to choose the one which applies at the moment to a particular person or to a particular group.

How he does this does not depend on his personal feelings, or personal likes or dislikes. It is fortunately much simpler than that—if I have something to do, or some impact to create on a person or on a group, at that moment in time I have no choice of the technique or tactic which I use.

Okay.

This is a very delightful situation and it's called "absence of choice." It's not lack of choice—I have millions of choices—but if I allow myself the luxury of thinking through all the choices, that instant of time has gone.

I try, usually, to create impacts in a reasonably conventional way; or, more usually, in a way that nobody notices. But if I do happen to do anything which is extremely unconventional, that doesn't automatically mean that I have gone mad. That is always a possibility — but fortunately we have enough psychologists and other people who would take care of me, I'm sure.

24.01.87

# RULES OR SECRETS OF THE NAQSHBANDI ORDER

## LEARNING THE TRADITION LIKE A LANGUAGE

There has been—and there will inevitably continue to be—much talk about various levels of activity or levels of teaching, as exemplified in the idea of "hidden" or "obvious" meanings or—to use a common phrase—the "outer shell" and "inner kernel" of the teachings. There has been a lot of talk about things like "hidden Masters" and "Sufic Masters" and various topics of that sort.

The teaching of the Tradition covers both the surface consciousness and also the deeper levels of consciousness within a person, in that—firstly and consciously—a person who reads something, listens to a piece of music or who performs an activity within the context of the Tradition is conscious of an action they are doing at that time.

As such, it is a conscious, thought-out action, undertaken deliberately and with some intent, which most certainly does get into the surface consciousness, remaining there to be thought about, or else to be consciously brought out and used. It influences people, as it is intended to do, and it also has an impact on people on a deeper level—not exactly on the level of the subconscious, but on their inner consciousness. There are things in books, activities and in music which are absorbed and noted consciously, and there are things which are absorbed or taken on unconsciously, and which find a place in the inner memory or inner being of the person, where they are remembered.

Nevertheless, it is not entirely correct, in a sense, to talk about a "hidden teaching"—because the use of the word

# LEARNING THE TRADITION LIKE A LANGUAGE

"hidden" presupposes that it is obscured in some deliberate way, in order to conceal itself from everybody except a chosen few.

Certainly, there are aspects—which can be called "secrets" within the teaching—that are deliberately hidden, and the business of which is deliberately concealed from people who are not working in the Tradition—for the very simple reason that, for some parts of the teaching, if the person were not prepared inwardly as well as outwardly, they would not be able to properly use or take advantage of that formulation, or the energy produced by a particular activity.

It is not so much that if any of the secrets, hidden purposes or hidden activity were to be used by somebody outside the Tradition, it would result in the person going up in a puff of smoke or being turned to stone—not at all.

What would happen is this—it is a thing which I strive continuously to try and reduce—if such elements were given or told to a person who is without the capacity to understand and use them correctly, it would result in confusion.

Confusion is one thing—I think it was Churchill who said: "up with which I will not put"—because it is a recipe for a lack of coherent thought and useful action, and a lack of action connected to a positive inner impulse. Confusion means something half-understood, and which is then acted upon with the best of intentions and under circumstances which seem propitious—but which, if not properly understood, cannot ever become part of a person's being or feeling—which means it is almost an alien activity.

If it is alien to people's activity, they will then carry out this activity or train of thought without much enthusiasm, with a certain reluctance, because they don't feel it to be part of them or harmonious to them. They may say "I'll go along with it and see what happens"—but there's a reservation there. They are only intending to commit themselves completely at a certain stage, or at certain stages, as they understand what this commitment means.

You can always say "I'm with it all the way"—fine, this is perfectly all right, but a person can only really say that when they have sufficient evidence to say it within their own particular terms of reference. But they first have to feel, or think, or to have understood enough to feel that there is some nourishment for them, for their inner selves, and that there is some harmony in the Tradition with which they can relate.

What happens at that point is not that they become "absorbed" or "taken over" into the Tradition like marionettes or dummies. They simply become part of the Tradition in the sense that the Tradition is a living thing which functions among and with people. Since the Tradition cannot function in the abstract or in a vacuum, the people involved in the Tradition become a part of the Tradition.

They do not—and are not expected to—rewrite or update the rules, or do anything extraordinary they might feel to be necessary for the 21st century.

The basis on which they take part in the activities of the Tradition is that there is an already laid-down discipline which is clear, and which has its rules and regulations. Also, unlike certain other philosophies, the Tradition has an aim, and the aim of the Tradition should be the same as the aim of an individual in the Tradition.

The Tradition exists for the purpose of enhancing one's understanding and comprehension, possibly elevating the consciousness and then sustaining that elevation of consciousness—not so that it peaks and drops according to people's enthusiasm or lack of it, but rather to build up a constant certitude of their own possible capacities. When this is put together with the rules, regulations and energy of the Tradition, they can then feel that this is, perhaps, not exactly an 'unbeatable' pairing or putting together, but it is pretty well as good as one can find.

The word "find" is particularly relevant here, because in the Tradition we say that when the person enters into the activities of the Tradition, they enter upon a "path" or that they are on a "voyage." This voyage—of a spiritual nature—consists of following certain well-defined guidelines using certain well-defined techniques, for the purpose of enhancing their capacities. It is a gradual thing, and it needs to be, because it must deal with a lot of the conditioning which has come before it.

So as they travel along this path—call it spiritual or esoteric—you'll find that a person does find certain things. Now where did these things which they find come from?

The impacts, motivations and encouragements come up, because, as like attracts like, so a person travelling on a well-defined path with a correct intention and enthusiasm will inevitably be drawn to certain areas of activity where they feel the harmony at its best.

As in any voyage, an individual has to have a fairly well-defined aim in view, in the sense of "I am going from A to B."

Let us say for the sake of argument that the aim of the Tradition is to elevate the consciousness of people, and that the intention of people working in the Tradition is to elevate their own consciousness, and to maintain that elevation of consciousness.

Therefore, in that any travel is full of what we will call 'chance occurrences,' let us take the analogy of traffic—there may be heavy traffic or less traffic, or light traffic, easy or difficult driving conditions—these are all conceivable situations. In the spiritual, inner or esoteric voyage, factors like the state of the traffic, bad weather conditions or poor road surface, are mirrored within a person. That is to say, just as one can get physically involved in a traffic jam where the traffic is not flowing properly, one can involve oneself or become involved in a similar sort of jam or block within oneself.

This is where we go back to the confusion factor. A person reads or hears something which is of some spiritual or esoteric interest, and perhaps they then carry forward a thought of this—in some (usually unconscious) way, they may put that impact or thought together with an activity in the context of the Tradition.

This is where the confusion factor starts to operate—it does so is a very simple, common and usual way. Take the analogy of a seed—you have a seed being blown by the wind— for that seed to germinate, it has to fall somewhere appropriate, say onto a piece of earth with a given amount of moisture and with proper light from the sun. It will then germinate, take root, and grow.

In that the Tradition tries to improve people's inward as well as outward discipline of thinking or way of thought—i.e., their terms of reference, their analysis, the way they react to things—in a certain way, this makes them vulnerable. Not dangerously so, but still vulnerable to little seeds of something of an "interesting esoteric nature" which take root and are perhaps unconsciously nourished by them, because they think "maybe it has some relation to" and therefore "I'll give it houseroom" in the sense of "I'll think about it" or "I'll try and relate it to ..." or "Isn't that interesting: I wonder if ..."

This factor can cause confusion, because if you take an activity from any goodness-knows-what other philosophy which is not based on a discipline within the Tradition, and add it to an activity in the Tradition, or even just keep it at the back of your mind as a "useful and interesting activity"—you can cause or produce a block or a confusion about it—because it is not operating on the same harmonic as the Tradition.

If you take a perfectly reasonable and possibly useful aspect of Zen, and introduce a Zen form of personal exercise into this context, it won't work. Because however laudable and useful that piece of Zen lore or technique may be, it is not vibrating on the same harmonic as the Tradition, and it will therefore become an encumbrance and an embarrassment, and, as I say, it can cause confusion to the person.

Where you get the spiritual or esoteric block or traffic jam is when a person is influenced by the Tradition while allowing certain impacts from other philosophies to come in at the same. There is simply no way to break through that barrier. Not that other philosophies are automatically alien or hostile, it is just that they do not mix.

Both oil and water are liquids—they don't mix.

Therefore if there is a state of blockage of thought or action, this leads to confusion.

The simplest and most useful way through confusion is to examine it clinically—don't think about it, don't try and force your way through it. Rather, detach the aspects which you consider may be causing disharmony from the confusion, and direct your activity and your intention along a more direct and more precise route.

# RULES OR SECRETS OF THE NAQSHBANDI ORDER

So why certain aspects of the Tradition are maintained as secret is because they can, in turn, cause confusion or become an embarrassment to a person if the person is not ready to receive, understand and use them. These secrets, such as they are, are usually of a nature that is—how shall I put it—they are, in fact, obvious.

In the teaching of the Tradition they are not emphasized as being 'secrets'—because, due to their conditioning and curiosity—people will automatically go straight to the index of a book and look up 'S' for secrets. They then disregard the rest of the book while reading up about 'their secrets.'

It is the ability to understand those secrets that is the prime basis for telling a secret to somebody. Telling a secret in order to show off—"I am so clever, I've got a secret, I will tell you if you're very good"—is a children's game. The only conceivable reason for telling a person any aspect of the secret teaching is that a) they are capable of understanding it, and b) to enable them to put it into practice. The two go hand in hand, they are inseparable.

If a person understands something of this sort and yet doesn't know what to do with it, it will remain abstract for him or her. Even worse, it will become an embarrassment to them, because if they have been told a secret and are nevertheless basically incapable of understanding how to use it, they will remain in a state of agitation or anxiety with this piece of knowledge in their hands, as it were, wanting to know what to do with it, where to put it, or how to use it.

It is therefore doing them no charity to impart a piece of knowledge to them which is better kept confidential until the time comes when it can be told to them in a form which they can comprehend, and in such a manner that they can both understand and use it.

# LEARNING THE TRADITION LIKE A LANGUAGE

So the way to discover or to find certain things—including finding oneself—is to travel a road which is well-known and marked and which has the backup of a technique which has been constructed for the purpose of the travellers' own clarity—not to be thought or debated about, not to be the subject of long discourses—but which was designed to be assimilated and become part of one's personality.

An inner development must always reflect in some ways upon the outer behaviour or conscious thought of the individual. To a certain degree, it means altering or taking on certain new terms of reference, certain different patterns of thinking and ways of acting, or reacting, to certain circumstances.

Again, this can only happen if there is a harmony between the person and the Tradition. If a person puts the Tradition on a different plane in their own existence, then the harmonic which should be generated does not vibrate, and it cannot function to the best degree possible.

When I refer to the Tradition, it does necessarily mean that we are measuring individuals in the Tradition, although a person might say "It's all very well to say that the Tradition is not on a different plane, but if you look at Jami, Hafiz, Saadi, Rumi and so forth, they were manifestly people of great development." Certainly, but they too started somewhere.

If they started somewhere and then codified and passed on the information, instruction and teachings which we still use up to this day—it proves that, irrespective of all these things like age, background and conditioning, an individual person can aspire to an elevated consciousness which can be used in both a conscious and unconscious way—otherwise you get a significant division between the conscious individual and that individual's inner being.

"The person may be useless or hopeless at their job or lazy or something, and yet, having worked upon themselves inwardly, they are a better person"—no, this imbalance should not occur.

The inner development of the person should be mirrored by some conscious and outward thought patterns, behaviour and feelings; otherwise you get switch-on, switch-off—"I am in the office, I am hopeless, stupid, lazy or this, that and the other thing, but when I get home and sit down to do my exercise, I am somebody completely different—calm, tranquil, without anxiety, and it is only my office or work self which is awful." No, this shouldn't be so.

As I have said before, one does not continually try to monitor the degree of what might or might not be one's own degree of development: "How much have I improved? Have I made any progress during the last six months?"

Or again, one asks oneself: "How and which way do I benefit from and take advantage of it?"

A person just has a feeling. It's a feeling of satisfaction, of interest, of harmony, of something good or useful, something positive or harmonious.

If they really need to, perhaps they can monitor themselves, as distinct from looking at themselves. But if they insist on monitoring themselves to try and find out whether they are better than they were "last week" or "yesterday" or "this time last year" and insist on this; it would be a pity, because it really is a waste of time.

If one is tempted to try and measure something like this, one should do so in terms of feeling and understanding: "In terms of what I did last week or a year or two ago, I think I

# LEARNING THE TRADITION LIKE A LANGUAGE

understand more than I did before"—but that is as far as one should go in terms of examining one's own degree of development.

The only person whose business it is to keep a score sheet and work out who is understanding what or using this or that function, is the person who is teaching you. It is his responsibility, not to guess, but to decide which aspect of the teaching should be dealt with, and with which individual or group at a particular time.

I am sure you will all notice that I usually speak of different factors, aspects or activities of the Tradition at different times, because the basis I work on involves two areas: that of my mandate or programme, and feedback in terms of the individual or group I am working with at that moment.

It would be intolerable for me, and incomprehensible to you, were I to deal with a subject about which you knew nothing. Firstly, it would cause confusion: "What the hell is he talking about?" Secondly: "We never heard about that sort of thing before." Thirdly: "Let's meet around the corner in the coffee shop and decide what we're going to do now" because "he wouldn't say anything."

As I say, this situation would be intolerable, ridiculous, inharmonious and unproductive—so therefore I have to maintain these three measurements very strictly.

Following the Tradition is not like following a course, in the sense of a first or second-year course of studies, and so forth. The Tradition is of a lifelong nature.

One works on oneself throughout one's whole life in the hope of achieving a level of consciousness, either of a permanent nature, or at least one according to which one can live or which

343

can be conjured up or attracted by putting oneself into a relationship with the Tradition—say in an exercise, or by listening to some sort of music.

I deal with different factors at different times, sometimes seemingly out of order. This is because each talk or activity I initiate is a result of a buildup of factors leading to a particular discourse or lesson—if you like—about something.

This is not scripted, in the sense that, as I say, it is a course with a first, second or third term. But it does build up to something like that.

The nearest equivalent conscious or worldly activity to the Tradition, I suppose, is learning a language. One starts learning a language from nothing. One learns the alphabet, the different accents, the spelling—starting perhaps with the grammar and a few rudimentary phrases—and one then begins to understand that language. This is the closest example to the development, coherence, or understanding to be found in the Tradition.

Both learning a language and achieving something in the Tradition do involve a lot of emotions and parallel situations.

Those of you who have tried to learn a foreign language know this. You may have gone doggedly on, day after day, week after week, month after month, mouthing these incomprehensible things, trying to get the pronunciation right, trying to learn the spelling—and then, I don't know if any of you have experienced it, one day you're sitting maybe in a café in the country of that language—and suddenly you start understanding what people are talking about at the tables around you. In terms of language, it is called a breakthrough.

You think "Well, it wasn't impossible, it was difficult and

# LEARNING THE TRADITION LIKE A LANGUAGE

I didn't understand beans at that time," but one is now using the linguistic abilities one acquired to be able to correspond with, relate to, and have contact with, other people.

Similar forms of breakthrough take place in the Tradition, which is why I use the term of 'finding' or 'having found' something. It is akin to a breakthrough in the sense that, even several years ago, one might have read, heard or seen something being done, and, thinking or reading about it, one will sometimes say, as a result of being in the Tradition, "That's what that was" or "That's what I now think it was".

These breakthroughs do not come at regular intervals, enabling a person to say: "It's about time I had a breakthrough because it's a quarter to nine." No, it's got to be something involuntary, otherwise people would say things like: "A whole week's gone by since my last breakthrough." They'd get disappointed, walk away, and wander off into some cult or something.

So the breakthrough is both functional and in many ways necessary, because the average human being requires some form of encouragement. They may be reluctant to take that encouragement from themselves, that is, to listen to oneself saying "I understood that." There is always a slight reservation in the sense that "one shouldn't be self-satisfied" or "turn inwards" or else, "What a terrible fellow I am" because "I am big-headed" and "this is not humility"—which means that they leave that whole side of themselves unexplored.

Along the path of the Tradition, people will feel impacts at certain irregular intervals, under circumstances which are not necessarily connected to the Tradition, but which nevertheless give them the satisfaction that something is coming to the surface and telling them "That is good" or "That can be good." It's a little encouragement, a little bit of a push or nudge, to give them adequate reason to feel satisfied with themselves— up to a point.

Not so self-satisfied that they will heave a big sigh of relief and lapse back into their old ways or old terms of reference after achieving something. No, first you achieve it, and then you maintain and increase it.

You are your own severest critic in all things, and you can take on that severity towards yourself in a humane way. You take that severity as being as close a measure as you can get to, in any form of development which you choose.

5.03.92

# SELECTED READING LIST

### Other books by Omar Ali-Shah

*The Course of the Seeker* (Tractus)
*The Rose Garden (Gulistan) by Saadi (translation)* (Tractus)
*Sufism as Therapy* (Tractus)
*Sufism for Today* (Alif )
*The Sufi Tradition in the West* (Alif)
*The Authentic Rubaiyyat of Omar Khayaam (translation )*(IDSI)

### Books by The Sirdar Ikbal Ali Shah

*Muhammed: The Prophet* (Tractus)
*Islamic Sufism* (Tractus)
*Lights of Asia* (Tractus)
*Selections from The Koran* (Octagon)
*Oriental Caravan* (Octagon)

### Books by Idries Shah

*Caravan of Dreams* (Octagon)
*The Commanding Self* (Octagon)
*The Sufis* (Octagon)
*Tales of the Dervishes* (Octagon)
*Wisdom of the Idiots* (Octagon)
*The Way of the Sufi* (Octagon)

### Books by Amina Shah

*The Assemblies of Al-Hariri (translation)* (Octagon)
*The Tale of the Four Dervishes of Amu Khrusru* (Octagon)
*Tales of Afghanistan* (Octagon)
and also:
*The Essential Rumi (trans. Coleman Barks)* (HarperCollins)
*The 99 Most Beautiful Names by Al-Ghazali* (Islamic Texts Society)
*Teachings of Hafiz* (Octagon)
*The Alchemy of Happiness by Al-Ghazali* (Octagon)

Other Books published by Tractus:

## LIGHTS OF ASIA
by
The Sirdar Ikbal Ali Shah

A simple and lucid introduction to the four main religions of the "Book"; Islam, Christianity, Judaism and Buddhism,as told in their own words, which completely eschews modern political-based debate about who's right or who's wrong. The four faiths are presented *in a vigourous almost passionate exposition*; in which *each religion speaks for itself without challenge, so that its full glow and warmth should be given to the reader.* It is a particularly timely book for an epoch such as ours where religion has been debased and used as a political weapon, and it is possibly one of the best books ever written on what the four religions are really about, by a man who is not without his own convictions, but who has no axe to grind.

## MUHAMMED: THE PROPHET
by
The Sirdar Ikbal Ali-Shah

This biography of the Prophet Muhammed reads like an exciting novel, since the Prophet himself led a life of almost incredible adventure, both in the spiritual area and at worldly level. The Sirdar does full justice to the sweep and drama of this life without any novelettish tackyness, and his narrative rises to the lofty heights of great poetry as he relates the life of an illiterate orphan who became a model for all mankind. As an introduction to Islam, it is a book that can hardly be bettered.

# SUFISM AS THERAPY
by
Omar Ali-Shah

This collection by the contemporary Sufi teacher Omar Ali-Shah bring together a series of talks made to congresses of medical and heathcare profesionnals who are interested in adding a dimension of traditional knowledge to their own therapeutic disciplines. Thus the Sufi Tradition is not considered here as a sort of magic miracle-cure, but as a very real and useful adjunct for people whose basic concern is to help others, or themselves.

# THE COURSE OF THE SEEKER
by
Omar Ali-Shah

This first collection of talks by the contemporary Sufi teacher Omar Ali-Shah was a milestone in Sufi literature because it was the first time a Sufi master was willing to openly share his "trade secrets" with his pupils, i.e., give a clear and uncluttered account of the various obstacles in contemporary life which prevent the seeker from achieving the lucidity we are all aiming for and which should be in our grasp. The present edition of the book is completed with the addition of five new chapters dealing with the master/pupil relationship, clearly the biggest hurdle to acceptance of the Sufi Tradition in the West, insofar as a Sufi envisages the intellectual mind rather like a artisan considers a tool, i.e., a good servant but a poor master.

# THE ROSE GARDEN / GULISTAN
## by
## SAADI
### (Translated and introduced by Omar Ali-Shah)

This great Persian classic collection of sayings, stories and poems is considered to be so important that chidren are taught ethics and behaviour with it in schools. They are so simple funny and accessible to all that there is hardly a Farsi-speaker alive that does not know some of them by heart.

Omar Ali-Shah's translation, hitherto only available in French, was the first to reveal the sufic dimension of this masterpiece, but children have instictively recognized it since time immemorial both in the East and in the West, insofar as the book acts as a kind of primer or exercise-machine of the spirit, because of the flexibility of mind it demands and obtains from its reader.


# THE WOMAN I LOVE
## by
## Augy Hayter

This is a collection of story-poems, loosely modelled on the oriental form of the diwan (as exemplified with far greater genuis above) which deal with the various forms that love can take, whether legitimate or illegitimate, friendly or hostile, joyous or depressed, which adds up to a kind of crossection of twentieth-century love customs whose sum may be considered greater than its parts.